D0568669

51

Mobile Web Design
FOR
DUMMIES®

Mobile Web Design FOR DUMMIES®

by Janine Warner and David LaFontaine

Wiley Publishing, Inc.

Library Resource Center
Renton Technical College
3000 N.E. 4th Street
Renton, WA 98056

Mobile Web Design For Dummies®

Published by
Wiley Publishing, Inc.
111 River Street
Hoboken, NJ 07030-5774

www.wiley.com

Copyright © 2010 by Wiley Publishing, Inc., Indianapolis, Indiana

Published by Wiley Publishing, Inc., Indianapolis, Indiana

Published simultaneously in Canada

No part of this publication may be reproduced, stored in a retrieval system or transmitted in any form or by any means, electronic, mechanical, photocopying, recording, scanning or otherwise, except as permitted under Sections 107 or 108 of the 1976 United States Copyright Act, without either the prior written permission of the Publisher, or authorization through payment of the appropriate per-copy fee to the Copyright Clearance Center, 222 Rosewood Drive, Danvers, MA 01923, (978) 750-8400, fax (978) 646-8600. Requests to the Publisher for permission should be addressed to the Permissions Department, John Wiley & Sons, Inc., 111 River Street, Hoboken, NJ 07030, (201) 748-6011, fax (201) 748-6008, or online at http://www.wiley.com/go/permissions.

Trademarks: Wiley, the Wiley Publishing logo, For Dummies, the Dummies Man logo, A Reference for the Rest of Us!, The Dummies Way, Dummies Daily, The Fun and Easy Way, Dummies.com, Making Everything Easier, and related trade dress are trademarks or registered trademarks of John Wiley & Sons, Inc. and/or its affiliates in the United States and other countries, and may not be used without written permission. All other trademarks are the property of their respective owners. Wiley Publishing, Inc., is not associated with any product or vendor mentioned in this book.

LIMIT OF LIABILITY/DISCLAIMER OF WARRANTY: THE PUBLISHER AND THE AUTHOR MAKE NO REPRESENTATIONS OR WARRANTIES WITH RESPECT TO THE ACCURACY OR COMPLETENESS OF THE CONTENTS OF THIS WORK AND SPECIFICALLY DISCLAIM ALL WARRANTIES, INCLUDING WITHOUT LIMITATION WARRANTIES OF FITNESS FOR A PARTICULAR PURPOSE. NO WARRANTY MAY BE CREATED OR EXTENDED BY SALES OR PROMOTIONAL MATERIALS. THE ADVICE AND STRATEGIES CONTAINED HEREIN MAY NOT BE SUITABLE FOR EVERY SITUATION. THIS WORK IS SOLD WITH THE UNDERSTANDING THAT THE PUBLISHER IS NOT ENGAGED IN RENDERING LEGAL, ACCOUNTING, OR OTHER PROFESSIONAL SERVICES. IF PROFESSIONAL ASSISTANCE IS REQUIRED, THE SERVICES OF A COMPETENT PROFESSIONAL PERSON SHOULD BE SOUGHT. NEITHER THE PUBLISHER NOR THE AUTHOR SHALL BE LIABLE FOR DAMAGES ARISING HEREFROM. THE FACT THAT AN ORGANIZATION OR WEBSITE IS REFERRED TO IN THIS WORK AS A CITATION AND/OR A POTENTIAL SOURCE OF FURTHER INFORMATION DOES NOT MEAN THAT THE AUTHOR OR THE PUBLISHER ENDORSES THE INFORMATION THE ORGANIZATION OR WEBSITE MAY PROVIDE OR RECOMMENDATIONS IT MAY MAKE. FURTHER, READERS SHOULD BE AWARE THAT INTERNET WEBSITES LISTED IN THIS WORK MAY HAVE CHANGED OR DISAPPEARED BETWEEN WHEN THIS WORK WAS WRITTEN AND WHEN IT IS READ.

For general information on our other products and services, please contact our Customer Care Department within the U.S. at 877-762-2974, outside the U.S. at 317-572-3993, or fax 317-572-4002.

For technical support, please visit www.wiley.com/techsupport.

Wiley also publishes its books in a variety of electronic formats. Some content that appears in print may not be available in electronic books.

Library of Congress Control Number: 2010933465

ISBN: 978-0-470-56096-9

Manufactured in the United States of America

10 9 8 7 6 5 4 3 2 1

006.7 WARNER 2010

Warner, Janine, 1967–

Mobile web design for dummies

About the Authors

Since 1996, **Janine Warner** has written more than a dozen books about the Internet, including *Web Sites Do-It-Yourself For Dummies*, *Dreamweaver For Dummies* (all eight editions), the last five editions of *Teach Yourself Dreamweaver Visually*, and the *Digital Family Album* book series (Amphoto Books).

Janine is the host of a growing collection of training videos for KelbyTraining. com in Web design, Adobe Dreamweaver, and Cascading Style Sheets. She's also a regular columnist for *Layers* magazine.

A popular speaker, Janine offers training in techy topics, such as Web design, and gives keynotes on Internet trends, the growing importance of the mobile Web, social media, and online reputation. Janine is fluent in Spanish and has given many speeches in Latin America and Spain.

Janine has worked on large and small Web sites. From 1994 to 1998, she ran Visiontec Communications, a Web design firm in Northern California, where she worked for a diverse group of clients including Levi Strauss & Co., AirTouch Communications, and many other small- and medium-size businesses.

From 1998 to 2000, she worked for *The Miami Herald*, first as its Online Managing Editor and later as Director of New Media. She left that position to serve as Director of Latin American Operations for CNET Networks, an international technology media company.

Since 2001, Janine has run her own business as a writer, speaker, and consultant. To find out more about Janine, find free Web design training materials, and get answers to common questions, visit DigitalFamily.com.

David LaFontaine's first cellphone came in a backpack and weighed about 20 pounds, and the closest he got to using gestures to control the phone came when it fell on his toe. Despite this early mishap, Dave remains fascinated with the promise of these little portable pieces of technology.

He has more than 20 years experience as a journalist, editor, and multimedia producer working on a variety of projects in film, television, print, radio, and the Internet. The Newspaper Association of America commissioned him to write two case studies about the promise of mobile advertising, which gave him a front-row seat on the tectonic shifts in what is now known as "the attention economy." He's also a popular blogger whose work can be found on Sips from the Firehose (www.sipsfromthefirehose.com) and the Mobile Web Design blog (www.mobilewebdesignblog.com). Dave is a partner in Artesian Media; to learn more, visit his personal site (www.davidlafontaine.com).

Dave has spoken to audiences around the world about the promise of mobile and set them loose on GPS-fueled scavenger hunts designed to teach them how to leverage the power of content everywhere, all the time. He continues to worry about what will happen when we're all able to plug digital content directly into our neo-cortexes, but figures that by the time this happens, there'll be an app for that.

Dedication

To all those who venture on the mobile Web, and to all who are working to make sure they find something of value when they get there.

Authors' Acknowledgments

Janine Warner: Over the years, I've thanked many people in my books — family, friends, teachers, and mentors — but I have been graced by so many wonderful people now that no publisher will give me enough pages to thank them all. In this book, I focus on the people who contributed directly to these pages, starting with the fantastic editorial team at Wiley Publishing: Rebecca Huehls, Leah Cameron, Jennifer Riggs, Susan Pink, Jeff Noble, and Steven Hayes.

Above all, I have to thank my brilliant coauthor and partner in all things digital and analog, David LaFontaine. Your sense of humor, your ability to tell a great story, and your passion for technology and communication have made this a better book, and me, a better person.

A heartfelt thanks to David Mitchell for providing the haven we escape to after impossible deadlines are finally done. And to my family, my parents, Malinda, Janice, Robin, and Helen, my brother Brian, and my brother Kevin and his family, Stephanie, Mikayla, Savannah, Jessica, and Calahan, for all their love and support.

Special thanks to Gail Rahn Frederick who wrote the section on HTML5 in Chapter 5. Gail is a mobile Web enthusiast, instructor of standards-based mobile Web development, and the creator of the site Learn the Mobile Web (http://learnthemobileweb.com). She's also the author of *Beginning Smartphone Web Development: Building JavaScript, CSS, HTML and Ajax-Based Applications for iPhone, Android, Palm Pre, BlackBerry, Windows Mobile, and Nokia S60* (Apress), an introduction to building standards-compliant Mobile Web sites for any mobile device.

Thanks to Lee Andron, Director of Information Design and Strategy for Ansible, Interpublic Group's full service mobile marketing agency. Lee generously spent hours on the phone with us, sharing his work and helping us develop a case study on the Microsoft Cloud Web site, which we feature in Chapter 6. For all his time, we also want to thank his new baby, Grace Elizabeth, and wife Tricia for sharing Lee with us. Thanks also to Sia Ea, Creative Director for Ansible, for all her design talent and for her time explaining her role in the Microsoft Cloud site project. Special thanks to Anouk Pape and Jamie Conner, Central Marketing Group, Microsoft, and the entire Microsoft Cloud Site team.

Thanks to Jonathan Thaler (www.whenimmobile.com) for sharing his experience creating multimedia sites for Tori Sparks (www.torisparks.com)
and Radio Paradise (www.radioparadise.com). Thanks to Andrew Taylor
(www.taopro.com) for his help with ecommerce site research. And thanks
to Mark Jenkins (www.mobilynx.net) for his expertise in mobile devices
and testing.

Most of all, I want to thank all the people who have read my books or
watched my videos over the years and gone on to create Web sites. You
are my greatest inspiration and I sincerely enjoy it when you send me links
to your Web sites. You can always find me at www.DigitalFamily.com.
Thank you, thank you, thank you.

David LaFontaine: I want to thank my parents, Gail and Dave, for making
trips to the library such a treat when I was young (and for the lifelong love of
the written word that those trips engendered), and my sisters Linda, Beth,
and Sara for the lively (ahem) discussions that taught me to always be prepared to examine and logically defend my conclusions.

A big shout-out goes to all the other ink-stained wretches of the Fourth Estate
working at newspapers all over the world, laboring to produce the daily
miracle; I hope that the spread of mobile content helps them regain so much
of what has been lost these past few years. I also want to thank all the panel
members, attendees, and innocent bystanders at industry events including
the Online News Association, OMMA, and Digital Hollywood that I have pes-
tered over the years; some of their patient wisdom is contained in this book.

But always and ever, I want to thank my wife and coauthor Janine, whose
easy grace and good-humored patience make the nerdy seem glamorous. *Esto
si es amor.*

Publisher's Acknowledgments

We're proud of this book; please send us your comments at http://dummies.custhelp.com. For other comments, please contact our Customer Care Department within the U.S. at 877-762-2974, outside the U.S. at 317-572-3993, or fax 317-572-4002.

Some of the people who helped bring this book to market include the following:

Acquisitions and Editorial

Project Editor: Rebecca Huehls

Executive Editor: Steve Hayes

Copy Editor: Jen Riggs

Technical Editor: Jeff Noble

Editorial Manager: Leah P. Cameron

Editorial Assistant: Amanda Graham

Sr. Editorial Assistant: Cherie Case

Cartoons: Rich Tennant
(www.the5thwave.com)

Composition Services

Sr. Project Coordinator: Kristie Rees

Layout and Graphics: Amy Hassos, Ronald G. Terry

Proofreaders: Laura Bowman, Jessica Kramer, Lauren Mandelbaum

Indexer: Infodex Indexing Services, Inc.

Special Help: Annie Sullivan, Stephen Worden

Publishing and Editorial for Technology Dummies

    Richard Swadley, Vice President and Executive Group Publisher

    Andy Cummings, Vice President and Publisher

    Mary Bednarek, Executive Acquisitions Director

    Mary C. Corder, Editorial Director

Publishing for Consumer Dummies

    Diane Graves Steele, Vice President and Publisher

Composition Services

    Debbie Stailey, Director of Composition Services

Contents at a Glance

Table of Contents

Introduction

In the nearly 15 years that we've written about Web design, we've seen many changes — from the early days when you could create only simple pages with HTML 1.0, to the elaborate interactive designs you can create today.

But just as the Web seemed to finally be coming of age, the rapid growth of cellphones and other mobile devices that connect to the Internet is simultaneously propelling everyone forward (because these devices make the Web available everywhere, all the time) and setting everyone back (because of the design limitations of small screens, the limited bandwidth, and other limitations most thought were left behind by now).

One of the challenges of Web design is that Web pages aren't only displayed on different kinds of computers; pages are also downloaded to computers with monitors that are as big as widescreen televisions and to devices as small as cellphones. As a result, creating Web sites that look good to all visitors is a lot more complex than it used to be, and standards have become a lot more important. That's why in this book, you find out not only how to use all the great features in Dreamweaver, but also how to determine which flavor of markup language best serves your goals and your audience when designing for the wide variety of screen sizes and display limitations of mobile Web browsers.

About This Book

We designed *Mobile Web Design For Dummies* to help you find the answers you need when you need them. You don't have to read this book cover to cover, and you certainly don't have to memorize it. Consider this a quick study guide and a reference you can return to. Each section stands alone, giving you easy answers to specific questions and step-by-step instructions for common tasks.

Want to find out how to test your designs when you don't have a dozen mobile phones of your own? Jump right in and go directly to Chapter 7 on mobile testing. Concerned about the simplest feature phones and what version of HTML they support? Jump to Chapter 5 for a review of markup languages, or go on to any other topic that interests you. Don't worry about getting sand on this book at the beach or coffee spilled on the pages at break-fast. We know that with your mobile device, you can read this book and test your Web pages anywhere, and we promise this book (and its authors) won't complain if you take it with you.

Conventions Used in This Book

Keeping things consistent makes them easier to understand. In this book, those consistent elements are *conventions.* Notice how *conventions* is in ital-ics? We frequently put new terms in italics and then define them so that you know what they mean.

When we include *URLs* (Web addresses) or e-mail addresses within regu-lar paragraph text, they look like this: www.mobilewebdesignblog.com. Sometimes, however, we set URLs on their own line, like this:

```
www.mobilewebdesignblog.com
```

That's so you can easily spot them on a page if you want to type them into your browser to visit a site. You can type domain names with all lower-case letters, all uppercase, or a mix. Domain names aren't case sensitive, but remember that you must match the case exactly for any part of a Web address that comes after the extension, such as .com or .net. So for an address, such as www.digitalfamily.com/videos, you must type *videos* in all lowercase.

We also assume that your Web browser doesn't require the introductory http:// for Web addresses. If you use a really, really old browser, remem-ber to type this before the address (also make sure you include the http:// of the address when you're creating links in Dreamweaver).

Even though Dreamweaver makes knowing HTML code unnecessary, you may want to wade into HTML waters occasionally. We include HTML code in this book when we think it can help you better understand how things work in design view. Sometimes it's easier to remove or edit a tag in Dreamweaver's code view than in design view. When we provide examples, such as the fol-lowing code which links a URL to a Web page, we set off the HTML in the same monospaced type as URLs:

```
<A HREF="http://www.mobilewebdesignblog.com">Janine's Blog
          about Mobile Web Design</A>
```

When we introduce you to a new set of features, such as options in a dialog box, we set these items apart with bullet lists so you can see that they're all related. When we want you to follow instructions, we use numbered step lists to walk you through the process.

Foolish Assumptions

Most of the Web pages on the Internet don't work well on mobile phones, a limitation that's increasingly important as more and more people surf the Web on BlackBerrys, iPhones, Droids, and other mobile devices.

If this is your first foray into Web design, this book may not be the best place to start. We've written several guides to Web design that are designed for beginners, including *Web Sites Do-It-Yourself For Dummies* and *Dreamweaver CS5 For Dummies*.

This book is designed for Web designers who already have a basic under-standing of Web design and want to develop new skills for designing pages for the mobile Web. That said, we don't expect you to be a *professional* devel-oper or to know everything there is about Web design. To make sure that you can follow along even with just a basic grasp of Web design, we include some basic material, such as an overview of XHTML and Cascading Style Sheets (CSS) in Chapter 4, to give you a review and to make sure you have a solid foundation before you move on to the more advanced chapters on which markup languages work best on mobile devices and how to work around the limitations of CSS on many cellphones.

We don't assume you're a pro — at least not yet. In keeping with the phi-losophy behind the *For Dummies* series, this book is an easy-to-use guide designed for readers with a wide range of experience.

If you're an experienced Web designer, *Mobile Web Design For Dummies* is an ideal reference for you because it gets you working quickly, starting with basic mobile Web pages and progressing to more advanced page features.

How This Book Is Organized

To ease you through the learning curve associated with any new material, we organized *Mobile Web Design For Dummies* as a complete reference. This section provides a breakdown of the four parts of the book and what you can find in each one. Each chapter includes an introduction to general concepts, step-by-step instructions, and tips to help you understand the vocabulary and basic rules of Web design as you go along.

Part I: Designing for Mobile Devices

Part I introduces you to how designing for mobile devices is different from designing for the Web, and helps you appreciate what makes mobile different and why following Web development standards is so important. In Chapter 1, you find an overview of the mobile Web and the trends that are shaping how — and why — Web designers are adapting their sites to so many devices. In Chapter 2, we give you an overview of the many approaches to mobile Web design, cover a range of design challenges, and introduce you to some of the common differences among mobile devices.

Part II: Following Mobile Web Standards

Chapter 3 shows you how to create a simple version of your Web site that will work on most mobile devices. Chapter 4 provides an introduction to using XHTML with CSS. CSS is *the* way to create Web page designs.

In Chapter 5, we take you further into markup languages and CSS, delving into the many challenges specific to mobile Web design with a review of WML, XHTML MP, and HTML 5.

In Chapter 6, we focus on the high-end of mobile Web design and feature a real-world case study on a complex mobile launch. We also review how device detection works and how you can automatically redirect visitors to the mobile version of your site.

In Chapter 7, we take you on a tour of the many ways you can test your mobile Web designs with online emulators and programs, such as Adobe Device Central, that make it possible to view how a design will look on a mobile phone, even if you don't have the phone. You also find out how to publish the mobile version of your Web site by using FTP features in Dreamweaver to put your site online.

Part III: Multimedia, Marketing, and E-Commerce

In Part III, you discover the limitations of mobile phones when it comes to multimedia, and how to get around those limitations with a few special tips that make it possible to add audio, video, and even Flash Lite. In Chapter 8, you find instructions for optimizing images for mobile and using tricks, such as using percentages instead of fixed widths, to make your images and multimedia more adaptable. In Chapter 9, you find out what it takes to make a blog mobile-friendly and discover the best mobile templates for WordPress and other blogging tools. In Chapter 10, we explore some of the best ways to market your mobile site after you launch it. From advertising to social media, mobile offers many new advantages with the ability to reach people based on geographic location, time of day, and more. In Chapter 11, you find out what it takes to make e-commerce work on the mobile Web and how Google Checkout makes it easy for anyone to add a mobile-friendly shopping cart to their site.

Part IV: The Part of Tens

Part IV features two quick references to help you develop the best mobile Web sites possible. In Chapter 12, you find ten design tips to help you over-come the challenges and take advantage of the best that mobile design has to offer. And finally, in Chapter 13, you find reviews of ten great mobile Web sites with screenshots that show how they look across multiple devices.

Icons Used in This Book

This icon reminds you of an important concept or procedure that you want to store away in your memory bank for future use.

This icon signals technical stuff that you may find informative and interesting but that isn't essential for designing a mobile Web site. Feel free to skip over this information.

This icon indicates a tip or technique that can save you time and money — and a headache — later.

This icon warns you of any potential pitfalls — and gives you the all-important information on how to avoid them.

Where to Go from Here

If you want to get familiar with the latest in mobile Web design trends and where things are going from here, don't skip Chapter 1. If you're ready to dive in and start making your Web site mobile-friendly right away, jump ahead to Chapter 2 or 3. If you want to find out about a specific trick or technique, consult the table of contents or the index; you won't miss a beat as you work to make those impossible mobile design deadlines. Most of all, we wish you great success in all your mobile Web projects!

Part I
Designing for Mobile Devices

The 5th Wave   By Rich Tennant

"Of course your current cell phone takes pictures, functions as a walkie-talkie, and browses the internet. But does it shoot silly string?"

In this part . . .

In this part, we discuss how the mobile Web is different from the standard Internet. We also discuss how to design for the mobile Web with those differences in mind.

Designing Web pages for cellphones and other mobile devices is a bit like going back in time to the early days of the Internet, when small computer monitors and limited bandwidth restricted what people could create. The mobile Internet is best served by creating a smaller, simpler version of your Web site, one that focuses on the information and services (such as directions to find your store or office) that are likely to be most important to someone on the go.

Chapter 1

Understanding What Makes the Mobile Web Different

*T*rying to predict the future is always dangerous, particularly when it comes to the mobile Web. Experts have been predicting that "this is the year of mobile" pretty much every year for the last decade. Cynics point to this as proof that the mobile Web is merely a mirage — that the iPhone, Droid, and their smartphone brethren are fun little toys, but that they'll never rival the Internet on a computer screen.

The problem with this pessimism is that it doesn't take into account all the advantages that come with the mobile Web, just the obvious limitations.

People put up with all the problems associated with the Internet, on top of the uncertain wireless connections, because the power and possibilities of having access to all the information — instantly available wherever you are, whenever you want — outweigh the little inconveniences. Although trying to use most current Web sites on the mobile platform can be an exercise in pain, frustration, and the barely suppressed urge to hurl an expensive device into the nearest junkyard car-crusher, the pace of technology puts the computing power that used to cost $10 million and fill an entire building at MIT into an 8-ounce chunk of plastic that fits in your shirt pocket.

In this chapter, we help you assess your mobile users' overall needs, recognize the limitations of the platform and the new functions available, and understand how your Web site can deliver the right resources in the right place at the right time — in a way that your visitors can access on any device.

Introducing the Mobile Web Audience

Designing for your audience has always been important, but designing for the mobile Web is even more complex because you have to design for so many different audiences and mobile devices — and do it all in a tiny space.

Your audience is growing

The sheer size of the potential audience for the mobile Web is staggering. Selling the first billion cellphones took 20 years; the next billion sold in 4 years; and the third billion sold in only 2. The next billion will be sold in a year, so that by 2011, more people on earth will have cellphones than those who don't.

Most of these last billion cellphones will be bought by people living in rural areas of developing countries; people who have never owned any phone in their lives, and for whom the prospect of being connected to the larger world is absolutely life-changing. This part of the audience will probably experience the Web for the first time on the 3-inch screen of a mobile device.

Already, sites like ESPN.com report that on weekends during football season, they receive more traffic to their Web site from mobile phones than they do from computers. Market researchers for Yahoo! find that in sports bars, surrounded by dozens of giant-screen high-definition (HD) TVs with 5.1 Dolby sound, fans had their heads bowed, looking at their cellphones — following the up-to-the-minute point totals of their fantasy football teams.

The convergence of this explosive growth in audience size and the restrictions (and amazing possibilities) of the mobile Web pose a unique challenge for Web designers.

Your audience wants to save time, kill time, or socialize

If the Internet was driven by the ability to access words, pictures, videos, and sounds, the mobile Web is driven by even more immediate needs. Speaking on a panel for the Online News Association, Nick Montes, president of the mobile gaming company VivaVision, told the audience that people are driven to use the mobile Web for three primary reasons:

- To connect with their friends and social group
- To save time or money
- To kill time

When users come to your site, they're reacting to one of these needs. If you want them to find you, to be able to use the content that you've so painstakingly crafted, and to use the two-way communication of the Web to interact with what you've done, you need to have a site optimized for the mobile Web. This means not only offering the right content, but also employing mobile Web design standards to organize that content in ways that mobile Web users will be able to use, which we cover throughout this book.

Your audience uses different mobile devices

Our goal is to help you design the best Web site you can to deliver the right resources in the right place at the right time. We say "the best Web site you can" because designing for the mobile Web is still an imperfect science and how far you go in making sure your site is optimized for all the mobile devices that might ever visit will depend on your budget, skills, time, and the return you can expect on your investment. As a result, we include a range of options and approaches in this book with the goal of helping point you in the right direction to make the best choice for you.

For many graphic artists and experienced Web designers, the restrictions imposed to create Web pages that work at the lowest end of the mobile Web can make them feel like Picasso being asked to paint bar charts and pie graphs using crayons.

But today, the biggest challenge of the mobile Web is not just designing within the constraints of the low end, it's designing mobile sites that take best advantage of both the low end and the high end of the mobile spectrum, which now includes iPhones, and even iPads, capable doing *almost* everything that works on the desktop Web, as well as many things that are only possible on a mobile device. (We explore some of the design challenges of the mobile Web in Chapter 2.)

Your audience may be any age

Never has the divide been more dramatic, or more blurred, among the generations. The Internet generation is made up of people who use the iPhone intuitively and trade instant messages 100 times a day with their friends. But grandparents today are different, too. The baby boomer generation may be slower to the Web and mobile, but they're catching on. And don't forget the moms and dads in between those two extremes, or the next generation that's coming along. Toddlers play games on mobile phones before they can talk.

Library Resource Center
Renton Technical College
3000 N.E. 4th Street
Renton, WA 98056

Evolving Standards: WAP, WML, and the Mobile Web

The first mobile Internet experience was very slow and came with hideously expensive digital data plans that were available only in certain large markets, and even then only in the densely populated areas with clear wireless signals.

Basically, the early mobile Web looked a lot like Prodigy, if you remember that early online service. Prodigy had eight bland colors, tiny photos, and only a few lines of text per screen. Paging through a story — or, if you were really daring and had a high pain threshold, a photo gallery — took both saintly patience and deep pockets.

Although the mobile Web seems to be forever moving forward, understanding how early mobile Web sites worked and the technology those sites were based on is helpful. You may run into the terms WAP and WML if you're redesigning an old mobile site, and the technologies in use today have evolved from these early technologies. The following sections explain what you need to know as you begin designing mobile Web sites.

Sizing up WAP, WML, and XHTML

The earliest mobile sites looked a little bit like pictures drawn on the old dot-matrix printers. The pages were designed within the limitations of Wireless Access Protocol (WAP 1.0) in the late '90s, when programmers first started thinking about cramming Web page functionality onto the cellphones of the time. (And no, WAP isn't the sound of designers slapping themselves on the forehead when confronted with the restrictions of the day.)

This is where things get a little confusing. Many mobile Web designers and experts (who should know better) have gotten into the habit of referring to anything related to the mobile Web as WAP. Others use WAP only to refer to the simplest, most bare-bones sites, calling them "WAP sites" because they were designed using the Wireless Markup Language (WML), which was part of WAP 1.0.

Unfortunately, just using the blanket term "WAP site" to refer to all sites designed for the mobile Web is both confusing and inaccurate. WAP is a series of rules and specifications, not design principles. These rules were updated in 2002 with WAP 2.0 to include support for XHTML MP, and just about every phone sold since 2004 supports this more sophisticated markup language. (You find more on the best markup language options for the mobile Web today in Chapter 5.)

Library Resource Center
Renton Technical College
3000 N.E. 4th Street
Renton, WA 98056

To make things even more confusing, very few mobile devices in use today support *only* WML content. Many mobile phones sold today support both WML and some variation of XHTML. At the high end, sophisticated smartphones like the iPhone display Web pages pretty well even if they're not designed with WAP standards. You could say that most mobile Web designers now work in a WAP 3.0 environment, but that term hasn't caught on, and clear standards for WAP 3.0 have not been agreed upon.

In this book, we decided to avoid all the confusion around the term WAP. Instead, when we distinguish between Web sites that are designed for mobile devices and those designed for computer screens, we use the phrases *mobile Web* and *desktop Web,* respectively. See the glossary in the "Mobile alphabet soup" sidebar in this chapter for a better explanation of these and some of the other terms we use throughout this book.

The browser wars and WAP

The browser wars on the desktop Web greatly shaped the development of the mobile Web. In the late '90s, Netscape Navigator leapt out to an early lead in market share — at one point, nearly 80 percent of the people accessing the Internet did so through Netscape. Then Microsoft started bundling Internet Explorer for free with every copy of Windows. The two companies struggled to dominate the market and competed to add features to their Web browsers ("Look! Here's a command to make the text blink on and off! Obnoxiously! How cool is that?") without paying attention to the security holes and bugs that often caused the program or the entire operating system to crash. Chaos, wild swings in stock prices, and antitrust lawsuits ensued.

The early mobile Web designers looked upon this carnage and shuddered. If that kind of Wild West mentality were to take hold on the mobile platform, it could strangle this new medium in the crib.

Broadly speaking, WAP 1.0 sites were all about functionality. The WAP 1.0 protocol was invented when phones had a minimum of buttons to use; trackballs or rocker switches were rare, and touch screens like on the iPhone were barely a gleam in Apple's eye. If you think of the kind of navigation controls you'd find on your ATM screen, well, that's a pretty good approximation of what early mobile Web design and use is like; there's a numbered menu, you press on keys to move up and down or input very basic data. Or you can press a 0–9 button to highlight the choices, and then press another button to select and move to the next screen.

Additionally, a lot of sites that were designed under the restrictions of WAP 1.0 were what are known as "walled gardens," maintained by the wireless carriers. Instead of being able to type a URL into an address bar to access the news site of their choosing, users were restricted to the content that the carriers allowed them to see, usually from content providers that had signed deals with the carrier. So while you'd be able to "Push 3 for Sports News" and get a list of the latest college football scores, you'd never be able to access a smaller, more specialized site like "Mid-Atlantic Hamster Racing Results" that wasn't part of the content mix the carrier figured would appeal to the widest possible demographic.

These days, nearly all mobile phones, even low-end feature phones, are capable of accessing the World Wide Web, and a growing number can display Web sites with complex features, including e-commerce, multimedia, and so much more.

Designing low-end mobile Web sites: Like Mozart forced to play a kazoo

Much of the look and feel of the mobile Web was established before touch screens and was designed to work within the limitations of up/down and forward/back navigation options. Unfortunately, there are still quite a few low-end feature phones on the market with these limitations, and although many of us hope they'll disappear completely in the next few years, it's too early to give up on them completely if you want to reach the broadest audience.

Navigation menus designed for feature phones often look a bit like the color-coded Homeland Security terror-alert charts. Multicolored bars are stacked horizontally; you either highlight the link you want to follow by pressing the buttons (or use a central rocker switch that you can push right/left or up/down) to move around the screen. If the Web designer was smart enough to use Access Keys (covered in Chapter 5), you might also have the option of pressing a number key to trigger the link you want.

Although the touch screens of today's high-end phones are vastly superior, the legacy of these early devices lives on. Thus, if you want to reach the broadest audience on the mobile Web, don't let your iPhone spoil you. Many people on the mobile Web today still suffer with very limited ways of interacting with Web pages.

When you review the statistics from many popular mobile sites today, you find that traffic comes from many different kinds of devices. For example, the Microsoft Cloud Site, featured in the case study in Chapter 6, attracts an audience of relatively high-end users, and not surprisingly, more than 40 percent of the audience views the site on a touch-screen device — iPhone (about 20 percent), iPod (about 10 percent, and nearly 10 percent more arrive via phones that use the Android operating system, which also supports many high-end Web features. After those three devices, however, the numbers drop off sharply and the list of more than 400 devices that represent less than 1 percent of the traffic to the site continues for seven pages of 10-point type, single spaced.

"The long tail is ridiculous when it comes to mobile devices," said Lee Andron, Director of Creative Development for Ansible Mobile, the company that built the Microsoft Cloud site. "We took the top 10 devices visiting across all of Microsoft sites and tested on those. We can assure you the site will look good on those 10 devices, but after that, you can expect diminishing results."

In fairness to Lee and the team at Ansible, the site held up quite well across all the devices we used to test it for this book. That's because Ansible, Interpublic Group's full-service marketing agency, has been developing mobile sites for a long time and clearly understands how to create sites that look great at the high end and still work at the low end. (Read the full case study in Chapter 6.)

If you've only surfed the mobile Web on an iPhone, iPod, Droid, or other high-end mobile device, you probably can't appreciate just how challenging it is to surf the Web on a feature phone.

To help you appreciate what it takes to design a site that works within the limitations, consider how the British Broadcasting Corporation (BBC) created a design that is optimized for the limited navigation options of low-end devices. On a well-designed mobile site like the one created by the BBC (shown in Figure 1-1), this is the kind of user experience you can expect:

Figure 1-1: The BBC's mobile Web site design is easy to navigate, even on a feature phone like the Motorola RAZR shown here.

1. You browse to the mobile version of a site by entering the URL into the device on a number keypad, which means that you have to press most keys multiple times to spell out all the letters in BBC.mobi.

The BBC site is designed with multiple mobile URLs, including `bbc.com/mobile/i` for the iPhone version. But like many well-designed mobile sites, if you enter the main URL (`bbc.com` or `bbc.co.uk`) into a mobile device, the server automatically redirects you to the best version of the site for the phone you're using.

On the main page of the BBC news site, you find the three top stories of the day/hour with tiny images and links, optimized to fit well, even on the 240-pixel-wide screen of the Motorola RAZR V9 shown in Figure 1-1.

2. Scroll down a little further, and you find a few more links with familiar section names, including More News, Sports, World, and Weather.

   Using short words as links and sticking to common, easily recognized terms are good practices on the mobile Web because you need to convey a lot of information in a very small space.

3. Click any section name to summon a submenu with links to a few more items in that category.

4. Clicking those links, in turn, leads you to more links or to the text and photos of each story.

   In this way, a well-designed mobile site guides you to the information you seek quickly because you only need to click links to two or three fast-loading pages to reach your destination.

5. If the story is long, you may have to scroll down a page or two or follow a link to continue reading.

   The amount of text on each screen is limited because scrolling can be challenging on low-end feature phones, such as the RAZR shown in Figure 1-1. On a RAZR, like many feature phones, you can only scroll a few tedious pixels at a time.

6. To move on to another story or another section, you can click the back button on the handset of most phones (even feature phones) to return to the previous list of links or move on if additional navigation links are provided, as they are on the BBC site.

It's good practice to offer at least a few navigation options on any mobile page. As the designer, you must find a delicate balance between enabling a visitor to easily find what they want and overloading each page with so many links that users have to wait a long time to load the content when they get to it.

If the desktop Web is the *information superhighway,* using low-end feature phones, even on sites that are designed for the mobile Web, can feel more like backing out of your garage, driving down your driveway, driving over to your neighbor's driveway, pulling into his garage, and then backing out into the street again, only to pull into yet another narrow driveway — while being at least partially blindfolded.

Mobile alphabet soup

Some handy definitions to keep in mind:

✔ **Feature phone:** An industry term that was originally used to distinguish mobile phones that had such advances as cameras or MP3 players built into them from the first wave of mobile phones that were only capable of sending and receiving calls. The term feature phone is now generally used to describe the simplest, low-end phones on the market, those that lack typewriter-like QWERTY keyboards, large display screens, or other more advanced technologies.

✔ **Smartphone:** When technology companies like Palm and RIM (the official name of the company that makes BlackBerry phones) rolled out devices that brought together the mini-computer functions of PDAs like the Palm Pilot with wireless phone functionality, the industry called them smartphones to differentiate them from the more limited feature phones. While the lines between "smart" and "feature" are blurring, broadly speaking, a smartphone is one with strong computer-like capabilities. It has a color screen, a keyboard that looks like a typewriter, and storage for music or video, and it can run applications or "apps" that allow it to do complicated tasks.

✔ **Touch-screen phone:** The most famous example is the iPhone, but in the years since Apple launched this device, many others with a dizzying array of capabilities have hit the market. Their distinguishing feature is that they have large, high-resolution color screens. Also, you can use your fingers to tap on the screen to type on a virtual keyboard, use two or more fingers to click and drag items or pinch and expand images, or flick your fingers to make Web pages scroll.

✔ **Dumbphone:** An industry term used for mobile phones that look like they have the hardware features of an iPhone, but lack the software to back it. A touch screen without a sophisticated Web browser, like the Safari browser on the iPhone, can be especially misleading because mobile sites designed for touch-screen phones won't work well on these poorly designed knockoffs.

✔ **Mobile Web:** Anything on the World Wide Web that can be viewed on a mobile device.

✔ **Desktop Web:** Used to describe Web pages designed to be viewed in Web browsers, such as Firefox and Internet Explorer, on desktop computers.

✔ **Open Mobile Alliance (OMA):** In June 2002, this international organization formed to develop specifications for the mobile Web. One of the things that distinguishes the OMA is that they bring together representatives from every aspect of the mobile industry, including mobile operators, device and network suppliers, information technology companies, and content and service providers. The goal, according to the OMA Web site, is to create "interoperable mobile data service enablers that work across devices, service providers, operators, networks, and geographies." Essentially, they want to create standards that work across all devices and services, a lofty goal that would definitely make the mobile Web a better place.

✔ **Wireless Access Protocol (WAP):** WAP basically sets down what a mobile Web browsing session is, how the phone is allowed to talk to the network, how the network is allowed to talk back, and how

(continued)

(continued)

that communication is to be kept (reasonably) secure. WAP 1.0, which restricted the mobile Web to very limited technologies, such as WML, has been replaced by WAP 2.0, which supports more advanced technologies, including XHTML.

✔ **Wireless Markup Language (WML):** The first of many programming languages used to design mobile Web pages. Documents in WML are known as *decks,* and the data in each deck is broken down into *cards* (or pages). WML allows information in a Web page to interact with the mobile phone, such as clicking a phone number on a WML page causes the mobile phone functions to wake up, kick in, and call that phone number. (You find more information about WML and other mobile markup languages in Chapter 5.)

✔ **eXtensible Markup Language (XML):** A set of rules governing how documents are encoded, with the goal of allowing documents created by different programs on different platforms to share data (such as Excel on a Mac sharing data with Word on a PC).

✔ **Wireless Universal Resource File (WURFL):** A configuration file that contains information about the capabilities of nearly every mobile device on the planet. You can download the WURFL file for free from `www.SourceForge.net` and use it to help you direct mobile phones to the best version of your site. (You learn more about WURFL and developing for multiple devices in Chapter 6.)

✔ **eXtensible Hypertext Markup Language (XHTML):** This is a stricter standard for HTML, which is the language that Web pages are created in. The goal of XHTML is to organize the chaos of the Web into a stricter set of standards that prevent pages from displaying so differently across browsers. (You find an introduction to XHTML and CSS in Chapter 3.)

✔ **XHTML Mobile Profile (XHTML MP):** A variation of XHTML designed specifically for mobile phones. (You learn more about XHTML MP and other mobile markup languages in Chapter 5.)

Assessing the Current State of the Web

If the early years of the mobile revolution were marked by a kind of bemused dazzlement that had people using early cellphones to call from unusual places ("Hey, I'm standing in the surf on the beach!"), the massive adoption of cellphones since then has made people regard them as essential to their survival. More than 40 percent of Americans have said that "they could not live without" their cellphones; these little devices are integral to life as we know it.

There's only one choice for the device most responsible for taking the mobile Web from the Nerds Only Clubhouse into the popular consciousness. And this device is the elephant in the room in any discussion of the mobile Web.

So here goes: In the mobile Web world, the *iPhone* changed everything. There. We said it.

Understanding the iPhone factor

From the moment Apple CEO Steve Jobs strode out on stage to introduce the iPhone (shown in Figure 1-2), a kind of over-the-top techno-frenzy enveloped the mobile phone industry. Lines of eager Mac fans crawled around city blocks waiting for Apple stores to open and sell iPhones on June 29, 2007. Before iPhones became available outside the United States, enterprising travelers could buy the iPhone for $300 and sell it on the streets of Moscow or Bangkok for $2,000 or more.

Figure 1-2: The iPhone deserves credit for driving the popularity of the mobile Web.

Within weeks of the iPhone's launch, copycat HiPhones appeared in the gray-market stalls all over China. Later models, such as the SciPhone shown in Figure 1-3, adapted Apple's design to the Chinese market, putting in slots for two SIM cards so that the owner could have, in essence, two separate phone lines in his pocket — one for business and one for personal use. The SciPhone costs a fraction of what the iPhone costs; however, like many other phones, dubbed "dumphones" by developers, it suffers from uneven quality.

Although those who style themselves to be true "mobile Web purists" often sneer at the iPhone as being more hype than substance, the iPhone really kick-started the mobile Web revolution into high gear. Apple applied for 200 patents for new technology for the iPhone. Obviously, something was breaking new ground.

Figure 1-3: The SciPhone is just one of many "dumb-phones" designed to look like the iPhone.

Compared to the clunky navigation of early mobile sites, the iPhone creates a new and delightful user experience for mobile content:

- ✔ The multi-touch screen wows people with game-changing interactive features, such as the ability to use pinching or opening motions with your fingers to shrink or enlarge Web pages, photos, and text.

- ✔ Scrolling is a breeze. Zipping your finger down a Web page or a list makes the contents spin past like the wheels in a slot machine.

✔ An accelerometer (a tiny gyroscope) can tell when the phone was moved, and in what direction, so shaking the phone can be used to do things, like randomly changing the song you listen to on the built-in iPod. The accelerometer also determines whether the phone is being held in portrait or landscape mode.

✔ The iPhone doesn't come with a manual. It's so easy to use, that most people learn by just playing around with it and figure out things as they go along.

The iPhone can be credited with a 500 percent increase in traffic to the mobile Web. It was the first mobile device that could display desktop Web pages as well as most desktop computers (except for the inability to play Flash or other rich-media video technologies). According to AdMob, by November 2009, the iPhone and iPod touch accounted for more than 40 percent of mobile data traffic worldwide — this despite the fact that the iPhone still wasn't available in most markets, and even in the United States, it accounted for less than 10 percent of the total phones in use.

Every other month, Apple's competitors roll out a phone that's billed as "the iPhone killer," with about as much success (so far) as the challengers to the iPod in the digital music-player space. If imitation is the sincerest form of flattery, the efforts to replicate Apple's success are almost embarrassingly fawning.

What this means to Web designers is that the other phone manufacturers, who have already copied the touch-screen format of the iPhone, want to replicate its browsing capabilities, in the hopes of draining some of its market share. And, as is inevitable in the technology world, what was once prohibitively expensive quickly becomes affordable — and eventually cheap.

Cellphone technology is a perfect example of this class-to-mass movement because the early "brick" phones (so called because the clunky things were the approximate size, shape, and weight of a brick) that were such rarities in the early '90s and cost a relative fortune have given way to disposable phones that are half the size of a deck of cards and so cheap you can throw them away when you're done with them. Most disposable phones are feature phones with shoddy construction that can be purchased without a service plan.

By 2011, the prediction is that more than half the cellphones in the United States will be the equivalent of *smartphones* — that is, phones that can browse the Web and run stripped-down versions of applications, such as Outlook, Excel, Word, or Apple's App Store.

The siren song of "apps"

Apple's ubiquitous marketing campaigns have ensured that anyone more connected than a Patagonian llama herder has heard of its App Store (www.apple.com/iphone/apps-for-iphone); no matter what you want to do, you hear, "There's an app for that." These commercials promising near-divine powers were even successfully parodied by the tourism board of Nova Scotia, which faked a Web site for its Pomegranate phone that purported to include a video projector, live voice translator, harmonica, coffee maker, and shaving razor (see Figure 1-4 or visit the site at www.pomegranate.com). Although the phone was completely fictitious, it's not hard to image that all these features are in some stage of development in some mobile testing lab even as we write this.

An *app* is a small computer program that runs on your cellphone and causes it to do things that the phone normally can't do. For instance, you can play games, use light versions of software programs (such as Word, Excel, or Photoshop), or use any of the more than 200,000 apps and counting to wow your friends and kill time.

Developers can give away apps for free, hoping to pay for the development cost through advertising, or they can charge for it. One early iPhone app — I Am Rich — cost $1,000 and did . . . nothing. Well, other than serve to prove that you had enough money to be able to waste $1,000 just to brag to other people that you could. Apple quickly killed the application but not before the developer raked in thousands of dollars from status-crazed app buyers.

Figure 1-4:
The Pomegranate phone Web site was created as a publicity stunt by the tourism board of Nova Scotia to show how the phone could brew coffee and even give you a shave.

Pomegranate 🝆 | NS08

Share   Release Date

COFFEE BREWING

Coffee Brewer

Privacy | Terms of Use | Cookies

Still, the media has been alight with stories about 14 year olds making a million dollars in a month from the sale of quirky apps. The iFart prank application made $10,000 a day, and it spawned other apps, such as Pull My Finger, and a long list of updates, including the Rock Band Fart Pack, which features the sounds of Fartwood Mac.

The revenues are no laughing matter. Within the first nine months of opening the App Store, Apple had 1 billion downloads, of which they take a hefty 30 percent cut.

The Android Market (`www.android.com/market`) and BlackBerry App World (`http://na.blackberry.com/eng/services/appworld`) app stores are hot on Apple's heels, and you can expect to hear a lot more about apps for the next year or so as developers chase this brand-new revenue stream.

But already there's backlash against apps; advertising agencies host How to Talk Your Client Out of Wasting Money on an App seminars. More than 200,000 apps are swimming around the App Store, with the number growing exponentially. This means that as the novelty factor wears off, people will realize that they're paying a premium to build what's essentially a Web-based experience that works only on one kind of phone. Similar to software programs that can work only on a Mac or PC, separate apps must be designed for each kind of phone. Thus, if you want to reach a broad audience with an app, you need to create one for the iPhone, another for the BlackBerry, another for Droid, and so on.

If you work the numbers, you quickly realize that it's much more cost-effective to create one Web site than to have an app or apps, even if you design different versions of your Web site for each phone. The bottom line is this: Apps are great for games and other highly complex programs, such as Photoshop for the iPhone, but for just about anything else, you're almost certain to get a better return on investment by creating a mobile version of your Web site.

Seizing the power of geolocation

One of the things that differentiates the mobile environment from the desktop Web is that location sensitivity is increasingly becoming part of the mix. From 2008 to 2009, local searches from mobile phones grew by more than 50 percent, as about 20.7 million users per month started using mobile browsers to find products and services near them. One of the buzz words of 2010 is *geolocation,* used generally to mean the act of assessing a location. It is a promising capability that is making smartphones smarter and more aware of their surroundings.

Now that GPS receivers are becoming as standard in cellphones as cameras are, the business opportunities inherent in local searches are exciting. One of the most persistent examples of what this could mean is the scenario in which a Web-enabled cellphone user walks through a mall, and her phone lights up and shows her special offers from stores nearby. Dozens of mobile consultants have trotted out footage from the movie *Minority Report* where the character played by Tom Cruise walks through a shopping mall and video screens in the shop windows start calling to him by name, telling him about specials tailored to his shopping history, his needs, and other data that is stored in a big database. The mobile consultants like to say that this is a preview of how the stores of the future will send ads, directly to your mobile phone, that use your name and mention that they noticed you were looking at new shoes recently. Groups concerned with consumer privacy and governmental agencies like the FCC have held hearings about the dangers of having companies know who you are, where you've been, who you've been with, and how long you spent with them. All this information is available to mobile carriers, who have solemnly promised that they will safeguard its use.

At this time, leveraging GPS data is a pretty advanced feature, and one that the iPhone, for example, has restricted by allowing only native apps to use this data. However, the much-anticipated HTML5 standards do include a `<location>` tag to take advantage of this function. It is expected that the next few years will see mobile device manufacturers rush to ensure that their products will be able to work with this advanced function.

The ability to add geolocation features is one of the most exciting additions of the latest markup language, HTML5, covered in Chapter 5. But even if you're not pushing the bleeding edge of Web design with the not-yet-fully-supported HTML5 specification, you can take advantage of the fact that most people with mobile devices are on the move, and many have maps in their pockets thanks to the basic features of their phones and Google Maps. In Chapter 2, you discover how even if you only create one simple mobile design, you should make sure to include your address and a link to a Google map.

Offering deals and data with QR codes

In Japan, the mobile advertising models are years ahead of the U.S. market, and they employ sophisticated technologies, such as *Quick Response (QR) codes.* These are 2-D bar codes — you may have seen them on FedEx packages — that look a little bit like a randomized checkerboard. They can contain up to 4,296 characters of information in them. Scan or photograph a QR code and it can launch a browser and navigate to a Web site, add contact information to an address book, or dial a phone number, among many other things. Putting thousands of characters of data or commands into a little picture means that advertisers can add rich detail and interactivity to print ads (you can find QR codes in a growing number of magazines already). In addition to enhancing an advertiser's message, mobile Web designers should take note of QR codes because they can free up users from having to type in complex and lengthy data on the small keypads of mobile devices. You can create your own QR code quickly and easily via free Web sites, such as `http://qrcode.kaywa.com`, shown in Figure 1-5, or Microsoft Tag, which provides similar functions, and is covered in Chapter 10.

Figure 1-5:
Free Web sites like Kaywa.com make it easy to create QR codes, which can deliver a wealth of data when they are scanned or photographed by mobile devices.

To use a QR code, you generally have to download a small application capable of interpreting the data. Then just point your phone's camera at the QR code and the application on the phone reads the code and automatically connects to the Web to unlock special content. Here are a few examples of how people use QR codes around the world:

- In Japan, QR codes are printed on escalator handrails in malls; you can point your phone at any code and get messages and discounts, like an offer for 20 percent off a haircut at a salon a couple of floors up.

- QR codes are huge, literally. In Figure 1-6, you see a QR code that was printed on the side of a skyscraper so you can easily access the Web site of the company that owns the building.

- In San Francisco, restaurants put the QR codes in their windows. Passers-by who are interested in the restaurant can point their phone at the code, click, and then receive reviews of the restaurant, descriptions of the menu, and a link to make a reservation.

Figure 1-6:
This giant
QR codes
makes it
easy for
people to
access the
Web site of
the com-
pany that
owns the
building.

Photo by Nicolas Raoul

✔ In England, Ford organized a mobile campaign to publicize its new Ka car. They printed stickers with QR codes on them, and when users pointed their phone cameras at them, up popped an image of the car on the phone's screen. As the users twisted and turned the phone, the car on the screen rotated and eventually revealed a secret code that led users on a scavenger hunt.

You learn more about QR codes and a similar technology by Microsoft called Tags in Chapter 10.

Watching video anywhere, anytime

The mobile phone has been termed the *third screen,* with television as the first and the computer monitor as the second. Already ads promise seamless experience of movies and TV shows from one screen to another — so that you can start watching a TV show on your big-screen HD monitor at home, walk out the door, keep watching it on your phone, and finish by gazing at the computer screen in your office or on your laptop at a coffee shop.

The growth of video on the mobile phone is something akin to the Loch Ness Monster — long rumored, but it somehow never quite shows up. Until now, that is.

In the last year, the growth in online video has been phenomenal. Forty-five percent of college students now shoot, send, and receive video on their mobile devices, and almost half the videos on Facebook are now coming in from mobile device uploads. This video production used to require $20,000 video cameras, control rooms full of technicians, and fenced-in yards of satellite dishes. Now, you can shoot video with your phone and stream it live to a worldwide audience, from anyplace that has a robust wireless signal.

Researchers measure time spent using media to see how popular various forms of media are with the public. As of 2009, college students spend about 2.5 hours per day watching TV — an amount that might seem low to parents of teenagers. But those same students spend 2.4 hours per day interacting with their mobile phones — texting, calling, surfing the Web, listening to music, watching video, playing games, or using apps.

Designers who want to add video to their sites have two basic choices:

✔ Rely on an online video-hosting site like Vimeo or YouTube that has carefully built up transcoders and detection scripts that allow it to serve up the appropriate format of video to the users' devices.

✔ Customize the video into formats appropriate for the most popular devices that will access the site, and use sophisticated detection scripts to route users to the appropriate version of the video for their devices.

You find more on adding video to your mobile Web designs in Chapter 8.

Appreciating privacy issues

The mobile phone is a very personal medium for each user. For instance, most people don't share their mobile phones, they take them everywhere they go, and their phones become an essential part of their lives. Research shows that users notice that they've left their phone behind in a restaurant or at a friend's house within an hour; in contrast, it usually takes about half a day before they realize that their wallet is missing.

Take a second and think about all the things that a modern cellphone knows about you:

✔ It knows who all your friends are — they're in your phonebook — how often and what time of day you call them, and how long you talk.

✔ If your phone has GPS, your phone knows where you live, where you work, how long your commute is, where you like to go out for lunch, and whose house you go to on weekends to watch football.

- ✔ If you use it to browse the Web, your phone knows what sites you like to visit and where you are when you access them.

- ✔ Like to take photos with your phone? It sees everything you see through the camera lens.

- ✔ If you use your phone to communicate, it knows what kinds of instant messages (IMs) and e-mails you send, and who you send them to.

- ✔ With advanced sensors in phones that allow you to talk via Bluetooth to your cars, your home entertainment systems, and even your shoes, your phone can tell what kind of car you drive, what movies or TV shows you like to watch, and how often you really go to the gym.

- ✔ If you use mobile coupons to shop, it knows your favorite brands and what kind of a discount it takes to make you change your mind and try a new product.

- ✔ If you've used the phone to check on your bank accounts, with the ever-more-popular mobile-banking applications, your phone knows what bank you're with, how much money you have in your accounts, what your passwords are, and what the routing and transfer numbers for your accounts are. Your phone even knows what stocks you follow, where your IRA or 401(k) is, and how involved you are in planning for your retirement.

Just listing all these data points that are trackable and recoverable from your phone should make you take a second look at the possible little snitch in your pocket.

Web designers will find that the next couple years are critical for privacy — the breaches of information security that lead to users' credit card numbers, Social Security numbers, and medical records leaking onto the Web are nothing compared to the damage that can be done with a hacked phone. Because the phone is connected to all kinds of information about you, identity theft is much more devious and harder to counter; it also makes it possible for governments, business rivals, or obsessed ex-spouses to track your every move and intrude on your life — to cyber-stalk you with ruthless efficiency.

Mobile Web designers need to be aware of the tightrope they walk with their users' privacy. While making Web sites as efficient as possible by tailoring them to a user's needs and preferences — time of day, place, situation, behavior and searches, *contextual awareness* (that is, searching for cardinals in a football stadium, in the Vatican, or in a forest) — designers must also ensure that all that information is safeguarded. Abusing your user's trust is the quickest way to get a whole bunch of people mad at you, and quite possibly a whole bunch of lawyers suddenly very interested in suing you.

Mobile Web designers should keep in mind that their users may lose their device or have it stolen, and, in response, they should build sites that don't automatically allow whoever currently has the device to log in to secure sessions without having to input a password. As you design Web sites, make sure you use a secure Web server, and if you collect personal data, include a privacy policy that informs visitors to your site how you may use their data.

Planning for the Future

Futurists, like Ray Kurzweil, have extrapolated the exponential increases in computing power and decreases in size. They predict that in 20 years computers will be as powerful as laptops and the size of blood cells, allowing Olympic athletes to run for 15 minutes without having to take a breath.

Although having a phone hardwired directly into your brain appeals to certain readers of cyberpunk science fiction stories, back in the real world, very few people are likely to want to have prank calls beaming into their frontal lobes at 4 a.m.

That said, the next generation of phones coming out stretches the limits of designers' imaginations. Just consider these examples:

- ✔ **A phone that's also a wristwatch:** Thought up by Japanese phone company NTT DOCOMO. To answer the phone, you snap your fingers and stick your finger in your ear. The sound vibrations are sent via the bones in your wrist and hands, through your fingers, and directly into your eardrum. You talk into your pinkie and hang up by snapping your fingers twice.

- ✔ **A phone with a screen that stretches like stiff Silly Putty:** If you want the image you're looking at to get bigger, you just grab the sides of the phone and pull.

- ✔ **Waterproof phones:** Designers apparently forgot that it's hard to say more than a sentence underwater without choking. Perhaps they're chasing the mermaid market segment.

- ✔ **Perfume dispensers:** The phone shown in Figure 1-7 looks like a melting bar of chocolate, and you can buy a perfume pack that makes it smell like one, too. These are nice in theory. The problem with this convenient design wasn't that women didn't want to be able to re-apply perfume before a hot date, it was that too many users hit the wrong key while texting and accidentally spritzed themselves in the eyes.

Figure 1-7:
NTT
DOCOMO's
F-02B phone
smells as
yummy as it
looks.

✔ **Built-in tasers:** See unfortunate accidents mentioned in the preceding bullet.

✔ **Phones built into the grip of a Glock semiautomatic pistol:** Again, see the earlier bullet.

✔ **A recyclable phone made out of organic components:** The phone was made out of hay sprayed with resins, but it dissolved into green goo when it rained, when users' hands were sweaty, or when it was humid.

✔ **A phone that extended little metal legs and used its camera, GPS, and face-recognition imaging to chase you around when people called:** Thought up by a Japanese company, the design was dropped when users reported epic nightmares of their phone coming to life, only to find that their phone had, in fact, come to life and was hunting them down like the Terminator.

Although no one can predict the future, by keeping up with the latest trends in mobile phone development (we'll let the aforementioned experiments speak for the themselves), you can identify some of the larger trends and extrapolate how these trends may impact what users want to accomplish on the mobile Web and start planning now how best to design sites that take advantage of these new features in the future.

Saving time or money with targeted searches

Even though the mobile Web is still in its infancy, the early adopters are quickly discovering that having a connection to all the information and entertainment on the Internet is changing their behaviors in fundamental ways. For example, people used to have arguments and just throw out facts or ask unanswerable questions. But so many people have taken to just whipping out their Web-enabled phone and looking up the facts on Google that newspaper columnists have written to decry the death of good arguments. Minor points that once formed the foundation for long disputes — say, "Who played 3rd base for the Dodgers in 1937?" — are now no longer the stuff of a good couple rounds of discussion at a sports bar.

Basically, people are turning into a nation of fact-checkers. If you want to know the answer to any question right now, right here, just pull out your phone and check it out.

This becomes especially important when you consider a growing function for the phones — that of price-checker and deal-finder. Indeed, the next big demographic group that marketers and politicians want to focus on is already being dubbed the iPhone mom (the latest in a series of mom-focused marketing campaigns that started with soccer mom). Blessed with both disposable income and purchasing power, the iPhone mom (or dad) stalks the aisles of any supermarket, pulling out a phone and using its bar-code reader to check whether the price on arugula is really a good deal. Enter that information into the Web and consumers are better armed than ever before to find mobile coupons and comparison shop until they save a few more bucks at the cash register.

If people find that the mobile Web can actually save them time and money, that's the strongest possible inducement to adoption. Users will rationalize away the costs of a slightly more expensive data plan as long as they can see the benefits in their daily lives.

Killing time with multimedia

If your site is dedicated to amusing people or has quirky information that helps people while away the time, mobile Web definitely figures large in your future.

All those hours spent waiting in line at the bank, the DMV, or doctors' offices, or for a chronically late friend are no longer exercises in counting the dots on the ceiling tiles or leafing through 10-year-old issues of *Aggregates and Roadbuilding* magazine.

Already, many hairdressers keep their patrons happy by placing a smartphone on the counter next to their stations, right next to the scissors and comb. The patron then can browse the latest celebrity gossip or watch the top-ten college slam-dunks of the week.

One overlooked space is the increasingly sophisticated entertainment systems included in many SUVs and minivans. Currently, most of these systems allow kids in the backseat to watch DVDs or play video games. But a simple connection to a fast wireless data network will allow kids to poke each other on Facebook, update their Twitter feeds, and play a *World of Warcraft* death match with the carload of kids in the adjacent lane.

Meanwhile, as data rates get faster, more and more video is consumed. In 2009, more than 25 percent of cellphone users reported watching video on their devices — much of this is *snacking* videos, or videos less than 5 minutes in duration. These are usually the kinds of things that your friends e-mail you to say, "Can you believe this? It's a roller-skating giraffe!"

With the growth of *Webisodics* (short video programs that appear at regular intervals) on the desktop Web, you can expect to see a rise in soap-opera-type programming for video for the mobile Web as well. Long and involved storylines tracking the trials and tribulations of long-suffering characters who look like they've just run a marathon and are panting for breath are sure to attract a following.

Again, this kind of rich content may be driven by the willingness of the audience to pay a subscription rate for this kind of entertainment on the mobile platform because it offers something worth paying for.

Connecting with people on social networking sites

We doubt you're surprised that the number-one most popular usage of smartphones is for Facebook. Rounding out the top ten are MySpace, Twitter, blogging software such as WordPress, and so on.

Just as the early Internet was dominated by users flocking to bulletin boards to trade insults on dialup modems, share Grateful Dead trivia, or express their inner poet, so too are early mobile Web users participating in the popular social sites in which they connect with their friends.

People naturally want to reach out and connect with others — well, the cellphone already made that possible through its voice services. But the mobile Web makes it more powerful for people to come together to do complex tasks, such as the street protests in Iran after the disputed election in June 2009. The crowds of protesters warned each other through Twitter updates sent from their cellphones where the police were massing and what kinds of violence were being used against them. The cellphone video shots of Neda Agha-Soltan dying in the street made her into an international symbol and martyr.

For mobile designers, this means the power of organic searches is growing. That is, rather than a user typing a query into Google, he asks a question on Twitter or his Facebook profile to see what his friends and social group have to say on the matter.

Word-of-mobile referral is a powerful force that can drive traffic to your Web site. Designers want to make it as easy as possible for users to share the content on their sites via social networking.

Having some kind of community/interactivity functionality in mobile Web sites is as important as ever because users are becoming accustomed to adding their input to what appears in the content.

Because the GPS capabilities of phones are growing, it's not hard to imagine that sites that allow users to see which of their friends are nearby or what other people have said about the restaurant they're about to enter, the park they're about to walk their dog in, or the office they're about to apply for a job in are going to see explosive growth.

Find out more about blogging and social media in mobile Web designs in Chapters 9 and 10, respectively.

Using smartphone functions in unexpected ways

Putting technology into the public's hands has always had unexpected consequences. The human impulse to tinker, modify, soup up, re-imagine, and tear apart can't be denied and will always result in usages that the original designers never could have anticipated. For instance, microwaves were born when scientist Percy Spencer walked past a radar emitter and noticed that the Hershey bar in his pocket melted.

The same kind of exploration is happening now with phones — and the products are as impossible to predict as the lunar rover would have been to Henry Ford. Here are a few examples of people finding novel uses for smartphone technology:

✓ **Medical diagnostics:** Scientists at UCLA recently discovered that when they removed the little glass lens from above the sensor in a cellphone's built-in digital camera, all kinds of exciting possibilities opened. When they put a droplet of blood directly on the sensor, they could then generate a microscopic 3-D image of the blood, showing whether viruses or parasites were present.

Efforts are underway to perfect this application because phones equipped with this functionality will be powerful diagnostic tools in remote areas; doctors in countries with shortages of medical devices could track disease outbreaks in real time and send medicine to head off outbreaks before they turn into pandemics.

It's not hard to foresee a time when your cellphone will constantly monitor your vital signs — like having TV's Dr. House in your pocket, constantly monitoring your heart rate and blood sugar levels, and calling an ambulance for you if you have a heart attack or are knocked unconscious.

- **Paying for goods:** Meanwhile, the money to pay for all these goods and services is also starting to migrate to the mobile platform. In Japan, commuters pay for their subway train rides by swiping their phone over sensors installed above the turnstiles and buy food out of vending machines by waving their phone over the control panel.

    Taxi drivers in Indonesia accept payment via phones and report that they are far happier this way because they're no longer at risk of being mugged for cash.

- **Transferring money to remote areas:** Manual laborers in Africa faced special challenges trying to support their families when they moved from the rural countryside to cities to find jobs. The village they came from didn't have any banks, and the amounts of money they earned weren't enough to open an account anyway. They could take a bus back home, but the ticket would pretty much eat up all their savings. They could pool the money and give it to a courier, but there was always the possibility that he'd disappear with their money or be robbed on the way.

    Under these pressures, they hit on an elegant solution — *sente,* or *sending money via airtime.* The worker buys a prepaid phone card and calls the person in his home village who has the mobile phone kiosk and reads the code on the phone card — usually about 10,000 Ugandan shillings or about $6.

    The owner of the phone verifies that the code works, checks to see that all the minutes are there, and then pays the man's family the money, minus a 10–20 percent charge. It's like an offshore bank account for people without the means to have an offshore bank account.

We don't know what the effects of this kind of radical innovation are going to be, but keeping up with the latest trends will obviously help mobile Web designers adapt their sites to take advantage of these kinds of advances.

The biggest imminent change in the United States is the rollout of 4G data connections to mobile devices. This means that users have Internet connection speeds in excess of 100 megabits per second (Mbps; by means of reference, the average top speed for a business-level cable modem is only about 8 Mbps). Uncompressed HD video requires about 10 Mbps.

Even the most technically savvy mobile analysts pale at the thought of the changes that such connectivity is going to cause. "We don't know what it's going to do, but it's going to be big," said Montes at a meeting of the Online News Association in Los Angeles.

Chapter 2

Designing for the Mobile Web

*1*n Greek mythology, Procrustes was a monster who notoriously forced people to fit in his iron bed. If you were too long, he cut off your feet. If you were too short, he stretched you until your body reached (uncomfortably) from the foot of the bed to the headboard. Today, *procrustean* describes things of different lengths or sizes that are forced to fit an arbitrary standard.

Transcoder is another term that seems inspired by the story of Procrustes. If you don't optimize your Web site for mobile devices, many mobile carriers do so for you through *transcoding,* which is a complex process of reformatting a page layout to make it display better on a mobile device. As you might imagine, the result of this type of automated reformatting often ends up looking like your site was put through the same sort of gruesome manipulations required to make everyone fit in the same iron bed.

If you've picked up this book, we have to assume you're at least considering developing a special version of your site for the mobile Web — the fact that transcoding can lead visitors to a distorted version of your site if you don't is just one of many reasons you're right to take an active role in designing a mobile version of your Web site.

In this chapter, we explore how to make sure your Web site fits well on mobile devices, without cutting off its feet or stretching it to within a pixel of its life. We also cover some of the key considerations in designing for mobile and some important design tips to keep in mind when you delve into the rest of this book.

Avoiding Unpredictable Mobile Designs

A couple of processes unique to the mobile Web work behind the scenes in your Web site code. One is transcoding and the other is the way mobile browsers process (or fail to process) mobile-specific style sheets. Understanding these issues when you begin can help you avoid many headaches down the road. We explain what you need to know in the following sections.

Transcoding: Forcing full-sized Web pages into tiny mobile spaces

If you don't develop a mobile design for your site, you run the risk that transcoders do so for you. *Transcoding* generally involves

- Stripping any video or multimedia.
- Shrinking photos.
- Breaking large Web pages into a series of smaller pages that link together. (These bite-sized pages load better over a low bandwidth connection in a way the carrier deems reasonable.)

 If you have any experience surfing the mobile Web, you probably aren't surprised to find out that this automated repurposing of a page's code provides disappointing results, at best, and embarrassingly terrible, unreadable results, at worst. If you just want to see how a Web page might look in a mobile device, you can enter any URL into Google's transcoder and you'll get a good idea of what the page will look like, even if all you have to test with is a desktop Web browser like the one used in Figures 2-1 and 2-2. In Figure 2-1, you see author Janine Warner's desktop site (`www.jcwarner.com`) in the Firefox Web browser on a Windows computer, and in Figure 2-2, you see the effect of the Google transcoder on the same site when it's automatically reformatted in the browser as it would be for mobile devices.

Keep in mind that transcoding is generally used only when someone uses a very limited mobile device and connects over a low bandwidth service. If you surf with a Wi-Fi network or use a mobile emulator on your desktop computer, you'll probably never see transcoding in action unless you use one of the transcoding services listed below.

If you want to get an idea for how transcoding works, you can enter the URL of any Web site into either of the following tools by replacing *yourdomain. com* with any Web address:

✔ **Google transcoder:** `http.//google.com/gwt/n?u=`
`http://`*yourdomain.com*

✔ **Skweezer:** `http://skweezer.com/s.aspx?q=`
`http://`*yourdomain.com*

Figure 2-1:
The desktop version of author Janine Warner's site looks different from the transcoded version.

Figure 2-2:
The site after the Google transcoder got done with it.

TIP

If you don't want Google or other transcoders to automatically reformat your Web site, you can direct users to an alternate page by including the following link tag in the Head area at the top of the HTML code of any Web page:

```
<link rel="alternate" media="handheld" href="alternate_
         page.html" />
```

Just replace `alternate_page.html` with another page on your site, and Google and most other transcoders direct users to that page instead of transcoding your main page. This tag doesn't automatically redirect all mobile traffic to the mobile version of your site, but it is a simple way to redirect many visitors to your site. You can read more about the options for redirecting traffic and creating multiple versions of your Web site in Chapter 6.

Designing mobile pages with the XHTML Mobile Profile markup language and using the corresponding doctype will also prevent most transcoders from reformatting your pages. You find a review of mobile markup language options and doctypes in Chapter 5.

Creating a mobile CSS file is not enough

If the challenges of designing for the mobile Web simply could be solved by creating a special style sheet for mobile, well, that'd be lovely. Unfortunately, it's not that simple. The rules for Cascading Style Sheets (CSS) include the option to create a mobile version, as well as special style sheets for printing and other uses, so many people who have learned CSS assume this will solve the problem.

In theory, creating a mobile style sheet makes great sense and is the clear winner in terms of efficiency. Because CSS makes separating content from style possible, you should be able to deliver the same page content to both a desktop computer and a mobile phone by simply using a different style sheet. For example, you could create a style sheet for the mobile Web that strips problematic features, such as big background images, and then have a different one that takes advantage of all that the desktop Web has to offer. Because you can link any page to more than one style sheet, you should be able to instruct mobile browsers to use your mobile style sheet instead of the desktop version.

Unfortunately, this approach falls short of the needs of many of the devices on today's mobile Web because:

✔ Many mobile devices don't support CSS at all.

✔ Other mobile devices don't distinguish correctly between the style sheet you create for a mobile device and the one that's used for desktop surfing.

Even in a world where CSS was supported universally (wouldn't that be awesome), consider your visitor's perspective. You're asking a lot of visitors on slow mobile networks to download an HTML page designed for the desktop. Even if you use CSS to hide some things that may not work on a phone, you're still making visitors download more than they need, which can cost your visitors more than wasted time — many pay access fees, a price too high to think you won't lose visitors with this approach.

You can use CSS in your mobile Web page designs; just don't rely on it exclusively. You can read more about when you can use style sheets in mobile Web design in Chapter 5.

Picking a Strategy for Different Devices

If you have the time, expertise, and budget, your best strategy is to design different versions of your Web site, each optimized for the different sizes and capabilities of various devices. Then set up a program on your Web server that detects what type of device each visitor to your site is using and directs them to the page that best serves their device. (You learn more about how device detection scripts work in Chapter 6.)

That doesn't mean you need a different design for every device, which is a good thing because your visitor may be using any 1 of an estimated 8,000 plus kinds of mobile phones and other devices in the world. No, even with this strategy, what most designers do is

1. Create a few categories, or profiles, of devices, based on screen size, JavaScript support, and so on. (More on that in Chapter 6.)

2. Create a few versions of the site optimized for each category, or adapt one version to work on many different devices.

You find out more about this approach to designing for different devices in Chapter 6.

In the sections that follow, we explore the most common approaches to designing for the plethora of devices that access the mobile Web.

Create a simple version of your site

If you want to make sure that the largest number of visitors to your site can at least get the most important information on your site (such as your phone number when they're on their way to your office), create a simplified version of your site designed to work on even low-end mobile devices.

This is the most cost-effective approach (after the do-nothing option), and it's especially important if you have a site that uses a lot of multimedia or is designed in Flash, which doesn't work at all on most mobile phones.

To make your site work, even on the most limited cellphone systems (think, unbelievably low bandwidth and a tiny screen that barely supports images, text, and links), you need to strip down your site to only the most important elements by limiting the home page to

✔ One or two tiny images (if you have any at all)

✔ A little text

✔ A few links

A good example of a very simple mobile site design is Mark Jenkin's Web site at `http://mobilynx.net` (shown in Figure 2-3). Mark, a specialist in mobile devices who helped with some of the testing for this book, designed the mobiLynx site to provide easy access to a directory of links to sites that are optimized for mobile phones. We explore this approach, creating one version of a site that works on most mobile devices, in Chapter 3.

Figure 2-3: This simple Web site design works on a variety of mobile devices.

Design multiple versions

The best mobile Web design strategy is to create more than one version of your Web site, optimized for different devices, and then automatically direct visitors to the best version for their device's screen size and features.

This high-level solution can be achieved by creating two or more completely different designs, each at its own URL, or by creating one design that can be altered on the fly to best serve each device. This increasingly popular approach to mobile Web design is called *content adaptation*.

If you're working for a site that needs to reach a broad audience — especially if you want to serve that audience with interactive features or multimedia — designing multiple versions of your site or using content adaptation is the best strategy for reaching the broadest audience most effectively. If you've guessed that these are also the most complicated options, you're right.

A growing number of large national and international companies have created multiple versions of their sites using content adaptation or separate URLs or both. If you design a site for a big company, such as American Airlines, that has to reach a broad, diverse audience and provide highly interactive features with advanced security and other complex options, you have to create different versions of the site to deliver a good mobile experience.

When you opt to create multiple mobile versions, you can decide how specialized you want those versions to be. Consider the following examples:

- **Broad categories:** Some companies create just three or four versions optimized for each of the main cellphone categories — smartphones, touch phones, and feature phones. (We describe these in more detail in the section "Considering Device Differences," later in this chapter.)

  If you just want to make sure your pages look pretty good to most people, you can generally get away with creating just a few variations that target the main categories of devices. As shown in Figure 2-4, the Geek Squad site — one of the better sites on the mobile Web — delivers the same design to both the iPhone and the Droid, but a different version is sent to the BlackBerry Bold 9700.

- **Specialized profiles:** Some mobile Web developers create as many as a dozen or more profiles for mobile devices based on screen size, multimedia capabilities, and other factors. This level of complexity is generally best managed by doing content adaptation. In this model, designers use dynamic site capabilities to design pages on the fly. For example, as each device is detected and identified, a page is created to match the features of that device. By drawing from a collection of elements in a database, such as images in various sizes and video and audio in different formats, you can generate as many different combinations as you need to suit the devices that are used to visit your site.

Apple iPhone

BlackBerry Bold

Motorola Droid

Figure 2-4:
The Geek
Squad site
on three
devices.

Design one high-end version

Many designers have decided that the only visitors who matter are the ones who've shelled out the money for a high-end phone, such as an iPhone, Droid, Palm Pre, or Windows Mobile device. Before you decide that looking good on smartphones is good enough, understand the arguments for and against this approach:

- **Argument for:** This strategy is based on usage statistics that show most of the people who actively surf the mobile Web today use iPhones, Droids, or other high-end smartphones.

- **Argument against:** The people using low-end devices still far outnumber the people using smartphones. Many people don't surf the Web on low-end mobile phones because most of the Web is unusable on them. As more Web sites are optimized for mobile devices, the world will become more accustomed to finding information when it's needed. If your site is still hard to access on the majority of low-end mobile devices, you'll be left out.

The evidence used to make these cases adds to the confusion. Here's an example: According to the mobile advertising network, AdMob, in April 2010, the iPhone was the device most likely to be used to surf your site, but it still represented only 19 percent of the global traffic to advertising on the mobile Web. That number approaches 30 percent when you add iPod users, and if you lump Droid phones into the mix, many sites now get close to 50 percent of their traffic from high-end phones.

But here's the rub. One of the most striking things about traffic reports to most mobile Web sites today is that the list of devices that represent only 1 or 2 percent of the traffic is really, really long. That means that reaching the high end is relatively easy — design for smartphones and you may take care of as much as 50 percent of your audience — but reaching the low end, effectively, requires a complex strategy that can meet the needs of dozens or even hundreds of different devices, each being used by less than 2 percent of your audience, but combining to represent more than 50 percent of the traffic to most sites today.

Although we don't think designing only for high-end smartphones is the best way for most Web sites to serve the broad mobile audience, if you know that your target market is likely to use a high-end phone, such as an iPhone or Droid, this may be a fine option for your Web site. Sites like Jasper Johal's photography Web site (see Figure 2-5) look great on an iPhone, and because his site is designed to showcase his work to creative directors and other design professionals who might hire him as a photographer, he's not overly concerned about providing an alternative design for people using feature phones or other low-end devices.

Figure 2-5: Jasper Johal's photography Web site looks good on an iPhone and a desktop computer.

Optimizing Mobile Web Site Designs

When you begin thinking about how best to design the mobile version(s) of your Web site, consider the unique challenges of the mobile Web covered in this section.

The key considerations to keep in mind while you design sites for the mobile Web are

- **Urgent need for information:** Many people resort to the mobile Web because they have to, because they're lost or late, or because they really need to know who won the Super Bowl in 1987 to win a bar bet.

- **Limited real estate:** Mobile designs need to fit on small screens.

- **Low bandwidth:** Limit images and text so pages load quickly even at slow connection speeds.

- **Interface limitations:** Create links and other navigation options that are easy to click with a (fat) finger, stylus, or other limited input options.

- **Limited processing power and memory:** Large files and scripts that require fast processors won't display well on most mobile devices.

- **Distracted users:** Navigating road or foot traffic is just one of many distractions that may compete for your users' attention.

- **Time and place:** Don't forget that your users' actions are likely to be affected by where they are, what time of day it is, and even whether it's raining. Make sure to include location-specific information, such as maps, and consider adding geolocation features, such as those included in the new HTML5 specification, covered in Chapter 5.

Designing for small screens

If every mobile phone had the same screen size, we might not have had to write this entire book about mobile Web design. Okay, there are many other considerations, but limited real estate is one of the most important to keep in mind. The chart shown in Figure 2-6 provides a quick reference to many of the shapes and sizes of the screens used to surf the mobile Web today. (There are actually even more, but these are the ones most mobile designers are targeting.) As you can see, there is no standard size for mobile devices.

Creating a single design doesn't work if you want to take best advantage of the real estate available on each screen. Even smartphones that are 320 x 480 can be rotated, so you can't assume that you'll always have 480 pixels of width when a visitor lands on your site. You can find more specific information about the screen sizes of different devices in the section "Considering Device Differences," later in this chapter.

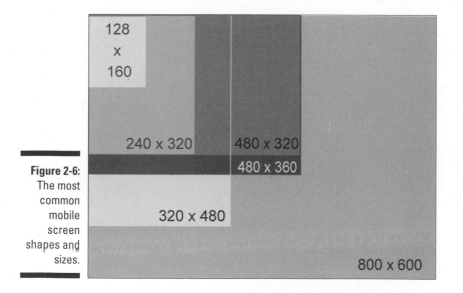

Figure 2-6: The most common mobile screen shapes and sizes.

Sticking to bandwidth limitations

If you've been online long enough to remember the days when modem speeds clocked in at 14.4 or 28.8 Kbps, think back to how frustrating it was to wait . . . and wait . . . for a page to load. Although the 4G network promises great download speeds on mobile devices, too many cellphone users still make their way through the mobile Web at molasses-slow speeds.

When you design for the Web, try to keep the page sizes small (that is, limit the amount of data the entire page contains and what your visitors have to download to access your site):

- **To reach low bandwidth users,** keep pages to no more than 10–25K (yeah, we know that's really, really small).

- **If you know your users have high bandwidth (3G or 4G networks),** you can get away with 150–200K, but that still makes it tough to include very much multimedia on your pages.

Navigating on mobile devices

If you've ever yelled at your computer in frustration knowing that it couldn't understand you anyway, you'll probably be delighted when you can start talking to it rationally instead, especially when it can fully understand you. That's coming to the mobile Web soon, but full voice recognition isn't here yet. In the meantime, keep in mind that mobile visitors to your site may have trouble navigating the links on your site if you don't make them easy to click.

Your mobile visitors are most likely

- Touching the screen
- Tapping the screen with a stylus
- Entering information through a wheel, buttons, or a keypad

That means you need to

- **Make links easy to see and easy to click.** If you design multiple versions of your site, make sure you optimize for the input options on each device. If your visitors use a stylus, they can click links relatively close together, but if they use a touch screen, you need to separate links with enough space between them to make it easier to tap them with a fat fingertip.

- **Limit the total number of links, especially on the low-end version of your site.** Help people move through your site by leading them from one short list of links to the next until they reach the content that best serves them.

- **Organize the levels of links.** Don't include too many levels with your links and consider adding breadcrumbs to help users find their way back through different levels of your site. *Breadcrumbs* are a list of links, usually added to the top of a page, that can help you identify where you are in the structure of a site with links to each section and subsection that appears above the page your are on in the site's structure.

The BBC uses breadcrumbs effectively on its mobile site. In Figure 2-7, you can see the breadcrumbs just below the BBC Sport logo. The links represent each section of the site that the user has navigated through to get to the page. In this example, you can see BBC Home (a link to the home page), BBC Sport (a link to the main page of the sports section), and finally Tennis (a link to the front page of the Tennis section, contained within the sports section).

✔ **Provide a navigation menu instead of a navigation bar.** Although most desktop Web sites include a navigation bar that links to all the main sections of a site at the top of every page, that's generally not the best use of the real estate on a small screen. Instead, consider including one link at the top of every page with a name like Menu, and then link to a navigation bar from that one link.

Including a list of links to all the main pages of your site on every page may not be worth the download time, but creating a small site map and including a link to that page from every other page on the site can provide a similar option. This strategy can also be used to include a list of links at the bottom of each page, with a Menu link at the top that "jumps" visitors down to the links at the bottom. (You find more on creating jump links in Chapter 5.)

✔ **Link from one site version to another.** Always good practice is to include a link on the front page of your mobile site to the desktop version and vice versa. Visitors to your mobile site may already be familiar with your desktop version and prefer to visit that full site, especially if they are using a smartphone, such as an iPhone or Droid.

Breadcrumb navigation

Figure 2-7:
The BBC
mobile site
design leads
visitors
through a
series of
links to find
relevant
content, and
adds bread-
crumbs to
make it easy
to return
to section
fronts.

Considering Device Differences

You're probably catching on that the world of cellphones and other mobile devices lacks standards (technical standards, at least), but it does have some common themes. As you consider how best to design the mobile version(s) of your site, it's helpful to start with at least a general understanding of the kinds of differences common among device categories.

Although some people opt for creating just one simplified version of their site for the mobile Web (a strategy covered in Chapter 3), keep in mind that unless you create multiple versions, you can't really meet the needs of the different kinds of devices on the market. The next sections describe some of the key differences among the most common devices (and device families) in use today. In Chapter 6, you find more information on how to design different versions of your site for different devices.

Apple iPhone: The game changer

Apple, with its "there's an app for that" ad campaign, captured the imagination of people around the world and made surfing the Web on a mobile device more appealing and more satisfying than ever.

Of all the mobile devices on the market, the iPhone (and its siblings the iPad and iPod touch) does the best job displaying desktop Web sites. The iPhone spoils you quickly if you use it to surf the mobile Web. Just keep in mind that not everyone on the planet can afford this fabulous device and that the Web looks far worse on most other mobile devices.

With the release of the iPhone 4 (as shown in Figure 2-8), the iPhone continues to improve, adding two cameras, mobile video conferencing capabilities, and a screen resolution that rivals anything else on the market. (Note: iPhone 4, sometimes mistakenly called the iPhone 4G because Apple called its predecessor the iPhone 3G, refers to the fourth generation of the product, not the speed of the network.) Therefore, if you design only for the iPhone, you have a great advantage. The mobile version of the Safari Web browser aims to display any desktop site as well as a desktop computer (and with the exception of the smaller screen size, it comes pretty darned close).

Specifications for the iPhone and iPad are

- **Screen size:** 320 x 480 pixels (rotates from portrait to landscape automatically)
- **Usable display area:** 320 x 480 pixels

- ✔ **Operating system:** Proprietary iOS

- ✔ **Browser (Safari WebKit):** Supports XHTML Mobile Profile (MP) and CSS2, as well as most of the HTML5 and CSS3 specifications.

- ✔ **Multimedia support:** GIF87, GIF89a, JPEG, PNG, MIDI, MP3, 3GPP, and MP4 (see Chapter 8 for more on multimedia formats and support)

Figure 2-8:
The iPhone deserves credit for generating interest in the mobile Web more than any other device on the market.

Google Android: Catching on fast

Although the iPhone has gotten all the hype in the last few years, Droid phones, which run on the Google Android operating system, started outselling iPhones in the first quarter of 2010 and are likely to continue to do so in the future. Many predict that Google could beat Apple with the Android operating system on the mobile platform in much the same way that Microsoft won on the desktop.

Because Android phones, generally shortened to *Droid,* can be created by many companies, they're cheaper and available on more networks. And although the iPhone has a head start with its famous App Store, the Droid world of apps is catching up, and support for the mobile Web is solid and improving all the time.

The list of phones that offer the Android operating system is growing, and one of the most popular phones today is the Motorola Droid (which can be used horizontally or vertically, and boasts a slide-out keyboard, as shown in Figure 2-9).

Specifications for the Motorola Droid are

- ✔ **Screen size:** 480 x 854 pixels (rotates automatically)
- ✔ **Usable display area:** 320 x 240 pixels
- ✔ **Operating system:** Google Android
- ✔ **Browser:** Supports XHTML MP and CSS2, and supports most of the HTML5 and CSS3 specifications
- ✔ **Multimedia support:** GIF87, GIF89a, JPEG, PNG, MIDI, MP3, 3GPP, and MP4

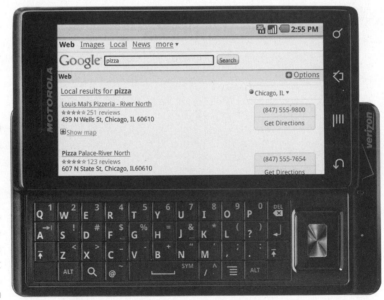

Figure 2-9:
The Motorola Droid can be used horizontally or vertically and boasts a slide-out keyboard.

RIM BlackBerry: So many to choose from

Unlike the iPhone, which is nearly identical from version to version in terms of screen size and support for everything from multimedia to markup language support, the RIM (Research in Motion) BlackBerry varies dramatically from version to version. And so far, there are 87 versions. In fact, many mobile Web designers complain that there are too many kinds of BlackBerry phones to design for them as one category of phone. Worse yet, BlackBerry phones give users many options about what kinds of content they want to view on the mobile Web.

As a result, many sites, such as GameSpot (see Figure 2-10), include a link and instructions for how to optimize a BlackBerry phone to best display its site. You see this link only if you visit GameSpot with a BlackBerry, but it's good practice if you include multimedia, JavaScript, or other high-end features on your pages.

Although we can't give one set of specs for the BlackBerry, we chose the BlackBerry Bold 9700 (as shown in Figure 2-10) as an example.

Specifications for the BlackBerry Bold 9700 are

- **Screen size:** 480 x 360 pixels (rotates automatically)
- **Usable display area:** 460 x 348 pixels
- **Operating system:** Proprietary OS RIM
- **Browser:** Supports XHTML MP and CSS2
- **Multimedia support:** GIF87, GIF89a, JPEG, PNG, MIDI, MP3, 3GPP, and MP4

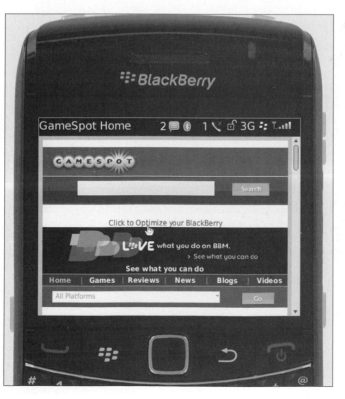

Figure 2-10: The GameSpot Web site includes a link to instructions for how to best optimize a BlackBerry phone when using its highly interactive mobile Web site.

Palm: A great OS with a little audience

Many developers would tell you that the Palm operating system is one of the best, but with such a tiny market share, it seems destined to the same obscurity suffered by so many other superior technologies over the years.

With the recent acquisition by computer giant Hewlett-Packard (HP), the future of Palm is even less certain. Today, 24 mobile devices are in the Palm family, including the Palm Pre, shown in Figure 2-11, but HP reports it won't make any new mobile phones, although it will continue to support the ones sold so far.

Instead, most industry analysts assume HP will use the Palm OS to develop tablet devices like Apple's iPad.

Specifications of the Palm Pre are

- **Screen size:** 320 x 480 pixels
- **Usable display area:** 316 x 480 pixels
- **Operating system:** Palm OS
- **Browser:** Supports XHTML, XHTML MP, and CSS2 and provides limited support for HTML5 and CSS3
- **Multimedia support:** GIF87, JPEG, PNG, MP3, 3GPP, and MP4

Figure 2-11: Many developers consider the Palm OS one of the best, but now that it's owned by HP, its mobile phone days are limited.

Windows Mobile: The Microsoft advantage

With the slew of new devices entering the market, Windows Mobile is getting more and more attention these days.

The number of mobile phones featuring the Windows Mobile operating system (such as the ones shown in Figure 2-12) is increasing, and this OS provides support for limited versions of Internet Explorer, Word, and other popular Microsoft programs.

Phones and other devices that run Windows Mobile generally support XHTML MP and CSS2, as well as audio, video, and JavaScript. Most also have large screen sizes, similar to the iPhone and Droid phones.

Figure 2-12: Expect to see more mobile phones with the Windows Mobile operating system in the future.

The Motorola RAZR and other feature phones

By many estimates, the majority of mobile phone users in the world are still restricted to low-end feature phones, like the Motorola RAZR. Although even these limited phones support XHTML MP, most display little or no CSS, and their low connection speeds can make multimedia nearly impossible to play.

In Chapter 13, we review ten sites we consider well designed for the mobile Web and include screenshots of those sites as shown on an iPhone, a BlackBerry Bold, and a Motorola RAZR. Looking through the figures in Chapter 13 will help you appreciate how limited the display area is on a small RAZR and why you should limit the content of your Web pages to just a few links and one small image when you design for feature phones.

Symbian: The global phenomenon

Outside the United States, the Symbian operating system is one of the most popular on the planet. If you want to reach the global market, you can't ignore the Symbian operating system, estimated to be used by the largest audience worldwide. Although some of the newest phones that run on Symbian offer high-end features and multimedia support, the vast majority of phones that run on Symbian are low-end feature phones.

One of the distinguishing features of high-end Symbian phones is that unlike the iPhone, they support Adobe Flash (at least the mobile version, Flash Lite).

The sheer number of people who use Symbian phones around the globe makes this low-end audience tantalizing because of the potential for volume. Although Short Message Service (SMS), or text messages, may still be the best way to reach most Symbian phones, they're improving in capabilities and increasingly supporting the mobile Web. (You find resources for conducting ad campaigns using SMS in Chapter 11.) We don't include specifications for Symbian phones because, again, they range so dramatically from phone to phone, but if you create a simple mobile site, covered in Chapter 3, you can reach most of this audience just fine.

Finding specifications for nearly any device at DeviceAtlas

We reviewed the specifications of some of the most popular phones in the previous section to give you a general idea of what you're up against and what you can expect visitors to use when they visit your Web site. But this is just a small portion of the kinds of devices on the market. If you want to know about more phones, check out DeviceAtlas at `http://deviceatlas.com`; see Figure 2-13. This Web site is a virtual treasure trove of mobile device data, including a comprehensive guide to the specifications of a wide range of mobile devices in use around the globe.

Figure 2-13: The DeviceAtlas Web site features a comprehensive guide to the specifications of most mobile devices.

Beware of dumbphones

One last word of warning when reviewing mobile phone specifications. *Dumbphone* isn't a term we made up; it's an actual industry term that refers to feature phones dressed up to act like smartphones (with a touch screen, fancy hardware, and so on) without really supporting everything they might appear to support.

Dumbphones almost always have browsers that claim to support Web standards but have such flawed implementations that even the best-designed mobile sites may not display well on them. Don't take it personally. If you run into dumbphones and they don't like your otherwise well-designed pages, send them a low-end version of your site as if they were feature phones.

Making a Mobile Site Search-Engine-Friendly

After you go to all the trouble of making your Web site mobile-friendly, don't forget to make it mobile search-engine-friendly as well. Although many of the same rules of search engine optimization (SEO) apply, you need to understand a few key differences and special additions, as well as a few things you shouldn't do on your mobile site if you want to be included in mobile search engines, such as Google's, as shown in Figure 2-14.

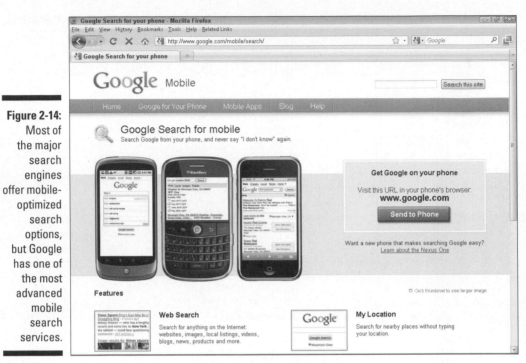

Figure 2-14:
Most of
the major
search
engines
offer mobile-
optimized
search
options,
but Google
has one of
the most
advanced
mobile
search
services.

Here are some do's and don'ts for mobile SEO:

✔ **Do add a meta tag that identifies your site as mobile.** Search engines, such as Google, are much more likely to find your mobile site, and deliver to mobile devices, if you include this piece of code in your pages. Just enter the code below, exactly as it appears, anywhere between the `<head>` and `</head>` tags at the top of your mobile-optimized Web page:

```
<meta name="HandheldFriendly" content="True" />
```

✔ **Do make sure your XHTML code is valid.** This is even more important on the mobile Web than on the desktop Web. Take the time to run your site through online validators, like the ones at the W3C, and make sure you code is up to snuff. (You find more on testing and using code validators in Chapter 7.)

✔ **Do register your mobile site with search engines.** Mobile search engines, such as Yahoo!, shown in Figure 2-15, feature mobile sites, but only if they know that they're there. Make sure to submit your mobile URL. (You find a list of mobile search engines in this book's Cheat sheet; see the inside front cover for details.)

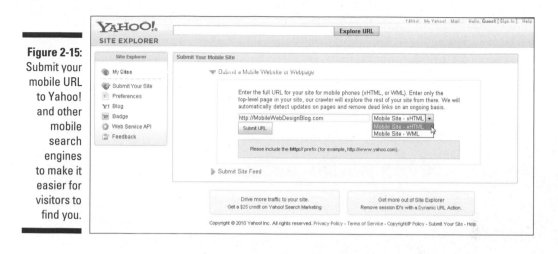

Figure 2-15:
Submit your
mobile URL
to Yahoo!
and other
mobile
search
engines
to make it
easier for
visitors to
find you.

✔ **Don't stuff in extra keywords.** Although keyword stuffing is a popular strategy in the world of SEO, it's increasingly frowned upon by search engines. Plus, it's downright self-sabotaging on the mobile Web where every word counts and adding extra words can cost you in valuable download times.

Part II
Following Mobile Web Standards

The 5th Wave   By Rich Tennant

"Other than this little glitch with the landscape view, I really love my iPhone."

In this part . . .

Designing a Web site that looks good on all the different Web browsers available for computers is a challenge, but creating a site for all the different kinds of mobile devices out there takes this challenge to an entirely new level. That's why in this part, we discuss why Web standards are so important, especially when it comes to mobile Web design. The more you follow standards, the more likely your designs will work well for the wide range of devices in use on the Internet.

Chapter 3

Creating a Simple Mobile Site

In This Chapter

▶ Planning a mobile version of your site

▶ Guiding visitors through your site

▶ Creating a simple mobile page design

*I*magine that you're on your way to a restaurant for a job interview with the coolest company on earth. You're late, and you're lost. You pull over and get out your phone to look for the restaurant's Web site. (You would pull over before trying to type into your phone, right?)

Now think about what you want to find on the restaurant's site. You probably wouldn't want a highly graphical, animated, Flash-based site complete with a virtual tour of the restaurant and a full-color menu. (And that would be a good thing because, at the time of this writing, Flash doesn't work on most mobile phones.) Like most people, you probably want the restaurant's phone number and address as well as a mobile-optimized map and directions. But you'd be surprised how many restaurant Web sites can't deliver these basic, crucial pieces of data to a mobile phone.

If you're creating one version of your site for the mobile Web, the most important lesson is to make sure to design it so that people can get what they need in a format they can quickly understand on their tiny phones. (By the way, in this fantasy, you find the restaurant, nab the perfect parking place, and arrive in plenty of time to impress your new boss and land the job, all because the restaurant hired a smart Web designer.)

Planning a Simple Mobile Design

Will you create multiple versions of your site optimized for different devices? Or have you decided to build a single simplified version of your site for the mobile Web? Either way, this chapter helps you create a simple version of your site that works on most mobile devices — even ones that aren't that smart. If you have the time and budget to create several versions of your site or are designing your mobile site only for the iPhone and other more sophisticated phones, you can get the basics from this chapter and then read other chapters to discover how to create more advanced designs with more complex layout options and technologies.

You can include more content and more complex features on a site designed for a high-end mobile device, such as an iPhone or Droid, than you can for a site designed for a low-end feature phone, such as a RAZR.

Streamlining the content on your pages

All the elements on the first page of your mobile Web site should total no more than 10K to 25K. Yes, 10K to 25K. Some mobile designers think that up to 100K is acceptable. But users of low-bandwidth mobile devices won't wait for such a slow site to load, especially when they're rushing to get somewhere, late for a meeting, or trying to check the site at a traffic light.

When you strip a site to something smaller than 25K, you're limited to only the most essential elements — a little text, a few links, and maybe one or two tiny, highly optimized images. Links offer more bang for the bandwidth hit than anything else you can include on the first page of a mobile site. Because links are just text, they download quickly. Five links on the main page of a simple mobile site work well; more than seven is usually too many.

Making ruthless decisions

If your goal is to design a simple site that works on most mobile phones, the biggest challenge isn't the limitations of the technology; it's the ruthless decisions you have to make about content.

Start by considering what is worth including in your site, from most to least important. Strip the features of your desktop site to the essential elements that are most likely to be important to someone using a mobile device. Think about visitors with an urgent need for what your site offers.

Following are a few guidelines for determining what you need to include on the simplest version of a mobile Web site:

✔ Include a small version of your company logo or a text version of the name of your company.

✔ Provide a way for people to contact you, including an e-mail address and a phone number on the front page, unless you don't take phone calls. (See "Making it easy for people to call," later in this chapter for how to make a phone number easier to dial on a mobile device.)

✔ If people visit your business in person, make sure the address is on the front page, as well as directions and a link to a map (see "Adding links to maps and multimedia," later in this chapter).

✔ Limit your design to one small or two or three tiny images. (See Chapter 8 for more information on using images on mobile devices.) Optimize the images so that they total no more than a few K. (For instructions on optimizing images, see Appendix B.)

✔ Never insert multimedia on the front page. If you feel you need to include a slide show, video, or audio file, link to it from the front page and let your visitors decide whether they want to view multimedia by following the link.

✔ If you don't have the expertise or resources to set up a device detection script to automatically route mobile phones to the best version of your site (covered in Chapter 6), add a link to the mobile version in the top-left corner of your desktop site. Browsers load pages starting from the top left, so including the link in the top-left corner means the link to your mobile site will load before anything else on your page, making it easier for mobile phone users to get to the mobile version faster.

✔ Include a link from your mobile site back to your desktop site. Smartphones display desktop sites reasonably well, and some visitors may prefer to view the site they're familiar with, even if it's a little harder to navigate on a mobile phone.

Guiding visitors through a mobile site

As you're planning what to include on the mobile version of your site, consider the most compelling reason why people would come to your site with their phone. For example, if you own an insurance company, you may be dealing with someone who has nothing left but the cellphone he grabbed as he ran from his burning house.

Including a phone number on the front page is almost always a good idea on a mobile site, but what might your visitors want to find next? How will you help them find the information they need, even if that info takes a while to download or requires advanced interactive features?

If you're an insurance company, the first page might have your contact information and perhaps links to two forms: one for current customers to use to file a claim and another for visitors who want to apply for a new insurance policy.

The first page needs to contain key information that everyone might need, such as your contact information, and then, in a few links, visitors should be able to move on to additional information. You want to guide people as quickly as possible to the information they need, keeping each page as fast-loading as possible.

A good example of a site that helps visitors find what they need quickly on a mobile device is the mobiLynx Web site (www.mobilynx.net), which provides a collection of links to sites optimized for mobile devices. The site was carefully designed by its creator, Mark Jenkins, to help visitors find what they need by organizing sites into categories and providing a series of links so users can find their way quickly to the site, or category of sites, that most interests them.

For example, in Figure 3-1, you can see how in just three links a visitor can get from the front page, to the travel section, to a specific airline. Mark didn't include images on the front page because he wanted it to load quickly, but he does include logos of the specific airlines to make it easy to identify the airline at a glance after visitors have progressed through the site to the airline page — a great example of designing for the distracted.

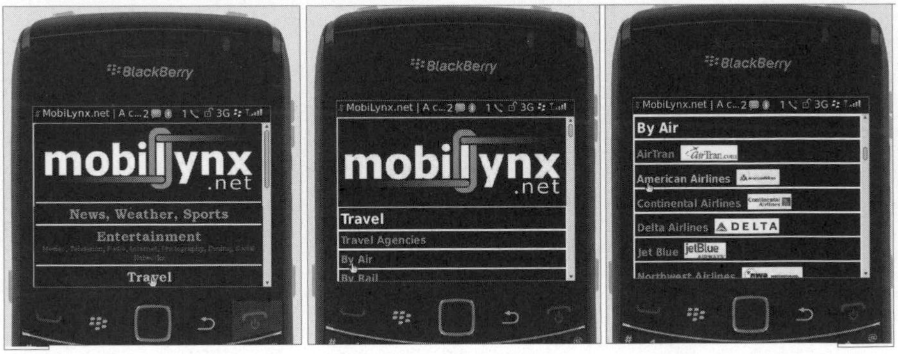

Figure 3-1: On the mobiLynx site, you can find a specific airline in just three clicks.

Creating a Simple Mobile Page Design

At the high end of the mobile Web design spectrum, experienced Web designers often create three or more versions of a Web page, optimized for different mobile devices. To direct visitors, they add a special script that detects each device as it arrives on a site, determines its capabilities, and then delivers a page optimized with the best images, multimedia, and other features for that device. (See Chapter 6 for more on detection scripts and designing for multiple devices.)

Those with a more limited budget, who must settle for one simple Web page, can still include valuable information and even multimedia by linking to Web sites that have already mastered the art of delivering content to mobile devices.

You don't have to do all the design work for your mobile site. By taking advantage of sites that are already optimized for the mobile Web, you can extend the capabilities of even a simple mobile site design. Among our favorite options: Upload a video to YouTube and link to it from your mobile site. Because YouTube has already developed a sophisticated system for delivering video to mobile devices, you don't have to worry about creating multiple versions of each video file — you upload one video to YouTube, and it converts your video into different formats and delivers the best one to each device for you. Similarly, you can link to a map on Google Maps or to directions on MapQuest and rely on the advanced mobile detection and optimization these sites have already invested in developing.

Case study: A simple mobile site for a multimedia company

When we were asked last year to create a Web site for XVIVO, a scientific animation company, we were excited about the challenge of creating a highly interactive multimedia site. XVIVO is well known for its beautiful, award-winning animations and capability to understand and interpret cutting-edge science.

Our biggest challenge after we created the desktop site (shown in Figure 3-2) was to help them create a simpler version that would work on mobile devices. In the sections that follow, you see two versions: a super-simple version and a slightly more complex version that includes CSS.

In addition to making it easy for anyone to find their phone number, address, and directions from nearly any mobile device, the partners at XVIVO wanted to showcase their demo video. The desktop version includes many large, colorful graphics, randomly loaded background images that change while you navigate through the site, and lots of videos in the Flash video format. These multimedia features provide a rich experience on the desktop but are problematic on most mobile devices, which can't display large background images or Flash files.

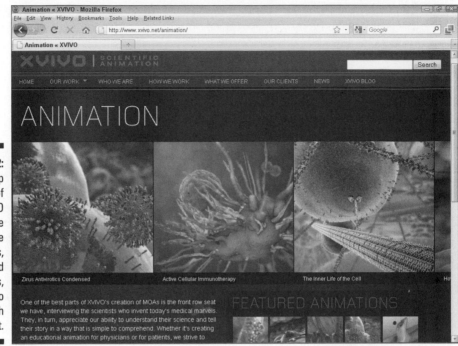

Figure 3-2:
The desktop version of the XVIVO Web site has large graphics, background images, and video in the Flash format.

When you create a mobile version of a complex Web site, the first step is to identify the elements to preserve. In this case, it was clear we'd have to give up the big images and Flash videos, but we still wanted to include some images and video. And like most Web design projects, we had a limited budget and time frame to develop the site. In the simplest version of the site (shown on a Motorola RAZR V9 in Figure 3-3), we used a tiny version of the company's logo, kept one small image to showcase their animation talents, and added a brief text description of the company's services. If you scroll down the page, you quickly find the company's main phone number and address, and a link to a map on Google.

We determined the best way to include their demo video was to upload the video to YouTube and link to it. The advantage of hosting their video on YouTube was that we uploaded one relatively high-resolution version of the video, and YouTube automatically optimized the video for different mobile devices. YouTube uses sophisticated device detection to deliver the best version of the video to each device. That means that two visitors to the XVIVO site using different devices may see a different version of the video when they click the link to view the demo on YouTube. For example, on an older iPhone, you see a more compressed version because YouTube recognizes that the iPhone version 1.0 has much slower download speeds. On an iPhone on the 3G network, you see a higher-quality version of the same demo.

Figure 3-3:
This mobile
version of
the XVIVO
Web site
was created
with simple
XHTML MP
code so it
displays
well even in
the limited
browser
on the
Motorola
RAZR.

We wanted to make it easy for clients and other visitors to find not only a
sampling of the company's work but also their offices, so we included the
address and a link to a Google map, another great third-party service for
including interactive features that work well on mobile devices. To make it
easy to call the phone number on the site, we formatted the number with the
link tag and a special attribute that enables users to simply click the number
to call. (You find detailed instructions for creating all elements featured in
this mobile site in the exercises that follow.)

Figure 3-4 shows how this same page looks when we used CSS to add background and text colors. Using CSS even in very simple mobile site designs
like this works because phones that don't support CSS ignore the style information and display the content formatted with XHTML, as shown in Figure
3-3. But the design looks best on more sophisticated phones, such as the
BlackBerry Bold 9700, as shown in Figure 3-4, which displays the background
color defined in a CSS rule.

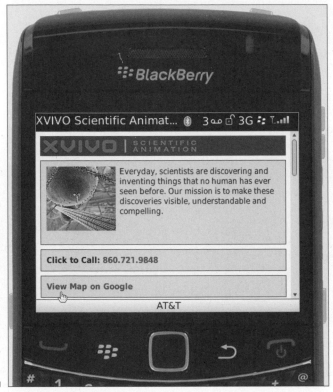

Figure 3-4: This version of the site uses CSS to add background and text colors, which display on the BlackBerry Bold 9700.

Using XHTML MP to create a simple mobile design

If you're creating just one simple mobile page, use XHTML MP (the Mobile Profile of the Hypertext Markup language, covered in detail in Chapter 5). Although there are still a few old, low-end mobile devices that support only WML (Wireless Markup Language), since 2004, the vast majority of mobile phones have supported XHTML MP and CSS2, and many smartphones, including the iPhone, already support HTML5. (You find a review and comparison of the various markup languages for mobile devices in Chapter 5.) As we write this, less than 5 percent of mobile devices in the United States are limited to WML, and studies show that most people with such limited devices don't even try to surf the Web, so we assume you don't need to design for that audience.

If you're still new to Web design and the basics of XHTML, pay special attention to the introduction to working with XHTML and CSS in Chapter 4. If all you want to do is create a simple Web page for your mobile site, the instructions that follow are all you need. If you don't have Dreamweaver, copy the XHTML MP code at the end of this exercise into any text editor and fill in the text and image references with your own content to make the page your own.

In Dreamweaver, follow these steps to create a simple page with XHTML MP that displays well on a variety of mobile devices:

1. **Choose File➪New.**

   The New Document window opens, as shown in Figure 3-5.

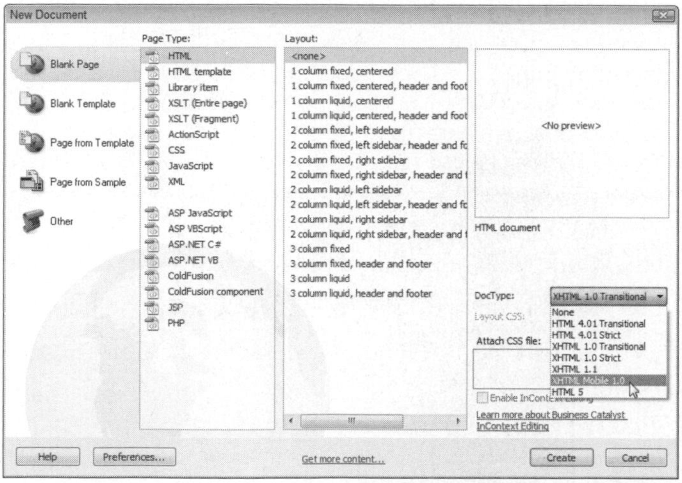

Figure 3-5: Adobe Dreamweaver makes it easy to create and format new Web pages using XHTML Mobile Profile.

2. **In the leftmost column, click the Blank Page tab.**

3. **In the Page Type list, select HTML.**

4. **In the Layout section, select <none>.**

5. **To make the code more mobile-friendly, choose XHTML Mobile 1.0 from the DocType drop-down list, as shown in Figure 3-5.**

   By default, Dreamweaver creates pages using the XHTML Transitional 1.0 doctype, which is the best option for most Web pages. If you're working on a site for the mobile Web, however, change this setting to XHTML Mobile 1.0, and Dreamweaver uses the correct doctype for the mobile Web page. (You find a list of doctype options and their best uses at the end of Chapter 5.)

6. **Click the Create button.**

   The New Document window closes, and a new blank page is created and opens in the workspace.

7. **In the Title field, at the top of the workspace, type a title.**

   Although the title isn't displayed in many mobile Web browsers (including the Motorola RAZR, shown in Figure 3-3), it's still good practice to include a title for mobile phones that do (such as the BlackBerry Bold, shown in Figure 3-4). Title text is also used when a visitor bookmarks a Web page.

8. **Choose File➪Save, navigate to the folder where you want to save the file, enter a name for the page, and click the Save button.**

   It's best to save the mobile version of your site in a subfolder with a name such as mobile, or simply m. Then name your mobile page the same as the main page of your site, such as index.html or index.php, depending on the technology you're using and your server. For example, suppose that you save the page as index.html in a folder named mobile. When you publish the mobile version of your site in its own folder, the address for your site is www.*domainname*.com/mobile. If you can create subdomains on your server, using an address like m.*domainname*.com is an even better option because low-end mobile phones, such as the RAZR, which are limited to a number keypad, make it difficult to enter a slash mark.

9. **Enter text on the page as you would on any other Web page.**

   Simply type to enter text into the main workspace in Dreamweaver.

10. **Format text with basic XHTML tags, such as heading tags, as shown in Figure 3-6.**

    It's good practice to use basic HTML tags, such as the heading tags, to format headlines. Similarly, you should separate images and sections of text with the `<div>` divider tag, `<p>` paragraph tag, or break tag `<br />`.

11. **Choose Insert➪Image and add one or two small images.**

    Use very small, optimized images that load quickly. (For more on the best image options for mobile Web design, see Chapter 8.)

12. **Specify the height and width attributes in the image tag.**

    If you've optimized the image to a small enough size to display well on all devices (220 pixels wide or less), you can safely include the height and width attributes, which Dreamweaver inserts automatically.

    Alternatively, you can use a larger image (320 pixels wide is a good option) and set the width to a percentage so that the image adjusts to the size of the device. In the example shown in Figure 3-7, we changed the width by entering 95% in the W (width) field in the Properties inspector. At this setting, the image will fill 95 percent of the available space in the display area of any mobile browser. You don't need to specify a height.

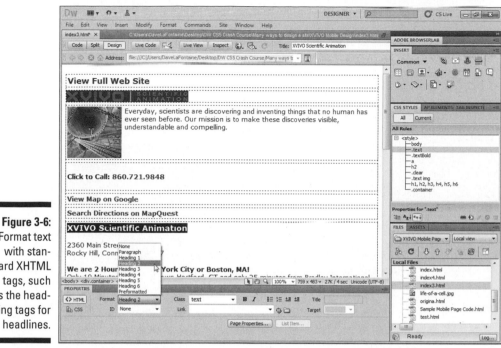

Figure 3-6:
Format text
with stan-
dard XHTML
tags, such
as the head-
ing tags for
headlines.

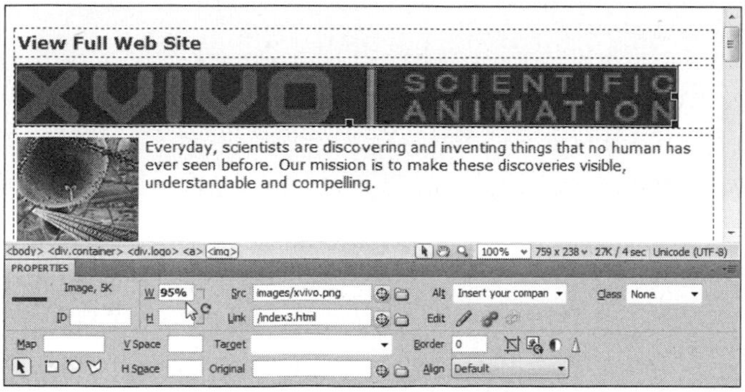

Figure 3-7:
Use a per-
centage for
the image
width so
that the
image auto-
matically
adjusts to
the display
area on
small mobile
devices.

13. Set your links:

   *a. Select an image or a section of text that you want to serve as the link
   and then choose Insert⇨Hyperlink.*

   The Insert Hyperlink dialog box opens.

   *b. In the URL field, enter the address of the page where you want the
   link to open.*

You can create links to other pages on your site or another site. You can also copy the URL to a Google map or a YouTube video and paste it into the Link field.

14. **To indicate that this is a mobile-friendly page, add a meta tag as follows:**

    a. *Choose Insert⇨HTML⇨Head Tags⇨Meta.*

    The Meta dialog box opens.

    b. *Select Name from the Attribute drop-down list.*

    c. *Type* **HandheldFriendly** *in the Value field.*

    d. *Type* **True** *in the Content field.*

    Your screen looks like Figure 3-8.

    e. *Click OK.*

15. **Choose File⇨Preview⇨Device Central and then click any device to view the page in one of the mobile device simulators in Dreamweaver (see Figure 3-9).**

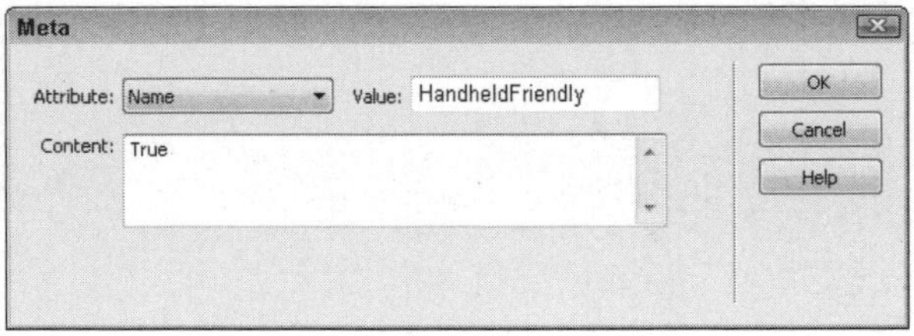

Figure 3-8:
The Handheld-Friendly meta tag tells search engines and others that this page displays well on mobile devices.

If you don't have Device Central, a simple way to test your HTML page is to reduce the size of your browser window to 320 pixels, or even to 240 pixels, to see how the page will display on a small screen.

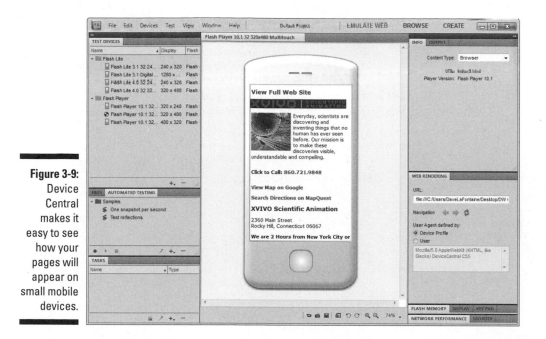

Figure 3-9:
Device
Central
makes it
easy to see
how your
pages will
appear on
small mobile
devices.

The best way to test your mobile page designs is to view them on real mobile devices. Simply reducing the size of a browser window gives you only a general idea of how the page will appear on a small screen, and even mobile simulators, such as the ones included in Adobe Device Central, can't replicate all the limitations of real-world mobile phones working over wireless carriers. Chapter 7 has tips for testing your pages and a list of resources, including more sophisticated mobile simulators than the ones included in Device Central.

Making it easy for people to call

Turning a phone number into a link that activates the dial feature on many mobile phones requires a simple piece of HTML code. The code is similar to what you use to turn an e-mail address into a link that launches an e-mail program and starts a message on your user's computer.

Follow these instructions to make a phone number *hot,* meaning users can click the number on their mobile device to initiate a phone call:

1. **Type the phone number into your Web page.**

2. **Turn the phone number into a link.**

   • If you're using Adobe Dreamweaver, select the phone number, choose Insert⇨Hyperlink, and enter the phone number in the Link field. Add the text **tel:** to the beginning of the number in the Link field, as shown in Figure 3-10. Note that there is no space between *tel:* and the number.

   • If you're using a text editor, type the following:

   ```
   <a href="tel:555-555-5555">555-555-5555</a>
   ```

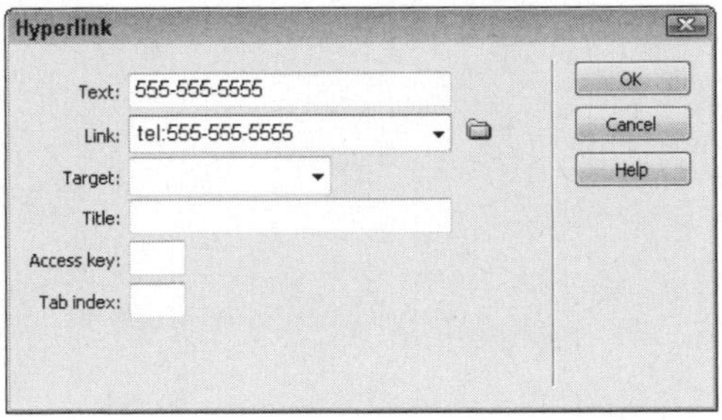

Figure 3-10:
Users can simply click the phone number to initiate a call.

Note that the only thing different from the standard link tag is the addition of *tel:* to make the telephone number active. This is similar to the code for an e-mail link, which uses *mailto:* before an e-mail address to make the e-mail address active.

Writing the XHTML MP code

Following is the XHTML code we created in Dreamweaver in the earlier section for the simplest XVIVO page layout with all the details removed (see Figure 3-11). You can type this code into any text editor or Web design program to create a simple mobile Web page. If you prefer not to do that much typing (or you don't want to risk making typos), go to www.digitalfamily.com/mobile and copy the code from there.

Although we used some CSS in the example shown in the figures in the earlier exercise, we left it out of this code example to keep this code simpler and easier to copy. You don't have to use CSS when designing for the mobile Web, but you have more formatting options in most mobile devices if you use CSS. On our Web site at www.digitalfamily.com/mobile we include both versions of this code, with and without the CSS, for your reference. (See Chapters 4 and 5 for more on designing pages with CSS.)

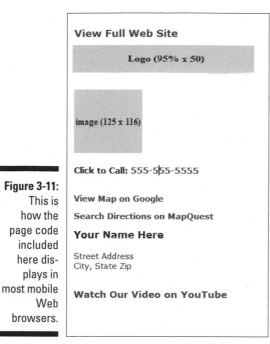

Figure 3-11:
This is how the page code included here displays in most mobile Web browsers.

Note that the text, links, address, and phone number have been altered to remove specific information. To create your own page, simply enter your own details as indicated:

```
<!DOCTYPE html PUBLIC "-//WAPFORUM//DTD XHTML Mobile 1.1//
        EN"
"http://www.openmobilealliance.org/tech/DTD/xhtml-
        mobile11.dtd">
<html xmlns="http://www.w3.org/1999/xhtml">

<head>

    <meta http-equiv="Content-Type" content="text/html;
        charset=utf-8" />

    <meta name="HandheldFriendly" content="True" />

    <title>Enter Title Here</title>

</head>

<body>
```

```
<div><h2><a href="http://www.placeyourfullURLhere.
    com">View Full Web Site</a></h2>
</div>

<div><img src="Enter image name and path here"
    alt="Enter Alternative Text here and change
    the width and height to match your image size"
    width="95%" height="50" /></div>

<div><img src="Enter image name and path here"
    alt="Enter Alternative Text here and change
    the width and height to match your image size"
    width="125" height="116" /></div>

<div><p><strong>Click to Call: <a href="
    tel:555-555-555">555-555-5555</a> </strong> </
    p></div>
    <div><a href="http://www.
    placelinktoGoogleMaphere.com">View Map on
    Google</a></div>
    <div><a href="http://m.mapquest.com/">Search
    Directions on MapQuest</a></div>
    <div>
<h2>Your Name Here</h2>
<p>Street Address<br />
City, State Zip</p>
</div>
<div><h3><a href="http:// www.
    placelinktoyourvideoonYouTubehere.com /">Watch
    Our Video on YouTube</a></h3></div>

</body>
</html>
```

Adding links to maps and multimedia

Even on the simplest mobile sites, you can include far more than just text, images, and links by linking to third-party sites for special features, such as videos and maps.

If your page has an address, include a link to its Google map or a link to MapQuest (www.mapquest.com) for directions so users can find you easily. Otherwise, users have to memorize or write down the address and then navigate to a map site and enter the address because most mobile phones don't allow you to copy and paste or to have more than one open browser window.

Save your users the hassle by simply entering your address into `http://maps.google.com` and then including a link to that page on your site.

You can include video, audio, and other rich multimedia, such as slide shows, through YouTube. YouTube delivers mobile-friendly content to a variety of mobile phones and other devices, and if you link to a video on YouTube, you can be sure that it will be optimized for your user.

Chapter 4

Understanding XHTML and CSS

● ●

In This Chapter

▶ Exploring HTML and XHTML

▶ Understanding mobile Web design and layout options

▶ Styling Web pages with CSS

● ●

Since the early days of the Web, one of the biggest challenges when designing Web pages is making them look good in all the different Web browsers in use on the Internet. The creators of Web browsers and the companies that create software for designing Web pages do not always agree on the same standards. That means that even on desktop computers a page that looks great in Firefox 3 may be unreadable in Internet Explorer 6.0 (widely considered one of the most problematic Web browsers on the Internet).

The mobile Web makes designing Web pages even more complicated because so many different types of cell phones and other devices exist and they use different kinds of software.

Most professional designers agree that the best way to create a Web page is to follow the latest in Web standards and use XHTML (eXtensible Hypertext Markup Language, a strict form of HTML) with CSS (Cascading Style Sheets).

In the next few chapters, we focus on the many versions of XHTML and CSS and why you might use one over another for designing mobile sites. But before we describe the variations that work best for mobile use, it's important to understand the basics of XHTML and CSS.

If you're already an expert in XHTML and CSS design, I recommend that you at least skim this chapter because the basic concepts covered here are the foundation for the more advanced topics that follow.

HTM-What? Exploring HTML and XHTML

Contrary to popular belief, HTML isn't a programming language. Rather, it's a *markup* language: That is, HTML is designed to "mark up" a page, or to provide instructions for how a Web page should look. HTML is written by using *tags,* markup instructions that tell a Web browser how the page should be displayed. For example, to make a section of text italic, you use the HTML tag <em>, which stands for *emphasis.* Most tags in HTML include both an open tag and a close tag, indicated by the forward slash /. Thus, to make the name of this book appear in italics, I would write the code like this:

```
<em>Mobile Web Design For Dummies</em>
```

XHTML is a stricter version of HTML and is the recommended language for Web design today. XHTML differs from HTML in several ways. For example, XHTML must be written in lowercase letters but HTML tags can be written in uppercase or lowercase. Also, XHTML, unlike HTML, requires that all tags include a close tag (more on that later in this chapter). All templates and code examples in this book follow the XHTML standard.

To see what the code behind a Web page looks like in most browsers, choose View➪Source. If you're using Dreamweaver, as shown in Figure 4-1, you can click the Split button (in the upper-left corner of the workspace) to see the code and the design areas of the program at the same time in *split view.*

Split view in Dreamweaver is a useful way to keep an eye on what's going on behind the scenes, and, as a bonus, it can help you learn a lot of XHTML.

Dreamweaver offers three view options:

- ✔ **Code:** In code view, you see only the XHTML and other code.
- ✔ **Split:** In split view, the page is divided so you can see the code in one part of the workspace and a view of the how the page should be displayed in a Web browser in the other part.
- ✔ **Design:** In design view, you see the page as it should appear in a Web browser.

Dreamweaver's split, code, and design views are integrated, so if you select something in design view, such as the headline you see in Figure 4-1, the same text is highlighted in code view, making it easy to find your place in the code.

If at first glance you think that XHTML code looks like hieroglyphics, don't give up too quickly. With just a little experience, you can start to recognize common tags, such as the <h1> (heading 1) tag that was used to format the headline on the page shown in Figure 4-2.

common.css front.css urchin.js snap_shots.js
Code Split Design Live View
Title: DigitalFamily.com | Free tutori
<div·id="dreamweaver">¶
····<h1>Welcome·to·my·Digital·Family</h1>¶
·····<p><img·src=
"Janine-Warner/Janine-Warner-Total-Training.gif"·alt="Janine·
Warner"·width="191"·height="180"·class="fltrt"·/>Hi,·I'm·
Janine·Warner,·author·of·more·than·a·dozen·books·about··the·
Digitalfamily.com
Home Bookstore Videos Dreamweaver Expression Web Free Tutorials
What do you want to learn today?
Welcome to my Digital Family
Hi, I'm Janine Warner, author of more than a dozen books about the Internet and a growing collection of training videos and free tutorials.
On this site, you'll find:
Adobe Dreamweaver
<body> <div#container> <div#mainContent> <div#dreamweaver> <h1>
100% 760 x 331 193K / 28 sec Unicode (UTF-8)

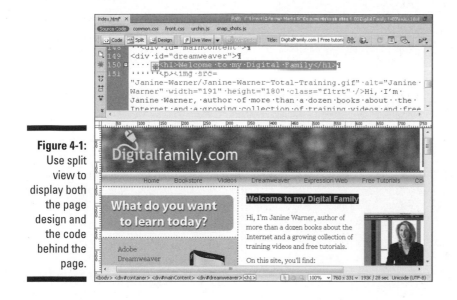

Figure 4-1: Use split view to display both the page design and the code behind the page.

<div·id="dreamweaver">¶
······<h1>Welcome·to·my·Digital·Family</h1>¶
······<p><img·src=
"Janine-Warner/Janine-Warner-Total-Training.gif"·alt="Janine·
Warner"·width="191"·height="180"·class="fltrt"·/>Hi,·I'm·
Janine·Warner,·author·of·more·than·a·dozen·books·about·the·

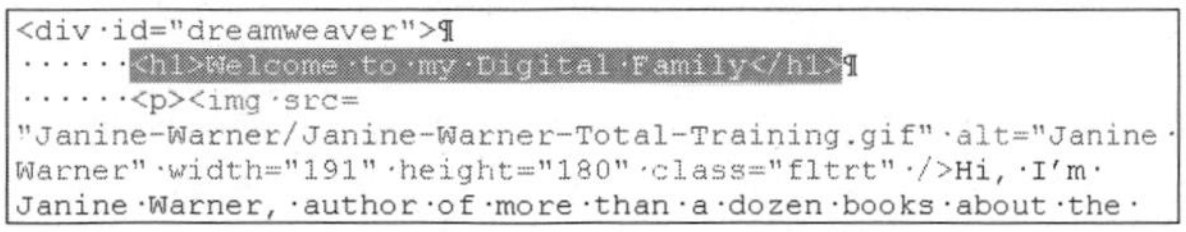

Figure 4-2: A heading 1 tag highlighted in Dreamweaver code view.

To help distinguish the code from the text in a Web page, Dreamweaver displays tags in a contrasting color, usually blue. You can change the size, color, font, and other features of the code in Dreamweaver's preferences.

Following are a few points to help you better understand XHTML:

- **In XHTML, all tags must include the closing slash.** XHTML tags, even those that stand alone such as the `<br />` tag, must have a close tag, and close tags always contain a forward slash (/). For example, the line break tag is `<br>` in HTML, but `<br />` in XHTML.
- **XHTML includes many hierarchical tags.** Examples are the `<h1>` through `<h6>` tags, which are ideally suited to formatting text according to its importance on a Web page. Reserve the `<h1>` tag for the most important text on the page, such as the top headline. `<h2>` is ideal for subheads or secondary headings, `<h3>` for the third level of headings, and so on. A headline formatted with the `<h1>` tag looks like this:

```
<h1>This is a headline</h1>
```

✔ **Some tags are complex, and the open and close tags don't always match.** More complicated tags, such as the tags used to create links or insert images into pages, are more challenging to use because they include link information, and the close tag doesn't always match the open tag. For example, the code to create a link to another Web site looks like this:

```
<a href="http://www.digitalfamily.com">This is a link
        to DigitalFamily.com</a>
```

At its heart, XHTML is just text, and believe it or not, you can write XHTML in a plain-text editor as simple as Notepad, SimpleText, or TextEdit. You have to be careful to type all the code perfectly because there is no room for errors or typos in XHTML. After writing code yourself, even to create a simple page, you're sure to quickly appreciate programs — such as Dreamweaver — that write the code for you.

One of the great advantages of using Dreamweaver is that you can specify formatting by clicking buttons or using menu commands instead of writing the XHTML code. For this and many other reasons, we use Dreamweaver in this book.

Creating Page Designs with HTML Tables

In the early days of Web design, most page layouts on the Web were created with tables. By merging and splitting table cells, and even adding background images, you could create complex Web designs with tables. CSS expands upon this concept by adding many new design options, including the capability to precisely add margins and padding around elements as well as better control over how and where background images appear.

How Web browsers work

Web browsers such as Internet Explorer, Firefox, Safari, and most microbrowsers for cellphones are designed to decipher HTML, XHTML, CSS, AJAX, and other code and display the corresponding text, images, and multimedia on a computer screen. Essentially, browsers read the code in a Web page and interpret how the page should be displayed to visitors.

Unfortunately, because Web browsers are created by different companies and the code they display has evolved dramatically over the years, not all Web browsers display Web pages the same way. Differences in browser display can lead to unpredictable (and often frustrating) results because a page that looks good in one browser may be unreadable in another. Add all the mobile devices on the Web and that challenge only gets worse. Much worse. For more information on testing your mobile page design to make sure it looks good to all your visitors, see Chapter 7.

CSS also enables you to keep formatting information separate from content, making it possible to use less code and create pages with smaller file sizes, which download more quickly. Using CSS also makes pages easier to update because you can streamline formatting changes. You can read more about CSS in the next section, "Designing with Cascading Style Sheets."

Figure 4-3 provides an example of an old-school site created with the HTML `<table>` tag. To help you appreciate how this page was created, I altered the original design to display the table borders. (Most designers turn off table borders to create a cleaner layout.)

If you visit the site at `www.chocolategamerules.com`, you can see how this same page was created using `<div>` tags and CSS. (I explain how `<div>` tags work within CSS in "Designing with Cascading Style Sheets" later in this chapter.)

Although tables are no longer recommended for creating page layouts, they're still considered the best way to format tabular data, like the data in a spreadsheet program. In mobile designs, however, it's important to limit the overall width of tables so that they fit on the smaller mobile screens. For example, you use tables to format a consistent collection of information, such as the photos and scores in the list of winners from the Chocolate Game Rules site shown in Figure 4-4, but when creating a page for the mobile Web, we would recommend you reduce the image size and use narrower columns than those used in the desktop page design.

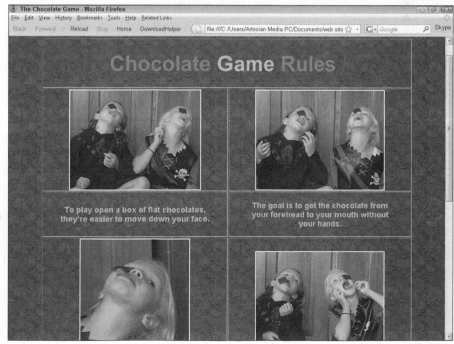

Figure 4-3: In the old days, HTML tables controlled text and image placement.

Don't even think about using HTML frames

Frames enable you to display multiple Web pages in one browser window. When you use frames, the URL at the top of a Web browser doesn't change, even when you click links and change the pages displayed within the frames. As a result, you can only bookmark, or create a link to, the first page of a site that uses frames. Worse yet, frames make it harder for search engines to index a site properly, which can diminish your search engine ranking. On a mobile device, frames are a very bad idea because there just isn't enough room to display multiple pages. For these reasons, we, like most designers, don't like frames.

I understand that many designers still find it easier to create layouts with tables, and not everyone has time to redesign their Web sites right away. However, I recommend using only CSS today for all your Web page layouts, except when you are creating a layout for tabular data. And in those tables, use CSS to add styling, such as background colors or padding.

In mobile Web design it's even more important not to use tables for layout because many mobile devices don't render tables well and tables with more than two rows generally won't fit on the mobile small screens.

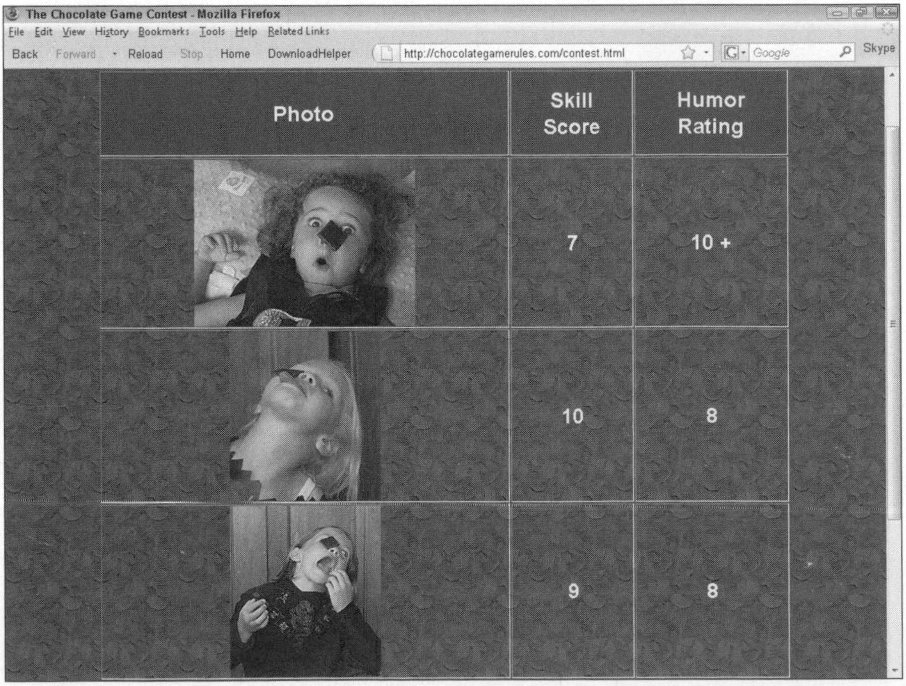

Figure 4-4: Tables are still considered the best way to display tabular data like the rows and columns of information here.

Photo	Skill Score	Humor Rating
	7	10 +
	10	8
	9	8

Designing with Cascading Style Sheets

The concept of creating styles has been around since long before the Web. Desktop publishing programs (such as Adobe InDesign) and word processing programs (such as Microsoft Word) use styles to manage the formatting and editing of text designed to be printed. In a word processor, you can create and save styles for common features, such as headlines and captions. In Desktop publishing and word processing programs, styles are great timesavers because they enable you to combine a collection of formatting options (such as Arial and bold and italic) into one style and then apply all those options at once to any selected text in your document by using only a single style. The advantage is that if you change a style, you can automatically apply the change everywhere you've used that style in a document.

With CSS, you can use style sheets for more than just text formatting. For example, you can use CSS to create styles that align images to the left or right side of a page, add padding around text or images, and change background and link colors. You can also create more than one style sheet for the same page — say, one style sheet that makes your design look good on computers, another for cellphones, and a third for printed pages. For all these reasons (and more), CSS has quickly become the preferred method of designing Web pages among professional Web designers.

Appreciating the advantages of CSS

A Web site designed with CSS separates content from design. Keeping the site content (such as the text and headings) separate from the instructions that tell a browser how the page should look benefits both the designers and your site visitors:

- ✔ **CSS simplifies design changes.** For example, instead of formatting every headline in your site as 24 point Arial bold, you can create a style for the `<h1>` tag that contains all the formatting information and then apply that style to the text in the XHTML file. You save CSS styles in the header section at the very top of an XHTML page or in a separate file that you can attach to multiple XHTML pages. If you decide later that you want your headlines to use the Garamond font rather than Arial, you simply change the style for the `<h1>` tag once.

- ✔ **Separating content from design enables you to create different style sheets for different audiences and devices.** In the future, separating content from design is likely to become even more important as a growing number of people view Web pages on everything from giant, flat-screen monitors to tiny, cellphone screens, as shown in Figure 4-5.

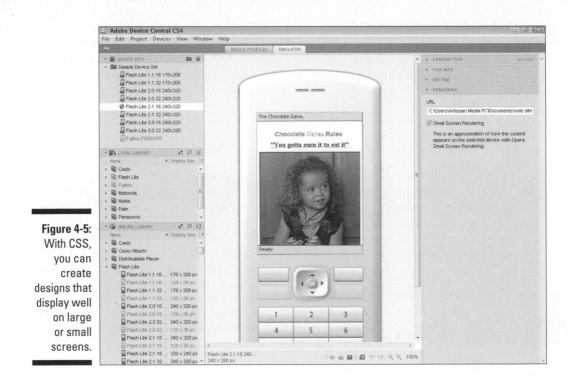

Figure 4-5:
With CSS,
you can
create
designs that
display well
on large
or small
screens.

✔ **Using CSS makes your site comply with the current standards.** Today, the *W3C,* which sets standards for the Internet, recommends using CSS for nearly every aspect of Web design because the best CSS designs are accessible, flexible, and adaptable.

✔ **Pages designed with CSS have cleaner, leaner code.** CSS is a more effi-cient way of designing pages than the HTML attributes we used to use because attributes had to be repeated throughout a page, even when you were adding the same formatting. In contrast, one defined style can be used many times throughout a site. The less code, the faster pages load, which is especially important when you're designing for mobile devices.

✔ **Web sites designed in CSS are accessible to more visitors.** Today, there's a growing movement among some of the best designers in the world to get everyone to follow the same standards, create Web sites with CSS, and make sure they're accessible to everyone.

When Web designers talk about *accessibility,* they mean creating a site that can be accessed by anyone who might visit your pages — including people with limited vision who use special browsers (often called *screen readers*) that read Web pages aloud as well as others who use special-ized browsers for a variety of other reasons.

> If you work for a university, a nonprofit, a government agency, or a similar organization, you may be required to create accessible designs. Even if you're not required to design for accessibility, it's still good to do so because pages that meet accessibility standards also tend to score better in search engines.

Combining CSS and XHTML

Most professional Web designers today recommend creating Web page designs by combining XHTML and CSS. How the two work together can be complicated, but you essentially do the following:

1. Use XHTML to create the structure of a page with tags, such as division <div>, heading (<h1>, <h2>, and so on), and paragraph <p>.

2. Create styles in CSS that specify the size of these elements, where they appear on a page, and a variety of other formatting options.

Similarly, you use XHTML to insert images and create links, and then add styles to change formatting options, such as removing the underline from your links or changing the color that appears when someone rolls a cursor over a link.

Creating page layouts with CSS and XHTML

The key to understanding how CSS works in page layout is to think in terms of designing with a series of infinitely adjustable containers, or *boxes.* This approach to Web design is commonly referred to as the *box model.* First you use HTML tags, such as the <div> tag or <p> tag, to create a box around your content. Then you use CSS to style each box, controlling the position and alignment of each box with attributes and specifying such settings as margins, **padding,** and borders.

Although you can use any XHTML tag as part of your page layout, the <div> tag is used most often to create the boxes for the main sections of a page, such as the banner area, main content area, sidebars, and footer. The <div> tag is like a generic container designed to hold text, images, or other content, or it makes a division on the page that separates one section of content from another. Unlike other XHTML tags, <div> has no inherent formatting features. Unless CSS is applied to a <div> tag, it can seem invisible on a page. However, the tag has a powerful purpose because any content surrounded by opening and closing <div> tags becomes an object (or a box) that can be formatted with CSS. When you create or edit a style that corresponds to a <div> tag ID, you can specify properties such as alignment, border, margin, height, and width to control how the <div> tag is displayed on the page.

In many CSS layouts, each `<div>` has an ID, which corresponds to a style in the style sheet (although you can use Class styles with `<div>` tags, it's common to use ID styles for the main `<div>` tags on the page). The ID appears in the XHTML within the `<div>` tag brackets so that the browser knows which style to use to control the formatting of that `<div>` when it displays the page. For example, all the templates have a `<div>` with the ID `container` that controls the overall size of the design area. In the code, the `<div>` looks like this:

```
<div id="container"></div>
```

In the corresponding style sheet, which you can easily access through the CSS panel in Dreamweaver, you'll find a style called `#container`, which controls the width and other settings for that `<div>`. If this is confusing, don't worry too much at this stage; my main goal here is to introduce you to the general concepts of XHTML and CSS.

You can find many more lessons on how to create, define, and edit CSS styles in *Dreamweaver CS5 For Dummies* (Wiley).

Understanding style selectors

When you create a new style, you need to know which selector to use for which job. You can use four main selector types when designing with CSS. If you're new to working with styles, understanding each selector and its respective restrictions and best uses is a good place to start. The descriptions of each selector in this section can help you understand your options before you move on.

Don't feel you have to memorize this information. Instead, refer to this list of selectors when you create and edit styles later.

Class selectors

The class selector is the most versatile selector option. You can use *class styles* as many times as you want to format any element (from text to images to multimedia on any page in a Web site).

Class style names begin with a period and cannot contain any spaces or special characters (for example, no apostrophes or exclamation points). ***Note:*** Hyphens and dashes are okay. Thus, you could create a style called `caption` for the text that appears after your pictures, but "my cool captions!" would not be a good name for a class style. Here's what a class style named caption should look like:

```
.caption
```

If you choose `class` as the selector type and forget to include a period (dot) at the beginning of the name, Dreamweaver adds one for you. *Note:* Don't include any space between the dot and the style name.

However, when you *apply* a class style to text or another element, the dot doesn't appear in the name when it's added to your HTML code. Thus, if you applied the `.caption` style to a paragraph tag to format the text below an image, it would look like this:

```
<p class="caption">This is a photo of an Egret in
          flight.</p>
```

Class styles must be applied to an element, such as the paragraph tag shown in this example. You can add class tags to elements that are already defined by other styles.

When you create a class style in Dreamweaver, the style is displayed in the CSS Styles panel on the right side of the workspace (shown in Figure 4-6). You can apply class styles by using the CSS drop-down list, also shown in the figure.

Figure 4-6: To create a style with a class selector, use the CSS drop-down list.

A common style is one that aligns images and other elements to the right or left of a page. In all our Web sites, we create two such styles to align images to the right and left of any page and name them `.float-right` and `.float-left`. These styles typically include margin spacing to create a little white space between an image and text when the text wraps around the aligned image (refer to Figure 4-6).

ID selectors

ID styles are the building blocks of most CSS layouts. You should use ID styles only one time per page, making them ideally suited to formatting `<div>` tags and other block-level elements that are used to create distinct sections in a design and appear only once per page.

ID styles must begin with a pound (#) character. Dreamweaver adds # to the beginning of the style name automatically if you forget to include it. As with a class style, don't include a space between # and the style name.

The ID selector option is a new addition to the CSS Rule dialog box in Dreamweaver CS4. (In CS3, you had to choose the Advanced option to create an ID style.) Like class styles, you can name ID styles anything you like as long as you don't use spaces or special characters (hyphens and underscores are okay). An ID style used to identify the sidebar section of a page might look like this:

```
#sidebar
```

The # isn't used in the HTML code when you apply a style to an element, such as a `<div>` tag:

```
<div id="sidebar">Between these tags with the sidebar ID
        style, you would include any headlines, text,
        or other elements in your sidebar.</div>
```

In the predesigned CSS layouts included in Dreamweaver, all the designs are created by combining a series of `<div>` tags with ID styles using names such as `#container`, `#header`, and `#footer` to identify the main sections of the design. Figure 4-7 shows a collection of ID and class styles displayed in the CSS Styles panel.

Tag selectors

The tag selector is used to redefine existing XHTML tags. Select this option if you want to change the appearance of an existing XHTML tag, such as the `<h1>` (heading 1) tag or `<ul>` (unordered list) tag.

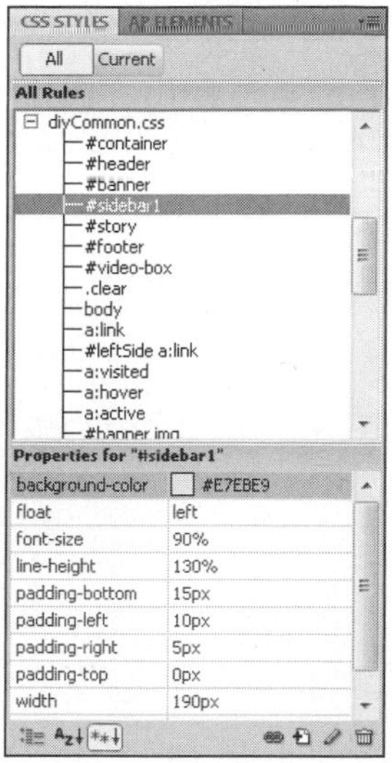

Figure 4-7:
Styles
created
with the ID
selector are
used only
once per
page and
are ideal for
creating a
CSS layout.

Redefining existing XHTML tags with CSS often has advantages over creating new styles. For example, the Web recognizes content formatted with the heading 1 tag as the most important text on the page. For that reason, many search engines give priority to text formatted with the heading 1 tag. Similarly, the hierarchical structure of the <h1>–<h6> tags helps ensure that text formatted with the heading 1 tag will be larger relative to text formatted with the heading 2 tag (and so on), even if visitors to your site change the text size in their Web browser.

Because you can change the appearance of headings and other tags with CSS, you can use common XHTML tags with all of the advantages they offer, while still being able to define the font, size, color, spacing, and other formatting options that you prefer in your Web design. When you use the tag selector to create a new style, the style definition you create for each tag is applied automatically to any text or other element formatted with that tag. For example, if you format a headline with an <h1> tag and then create a new <h1> style, the new style (and its formatting) replaces the original style of the <h1> tag.

When you use Adobe Dreamweaver to create a new style, the New style dialog includes a drop-down list where you can choose a tag selector type. If you choose the tag selected, a long list of XHTML tags appears in a drop-down list in the New CSS Rule dialog box. This list makes it easy to select the tag style you want to create, such as the <h1> tag shown in Figure 4-8.

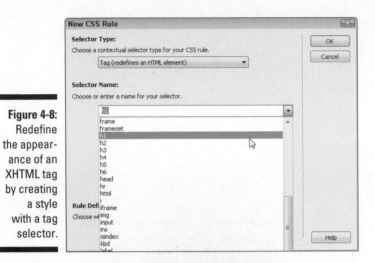

Figure 4-8:
Redefine
the appear-
ance of an
XHTML tag
by creating
a style
with a tag
selector.

Creating compound styles

You use the compound selector to combine two or more style rules. The advantage of compound styles is that you can create style definitions that control the formatting of elements in one part of a page differently from the way they are formatted in another because compound styles only work in places were a defined style is contained within another style. Compound styles are useful when you want to do something like use the heading 1 tag multiple times to format headlines in different ways on the same Web page. For example, you could create one style for headlines that appear in the main story area of a page and another style for headlines that appear in the sidebar on the page but use the heading 1 tag to format both.

To create a compound style, you combine the ID, class, or tag styles. For example:

```
#sidebar1 h1
```

Figure 4-9 shows you how an <h1> style defined within a #sidebar1 ID style looks in the New CSS Rule dialog box. Note that in a compound style, you must include a space between each name or tag in a compound style, and you don't include the brackets around the tag. In this example, the style definition applies only to <h1> tags that appear within another element, such as a <div> tag with an ID style #sidebar1.

If a compound style combines more than one tag, it's written like this:

```
#sidebar1 h1 a:link
```

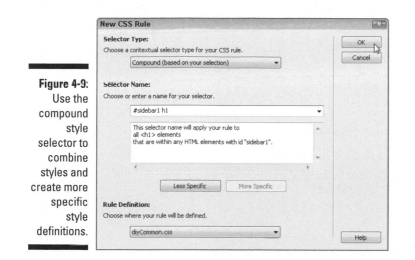

Figure 4-9:
Use the
compound
style
selector to
combine
styles and
create more
specific
style
definitions.

Again, you must include a space between each name or tag. In this example, you see a style that defines the appearance of the active link tag only when the link is located inside an element formatted with the <h1> tag inside an element formatted with the #sidebar1 ID. A compound style like this makes it possible to create links that look different in a headline in the sidebar of a page and in another part of the sidebar.

Here's another example of a compound style that includes styles created with an ID and class selector. This style would specify the way the class style .caption should appear only when it is contained within the <div> tag styled with the ID #sidebar. Note that there is a space between each style name and that the punctuation used in class and ID styles is maintained.

```
#sidebar .caption
```

Understanding rule definition options

In CSS, you have the option of creating internal, external, or inline styles. You can also use a combination of these options, or attach multiple external style sheets to the same Web page. Following is an explanation of these options:

  ✔ **Internal styles:** If you create internal styles, the CSS code is stored in the <head> area at the top of the HTML page you're working on, and the styles can be applied only to the page in which they were created. If you're creating a one-page Web site or creating styles that will be used only on one page, an internal style sheet is fine, but for most sites, external style sheets offer more advantages.

✔ **External styles:** If you save your styles in an external style sheet, they're stored in a separate file with the .css extension. External style sheets can be attached to any or all pages in a Web site in much the same way that you can insert the same image into multiple pages. You can also attach multiple external style sheets to the same page. For example, you can create one style sheet for styles that format text and another for layout styles. You can also create external style sheets for different purposes, such as one for print and one for screen display. One of the biggest advantages of external style sheets is that they make it faster and easier to create new pages, and they make it possible to update styles across many pages at once. ***Note:*** You can attach more than one external style sheet to the same Web page.

✔ **Inline styles:** Inline styles are created in a document where the style is used and applied only to the element it's attached to in the document. These styles are the least useful of the three style sheet options because any changes to the defined style must be made to the code that contains the element, which means you lose many of the benefits of styles, such as the ability to make global updates and create clean, fast-loading code. For example, creating one style for all your headlines and saving it in an external style sheet is more efficient than applying the style formatting options to each headline separately using inline styles.

At the bottom of the New CSS Rule dialog box, shown in Figure 4-10, you find a Rule Definition drop-down list. Use this list to specify where and how you want to save each new style that you define. The options are

✔ **This Document Only:** Create an internal style that can only be used in the open document.

✔ **New Style Sheet file:** Create the new style in an external style sheet and create a new external style sheet simultaneously.

✔ **An existing external style sheet:** Choose any existing external style sheet attached to the page by selecting the name of the style sheet from the Rule Definition drop-down list (see Figure 4-10, in which the existing style sheet named main.css is being selected).

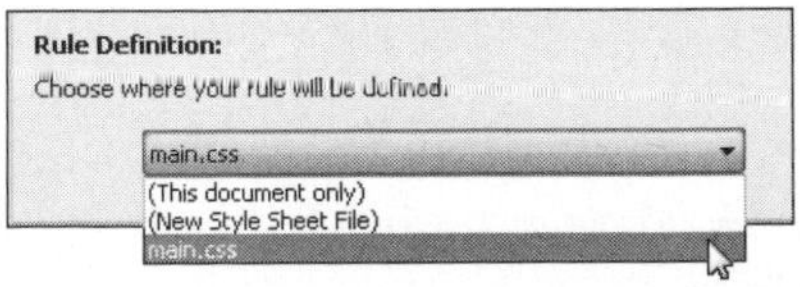

Figure 4-10:
When defining a new CSS rule, save it in an internal or external style sheet.

Why so many fonts?

Although you can specify any font you want for text on your Web pages, you don't have complete control over how that font appears on your visitor's computer because the font you apply is displayed properly only if your visitors have the same font on their hard drives. To help ensure that your text appears as you intend, Dreamweaver includes collections of the most common fonts on Windows and Macintosh computers, grouped in families, such as Arial, Helvetica, sans serif, and Georgia, Times New Roman, Times, and serif.

When you apply a collection of fonts like these to your Web page, the browser displays the formatted text in the first font available in the list. For example, if you choose the Georgia font collection and your visitors have Georgia on their hard drives, they'll see your text in Georgia. If they don't have Georgia, the text will be displayed in the next font on the list — in this case, Times New Roman — if your visitors have that font. If they don't have that font either, the text is displayed in Times; if they don't even have Times (which would be unusual), the browser looks for any serif font. (A *serif* font, such as Times, has little curly things on the edges of letters; *sans serif,* such as Arial, means no curly things.)

You can create your own font collections by selecting the Edit Font List option at the bottom

of the Font-Family drop-down list in the Property inspector or the Type category of the CSS Rule Definition dialog box. Use the plus and minus buttons at the top of the Edit Font List dialog box, shown here, to add or remove a font collection. To add individual fonts to a collection, select the font name from the bottom right of the dialog box and use the double left arrows to add it to a font list. (Use the double right arrows to remove a font from a collection.)

The only way to ensure that text appears in the font you want is to create the text in a graphic in a program, such as Photoshop or Fireworks, and then insert the graphic with the text into your page. That's not a bad option for special text, such as banners or logos, but it's usually not a good option for all your text because graphics take longer to download than text and are harder to update.

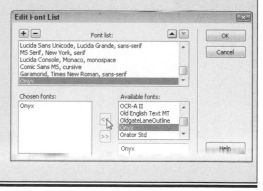

 If you're creating a style that you'll likely want to use on more than one page in your site, save the style to a new or existing external style sheet. If you save a style in an internal style sheet and later decide you want to add it to an external style sheet, you can move the style by dragging the style into the external style sheet list in the CSS Styles panel.

Looking at the code behind the scenes

Even if you *prefer* not to look at the code behind your Web pages, it's helpful to at least have some familiarity with different kinds of tags, CSS, and other code that Dreamweaver creates for you when you design Web pages. The following examples show what the CSS code in an internal or external style sheet looks like in Dreamweaver for the following styles:

✔ An ID style created with the ID selector named `#container` and defined as 960 pixels wide with the left and right margins set to auto (a cool trick for centering a CSS design).

```
#container {
        width: 960px;
        margin-right: auto;
        margin-left: auto;
}
```

✔ A style created with a class selector named `.caption` and defined as Verdana, Arial, Helvetica, sans serif, small, italic, and bold.

```
.caption {
        font-family:  Verdana, Arial, Helvetica, sans-
         serif;
        font-size: small;
        font-style: italic;
        font-weight: bold;
}
```

✔ A style created with a tag selector to redefine the HTML tag `<h1>` as Arial, Helvetica, sans serif, large, and bold. (***Note:*** Because the heading tags already include bold formatting, it's not necessary to include bold in the style definition.)

```
H1 {
        font-family: Arial, Helvetica, sans-serif;
        font-size: large;
}
```

Chapter 5

Comparing Mobile Markup Languages

---

*I*n a recurring story line in the popular *Peanuts* comic strip, Lucy pulls the football away from Charlie Brown, just as he's starting to kick. He ends up on his back every time, and every time he seems surprised. If you've read the comic strip and seen this exchange repeated, you may have trouble imagining how Charlie Brown could keep coming back to the field and falling for Lucy's prank. Unfortunately, many who have been trying to choose the right markup language for mobile Web design are starting to feel a special connection to Charlie Brown.

Although no one is trying to prank you on the mobile Web (at least as far as we know), the number of markup languages that have come and gone and the inconsistent support you'll find among the different devices may make you feel like the ball is getting yanked away just as you are about to kick it through the end zone.

At the risk of leaving you feeling tricked yet again, the best option for most mobile Web designs is the XHTML Mobile Profile (or XHTML MP), and there is growing reason to be optimistic about using HTML5 in the future. Indeed, if you have the luxury of designing multiple sites or you're focusing your efforts only on designing for high-end smartphones, you can go ahead and use HTML5 right away.

In this chapter, we explore the range of mobile design options, from the early days when WML (Wireless Markup Language) was the soup du jour, to a glimpse of what the future and HTML5 have to offer. Although the basic concepts of HTML and CSS, covered in Chapter 4, remain the same on the mobile Web, which version is best to use still depends on the devices for which you're designing. Many mobile designers create more than one version of their mobile Web site, which is why we cover the range of options in this chapter.

Reviewing Markup Languages

To help you keep all the options in markup languages in perspective, we begin with a quick review of how everyone got to where they are today. The World Wide Web was built on good old *HTML,* the Hypertext Markup Language, which was born out of *SGML,* the Standard Generalized Markup Language, which dates all the way back to 1986 — the same year the song, "That's What Friends Are For," sung by Dionne Warwick, Elton John, and Gladys Knight, topped the pop charts. (Yeah, it's nice to have friends to lean on when you're figuring out all this techy stuff.)

XML, eXtensible Markup Language, was also born out of SGML. And if you're starting to think that all these acronyms would make a good skit on SNL (the *Saturday Night Live* comedy show), we'd love to consult with you about script ideas. XML caught on so well that it became a standard for sharing data across all kinds of documents and systems.

The popularity of XML led to the evolution of HTML to XHTML. Essentially, XHTML is a more restrictive subset of SGML, one that can be read better by XML parsers because it follows the rules so strictly. If you can picture the typical "odd couple," HTML is the sloppy roommate, and XHTML keeps the contents of the medicine cabinet in alphabetical order.

You could think of HTML5 as what happens when HMTL grows up, gets a job, and has to start wearing socks, at least most of the time. HTML5 is not as strict as XHTML (slobs never clean up completely), but it has some grown-up features, such as better ways of presenting multimedia and location aware-ness, which make it especially exciting in the mobile world.

This five-minute version of the history of XHTML, however, is only part of the story of how people got to where they are today. In what many now consider a misguided effort, the makers of the first mobile Web browsers created another markup language, WML. Perhaps an understandable reaction to the limited options of early feature phones, WML is quickly being discarded today.

And while we're introducing acronyms, we should note that *Wireless Application Protocol (WAP)* describes everything related to the mobile Web. WAP 1.0 represents the earliest attempts at mobile Web design, including sites created with WML.

When the mobile Web evolved to WAP 2.0 in 2002, most mobile devices could display pages designed in *XHTML Basic* (a subset of XHTML that has no support for CSS). Since 2004, most phones can handle XHTML MP, which supports CSS2 (at least mostly).

C-HTML is yet another mobile markup language you may run into on the Web. C-HTML was designed to be used on NTT DOCOMO's phones in Japan, but most mobile designers in Japan now predict that the iPhone's growing popularity in Japan means C-HTML will eventually be replaced by XHTML MP.

If your head is spinning from all these acronyms, don't worry. What follows are more detailed descriptions of the markup languages you're most likely to need for your mobile designs. You also find a few tips to help you manage the transition from WML to XHMTL MP to HTML5.

The good news is that all the code designed for the mobile world is based on good old HTML. So if you have a background in HTML, you're off to a great start.

Comparing WML and XHTML MP

The limitations of the early mobile Web led to the creation of WML and then XHTML MP. Both WML and XHTML MP are more limited than XHTML, but they also add new capabilities specific to mobile design. What can be confusing is that WML and XHTML don't follow the same rules, so if you've been working with WML, update to XHTML MP, which we cover in the next section.

Here's an example. XHTML MP includes attributes, such as `tel:`, which is a great little addition to the `link` tag that turns a phone number into a link that you can click to dial automatically. Here's what the code looks like in XHTML MP:

```
<a href="tel:+1-555-555-5555">+1-555-555-5555</a>
```

But WML, which came before XHTML MP, has its own code for turning a phone number into a link. In WML, the code for a phone number that can be dialed automatically looks like this:

```
<a href="wtai//wp/mc;+1-555-555-5555">+1-555-555-5555</a>
```

Today, only really old mobile devices are more likely to support the WML option: `wtai`. Newer phones (those made after 2002) all support XHTML MP. Unless you design for populations likely to be using very old or recycled phones, most mobile designers agree that XHTML MP is the best choice.

In the sections that follow, we explore some of the differences between these markup languages and which tags are specific to each. At the end of this chapter, you find instructions for adding the correct doctype to your code so that browsers know how to render your pages.

In Chapter 6, you discover more about designing multiple versions of a mobile site and how to deliver the right version to each device.

Replacing WML with XHTML MP

WML was introduced in the late '90s, so it's really old in Web years. Early mobile sites were designed with WML, but spending much time on WML today seems about as important as going back to HTML 1.0. Some devices still support WML, but the few that support *only* WML are becoming obsolete, and every mobile designer we've spoken to agrees that WML has no future.

Replacing WML with XHTML MP offers many advantages, including the following:

- You can use CSS when you use XHTML MP, which makes it possible to separate content from design and create mobile pages with many of the same advanced design features of today's desktop sites.

- Desktop sites designed in XHTML and CSS can be converted to mobile site designs in XHTML MP with minimal changes.

- You can use the same software to develop desktop and mobile sites. (Dreamweaver is our top choice for all Web design, but you can also use Microsoft Expression Web or any other programs that support XHTML and CSS.)

- If you already know XHTML and CSS, you can develop mobile sites right away because designing pages with XHTML MP is similar.

- You can use desktop Web browsers to view mobile sites designed in XHTML MP, a handy way to test while you're developing — just make sure you test using emulators and real mobile devices before launch (see Chapter 7 for more on testing).

Working with XHTML MP instead of WML has many clear advantages but also some tradeoffs. In addition, some mobile developers miss the mobile-specific features in WML.

Table 5-1 lists some of the most important WML features that aren't supported in XHTML MP as well as the closest equivalent you can use as an alternative.

For a detailed comparison of supported tags in XHTML Basic, XHTML MP, and XHTML Strict, visit the W3C Mobile Web Initiative site at www.w3.org/2007/09/dtd-comparison.html.

Table 5-1	Comparing WML and XHTML MP
WML Feature Not Supported in XHTML MP	*XHTML MP Alternative*
Decks and cards	Use anchors and jump links for a similar effect.
Timers	Use the HTML refresh tag to load a new page after a specified time period.
Events	WML supported four events: ontimer, onenterbackward, onenterforward, and onpick. The HTML refresh tag can replace ontimer, but XHTML MP has no equivalent for the other events.
Variables	XHTML MP does not support variables, but you can do similar processing on the server.
Client-side scripting	You can use server-side scripting or JavaScript on devices that support it.
Programmable softkeys	You can use access keys, described later in this chapter.
<u> tag	Most Web designers avoid the <u> (underline) tag because underlining should be restricted to use with links. If you need to underline text, you can create a CSS text decoration rule.
Posting data using anchor links	Use the submit button to post form data.

Following the rules of XHTML MP

As mentioned, if you already have a background in XHTML, XHTML MP is relatively easy to figure out. (We include a crash course in XHTML and CSS in Chapter 4.) Mostly, you just need to subtract a few tags that aren't allowed in XHTML MP (we provide a list of those tags at the end of this section) and add a few new options that are useful on the mobile Web, such as the tel attribute described in the section, "Comparing WML and XHTML MP," earlier in this chapter.

When you develop pages with XHTML MP, you must follow the rules to the letter. Mobile Web browsers are even more unforgiving about errors in code than most desktop Web browsers. Even a simple omission, such as a missing close tag or a misspelled tag name, can cause a mobile browser to reject your page.

In the sections that follow, we describe some of the most important rules of XHTML MP.

Don't include comments and empty spaces

Most Web designers don't worry about including extra spaces in XHTML code because blank spaces and line breaks aren't displayed in Web browsers (mobile or desktop), unless you use the <p> (paragraph) or
 (break) tag.

Similarly, you can create comments in XHTML MP just as you would in any other XHTML document. However, in XHTML, never include double dashes within the body of a comment, only at the beginning and end. Here's an example of a properly formatted comment:

```
<!-- You can add notes to your code by using the comment
          tag in XHTML MP -->
```

Although spaces and comments aren't displayed in mobile browsers, the memory they require adds up. Every byte counts on the mobile Web, where you often want to keep page sizes 7K to 25K. Use extra spaces and comments sparingly in XHTML MP or strip them before publishing your pages to the server.

Set links with the anchor tag, but don't target links

Links work nearly the same in XHTML MP as in XHTML, but you can't use the target attribute in XHTML MP to open a link in a new window or tab because most mobile devices don't support tabbed browsing. You can, however, use the anchor tag (also called a jump link) to link to elements within the same page, an increasingly popular option for managing navigation in a limited space. For example, in the Microsoft Cloud site, shown in Figure 5-1, the Menu button at the top of the page links to the navigation options at the bottom.

Figure 5-1: Using the anchor tag, you can create links to elements on the same page.

If you generally use a touch phone, jump links may seem an unnecessary extra because it's so easy to scroll by sliding your finger down the screen. Feature phones, however, can scroll only a few pixels at a time, so jump links make navigation less tedious.

The following example is the markup for a page that has a link from the Menu button at the top of the page (<a href="#menu">) to the anchor at the beginning of the list of links (<a id="menu">). At the bottom of the page, the link labeled Back to top returns the user to the anchor at the top of the page <a id="top">. Here's how the code looks:

```
<p><a id="top"><h1>Our Company Logo</h1><a
        href="#menu">Menu:</a></p>Page content would
        go here, but remember, don't make your mobile
        pages too long.
<a id="menu">
    <ul>
      <li><a href="/mainpage.html">Menu Link 1</a></li>
      <li><a href="/secondpage.html ">Menu Link 2</a></li>
      <li><a href="/thirdpage.html">Menu Link 3</a></li>
    </ul>
    <p><a href="#top">Back to top</a></p>
```

Add access keys to links

Access keys make it possible to activate a link by pressing a key on a keyboard instead of clicking the link with a mouse and are generally used in desktop Web design to make a site more accessible for people with disabilities.

In XHTML MP, you can add access keys matched to the numbers on a phone pad or keyboard. Numbered shortcuts can be associated with links, so instead of clicking an image or a block of text, users can simply press a numbered key (1–9) to activate a link.

Following is an example of an `accesskey` attribute added to link code. The basic link tag is `<a href>`. By adding the `accesskey="1"` attribute, users can click the text of the link or enter the number 1 to trigger the link:

```
<a accesskey="1" href="chapter1.xhtml">Chapter 1</a><br />
<a accesskey="2" href="chapter2.xhtml">Chapter 2</a><br />
<a accesskey="3" href="chapter3.xhtml">Chapter 3</a><br />
```

Close all tags

Closing all tags is a rule that applies to all XHTML, but it's especially important that you follow the rules when you create mobile Web sites because mobile Web browsers are even less forgiving of code errors. If you start a paragraph with a `<p>` tag, for example, make sure you end it with a close `</p>` tag. If you use one of the few tags that doesn't include a close tag, such as the image tag, include a space and a forward slash at the end of the tag, like this:

```
<img src="/images/logo.jpg" />
```

Lowercase all tags and attributes

As with XHTML, all code should be lowercase in XHTML MP. Similarly, all attributes must be enclosed in quote marks. Here's an example of correct XHTML MP code to create a link (note that it's okay to use capital letters in the URL in the text that serves as the link and is displayed in the page):

```
<a href="http://www.digitalfamily.com">http://www.DigitalFamily.com</a>
```

Tags must be nested properly

Nesting refers to the order of tags, and getting this order wrong can cause problems in Web browsers.

The following nesting is correct:

```
<p><strong>A bold paragraph</strong></p>
```

Do not use this type of nesting:

```
<strong><p>A bold paragraph</strong></p>
```

Use heading tags, but don't expect six levels of formatting

The heading tags, which include the <h1> through <h6> tags, are the best choice for formatting headlines on any Web page. Stick with the <h1> tag for the most important headline, <h2> for the next most important, and so on. However, not all mobile devices support enough different text sizes to distinguish all six levels of heading tags. For best results, stick with heading tags 1–3; heading tags 3 through 6 are likely to display in the same size on most mobile devices.

Style text with CSS, not attributes

Attributes such as font face and font size aren't recommended in XHTML and are not supported by mobile devices. You can use the <small> and <big> tags in XHTML MP, but our best recommendation is to use CSS for formatting because you can create cleaner code that better follows modern Web standards.

Format lists with the ordered and unordered list tags

It's good practice to use list tags for lists of links and other items because the list tags, like the heading tags, are well recognized HTML tags and add additional meaning to your page code. XHTML MP supports both the *unordered* <ul> list tag, which creates a bulleted list, and the *ordered* <ol> list tag, which creates a numbered list. In XHTML, you must include a close tag for the list item (<li>) tag, even though doing so was not necessary in earlier versions of HTML.

The only attribute of the list tags that is supported is start, which can be used to specify the number to use to begin an ordered list. For example, <ol start="5"> starts an ordered list with the number 5. To change the style of the bullets in an unordered list, you need to use CSS.

Avoid tables or only use small, simple tables

Many feature phones don't support the <table> tag, so if you're designing for the low-end market, you may want to avoid them. That said, XHTML MP does include the <table> tag, and tables will work on many mobile devices. Where supported, you can include the <tr> (table row), <th> (table header), <td> (table data), and <caption> tags within open and close <table> tags. The colspan and rowspan attributes can be used with the <th> and <td> tags, but none of the other table attributes, such as cell padding, are supported.

If you want to add padding, spacing, or a border, use CSS because table attributes aren't supported. Also keep in mind that setting a table width can be problematic, especially if it exceeds the available space on a small mobile screen. Many mobile devices aren't wide enough to display a table and its contents, especially if it has more than two or three columns.

Don't use tables to create page designs. Tables should be used only for tabular data (such as the contents of a spreadsheet); you shouldn't cram too much content into table cells. On some devices, table cells that don't fit in the display area are reformatted to display vertically in a narrow cell, instead of horizontally, making the text hard to
r
e
a
d.

Separate content with the div and paragraph tags

As on a desktop site, the best way to separate content on a mobile site is to use block-level tags, such as the `<div>` (divider) tag or the `<p>` (paragraph) tag, especially if you want to use CSS to format that content. You can also use the `<span>` tag to assign a style to text that appears in line with, or within, a paragraph or other block element.

Use HTML entities for special characters

You can add a copyright symbol to your mobile Web pages, but make sure you use the HTML entity `&copy;` and not the © symbol. Similarly, you need HTML entities for accents and other foreign language characters.

In Dreamweaver, you can insert HTML entities by choosing Insert➪HTML➪ Special Characters, and then selecting the character you want to add to your page. (Select Other to find a more extensive list of options.)

You can find a comprehensive list of entities on the Digital Family Web site at `www.digitalfamily.com/dreamweaver/special-characters.html`.

Insert images with the image tag and add Alt text

The image tag is supported by nearly all mobile devices, and most devices display PNG, GIF, and JPEG images. Some mobile devices even support animated GIFs. Make sure to include the Alt attribute so that your alternative text is shown if the image is not displayed. Also include the height and width of each image so browsers can load the page more efficiently.

```
<img src="logo.gif" alt="Company Logo" height="55"
        width="120" />
```

Add multimedia with the object or param tags

You can link to multimedia files, including audio and video files, just as you link to any other files using the hyperlink tag <a href>. You can also insert multimedia directly into a mobile Web page using the <object> and <param> tags, which are supported in XHTML MP. The biggest challenge with multimedia is that support for audio and video formats varies dramatically among devices. See Chapter 8 for instructions on adding multimedia to a mobile Web page.

Use the script tag only for high-end mobile browsers

Although you can use the <script> tag to add JavaScript to pages created with XHTML MP, only the most advanced smartphones support scripts, even for relatively simple actions, such as rollovers and image swaps. If you use scripts, make sure the page design is readable if the script doesn't work on a low-end phone.

Create forms for user input

The basics of creating HTML forms are the same for mobile pages as for pages designed for the desktop Web. You can use forms to collect data from visitors to your site and create a variety of interactive features. For example, the American Airlines site includes pages where users can check to see what gate their flight is departing from. Figure 5-2 shows a page on a BlackBerry Storm, and Figure 5-3 shows the same page on an iPhone. Note that form fields where users input data are displayed quite differently from one device to another based on the type of phone.

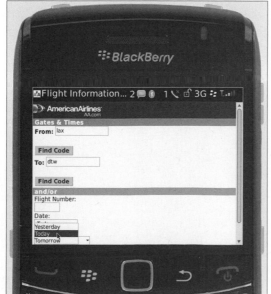

Figure 5-2: The American Airlines gate information page on a BlackBerry Storm.

Figure 5-3:
The same
American
Airlines
page on an
iPhone.

XHTML MP supports the `<form>` tag as well as the following form field tags: text field, password field, check box, radio button, selection list, hidden field, and submit button.

When designing a form, you must specify a method (`get` or `put`) in the `<form>` tag, as well as an action, and you must be able to execute a script on your Web server to complete the action. Check with your Web hosting service or system administrator to find out more about how to set up scripts on your Web server.

Use the right doctype

Any well-crafted Web page (for the mobile Web or the desktop) should begin with a doctype that identifies the kind of markup used in the page. If you design your mobile pages with XHTML MP, make sure you use the corresponding doctype. (You find more on this topic in the "Using Mobile-Specific Doctypes" section, later in this chapter.)

Use the head, body, and title tags

The `<head>` and `<body>` tags work the same in XHTML MP as in other versions of HTML, although you shouldn't use attributes of the `<body>` tag, such as background color. (If you want to specify background and text colors, use CSS.) It is good practice to include a short, descriptive title in the `<title>` tag of each page, even though many mobile devices don't display the contents of the `<title>` tag. Some mobile phones include the page title at the top of the browser window, and most will use it if the page is bookmarked.

Avoiding tags not included in XHTML MP

If you have a background in XHTML, you may find it helpful to know about the tags that you can't use when designing with XHTML MP. Following are some of the common tags that you should cut out of your markup language skills when you design with XHTML MP:

- ✔ **`<applet>`:** Although many mobile devices can run Java applications, they don't support Java applets in the Web browser.

- ✔ **`<basefont>`:** Mobile devices have limited font options, so you should use CSS to specify fonts for devices that support CSS.

- ✔ **`<button>`:** The generic button tag for forms is not supported, but you can use the submit button option.

- ✔ **`<frame>` and `<iframe>`:** Frames, which are used to divide the browser window into multiple pages, are no longer recommended for the desktop Web, and they're a definite no-no for the mobile Web. The same is true for iframes. Mobile screens are small enough; don't try to stuff more than one Web page into them at once.

- ✔ **`<center>`:** We know it's hard to break the habit of using the center tag and center attribute, as in `<p align="center">Some people love to center text</p>`. Instead, use CSS to center text and other elements.

- ✔ **`<dir>`, `<menu>`:** Although XHTML MP supports the ordered list `<ol>` and unordered list `<ul>` tags, the Directory and Menu List tags are not included in the XHTML MP specification.

- ✔ **`<map>`, `<area>`:** Image maps are not supported.

- ✔ **`<u>`:** The underline tag is not supported and should be removed from all the other variations of markup languages, too (in our opinion). Underlining should be reserved for links; there are better ways than underlining to make text stand out on a Web page, mobile or otherwise.

Test your XHTML MP skills

Following is an example of some badly written code in a seemingly simple XHTML MP page. Can you find the mistakes?

```
<!DOCTYPE html PUBLIC "-//WAPFORUM//DTD XHTML Mobile 1.0//EN"
"http://www.openmobilealliance.org/tech/DTD/xhtml-mobile12.
   dtd">

<?xml version="1.0" encoding="UTF-8"?>
<html xmlns="http://www.w3.org/1999/xhtml">
<meta name="HandheldFriendly" content="True" />

<head><title>Fun and Games</title>
</head>
<body>
<h1>Play this Way<H1>
<p>I love playing games<br>
Sometimes it's <em>really<strong>fun</em></strong>
<caption>My Favorite Games
<UL>
<li>The chocolate game at <a href=" http://chocolategamerules.
   com/>ChocolateGameRules.com</a>
<li> <a href=" http://www.digitalfamily.com/games/goldengate-
   puzzle.html">Play the puzzle games at Digital Family</a>
</ul>
      </body>
</html>
```

Did you find all the mistakes in this XHTML MP document? Check your answers with the following:

✔ The close heading tag `</h1>` should not be uppercase.

✔ There is no close `</p>` tag to complete the open `<p>` tag.

✔ The break tag should include a close tag within the break tag, like this: `<br />`.

✔ The `<em>` and `<strong>` tags are not nested properly.

✔ There is no close `</caption>` tag.

✔ The `<ul>` tag, like all tags, should not be capitalized.

✔ The `<li>` tags must include close `</li>` tags in XHTML.

✔ In the link to the Chocolate Game Rules site, the end of the URL is missing its quotation mark. See the link just after that link, with the text "Play the puzzle games at Digital Family" for the correct use of quotations.

Note: The doctype and other info at the top of the document are correct.

Styling with Cascading Style Sheets

Further complicating the many ways to design mobile Web sites is the fact that multiple versions of CSS are available. Because most mobile devices that support XHTML MP also support at least some CSS, the two work well together on the mobile platform, just as they do for desktop Web sites. However, many mobile phones provide only limited support for CSS, and you will find that the display of CSS varies among mobile Web browsers.

As we write this, most desktop sites are designed with CSS 2, and most mobile devices that support XHTML MP support most of the CSS 2 specification. For older mobile devices, you may want to limit your designs to the CSS options in more mobile-specific flavors of CSS, including CSS MP and Wireless CSS, which are both subsets of CSS 2.

Working within the limitations of CSS on mobile devices

Both CSS MP and Wireless CSS follow the basic rules of CSS2, but with their own variations. The Open Mobile Alliance (OMA) developed the Wireless CSS standard, and the W3C is responsible for CSS MP. Fortunately, the two groups say that they are now working together to merge the two specifications into one, which will probably be named CSS-MP. Keep any eye on the W3C site at `www.w3.org/TR/css-mobile/` (shown in Figure 5-4), as well as the OMA site at `www.openmobilealliance.org` for more details.

When using CSS on the mobile Web, you have to work within a more limited set of rules than you have available on the desktop Web and follow more strict standards. For example, although you can define sizes in CSS without identifying the measurement and the style will still render properly in most desktop browsers, mobile devices often choke on this omission.

For example: `margin-top: 10` renders fine in most desktop browsers, but you need to include a measurement, such as pixels (here's an example, `margin-top: 10px`), for mobile browsers.

Similarly, use of the `float` option in CSS to align images and other elements doesn't always work. Sometimes the tag isn't supported by the browser; other times the mobile screen doesn't have enough room to display an image aligned to the left or right with text wrapped around it.

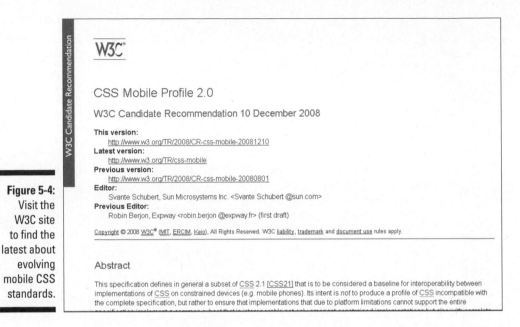

W3C Candidate Recommendation

Figure 5-4:
Visit the
W3C site
to find the
latest about
evolving
mobile CSS
standards.

As mobile browsers begin to support HTML5 (covered in the section "Using HTML5 with Mobile Browsers," later in this chapter), they will probably also support at least some of the CSS 3 specification. However, using these technologies today is still premature.

Using internal, external, or inline style sheets

As with most things in mobile Web design, the question of whether it's best to use internal or external style sheets (introduced in Chapter 4) depends on the capabilities of the device that displays your pages.

On the desktop Web, most designers prefer external style sheets because using the same external style sheet linked across multiple pages of a Web site is more efficient. The same is true in most mobile Web designs but with some limitations. Depending on how the mobile browser supports CSS and how the device manages caching, using an external style sheet may require that the device connects to the server to download the styles with each new page. If that's the case, styled pages would download more quickly if you use an internal style sheet rather than an external one.

Inline styles should be used sparingly, if it all. Like the desktop Web, internal and external style sheets are more efficient because they keep content separated from style, whereas inline styles can complicate code because they must be included with each tag you style.

Identifying levels of support for CSS

No definitive guide lists which devices support which CSS rules. However, to find out more about designing with CSS for specific types of devices, do the following:

- ✔ Visit the CSS Mobile Profile page on the W3C Web site at `www.w3.org/TR/css-mobile`.

- ✔ Review the documentation provided by mobile device manufacturers.

- ✔ Visit the DeviceAtlas Web site (`www.deviceatlas.com`), which offers a comprehensive collection of reports on mobile devices. Although these reports often include little or no data specific to CSS (at least at the time of this writing), the mobile phone profiles on DeviceAtlas do include the type of HTML supported and it's generally safe to assume that devices that support XHTML MP also support CSS2.

The best way to make sure that your CSS works well for your intended audience is to test your page designs across the devices you think will most likely be used by your visitors. You can find resources and tips for testing your mobile page designs in Chapter 7.

Using HTML5 with Mobile Browsers

HTML5 is the next major revision of HTML and is a big deal, especially for mobile browsers. If all draft features are present in the final version, HTML5 will standardize document structure, offline browsing, canvas animation, and location-based services in supporting mobile browsers.

HTML4, the previous version of the Web's markup language, was finalized in 1999 but never formally accepted as a W3C standard. (It remains in limbo as a recommendation. Go figure.) Eleven years later, HTML5 proposes an overhaul of Web document structure, interactivity, and offline behavior.

The HTML5 standards effort kicked off in 2007 and is not expected to conclude until at least 2011. W3C and technology industry working groups are working together to develop and refine the standard. They have worked for more than three years (as of this writing) to craft a major restructuring of the foundational markup language of the Web.

Killer features for mobile Web design

HTML5 is great news for the mobile ecosystem. Mobile users get richer Web applications and improved usability. Mobile browsers reclaim the rendering of rich Web content from third-party plug-ins. Mobile developers get testable, cross-platform and standards-based interfaces for content development.

The new features of HTML5 standardize technologies that are common in smartphone-optimized mobile Web applications. In today's mobile Web XHTML MP or HTML4 documents, these killer features are implemented using proprietary device and browser APIs. With HTML5, advanced Web application features are available in all mobile browsers supporting the markup language, using the same standard syntax and displaying the same standard behavior.

The following are the most important HTML5 features for mobile browsers:

- **Location awareness:** The geolocation API makes the mobile device's geographic location available to a Web application. In the past, obtaining device location was possible only by using proprietary extensions to JavaScript or server-side integration with a mobile operator API.

- **2D animation API:** The new `<canvas>` element and the JavaScript API allow two-dimensional drawing, graphics, and animations. Cross-platform games are now possible in mobile browsers. (***Beware:*** Script execution effects battery life on mobile devices.)

- **Persistent storage:** The Web Storage API allows documents to persistently store data in a mobile browser. Mobile browsers can write data in one browsing session and read it in the next session.

- **Offline application caching:** Network connectivity may be intermittent for mobile devices as they roam in and out of coverage areas. In HTML5, the user can interact with a cached mobile Web application while out of coverage. Web documents list all external resources (such as CSS files and JavaScript libraries) required for the document to be completely displayed and usable. Mobile browsers that support HTML5 can use this list to cache an entire Web application for offline use.

- **Structural elements:** New `<header>`, `<footer>`, `<nav>`, `<section>`, `<article>`, `<figure>`, and `<aside>` elements were added to HTML5 to make it easier to design Web pages with a logical structure. Structural elements make it easier for mobile browsers to navigate document components and display partial documents.

- **Native media support:** New `<video>` and `<audio>` elements embed multimedia into a Web document without using third-party browser plug-ins. Mobile browsers may natively control multimedia display, user interfaces, and *codecs,* which encode or decode data for playback.

HTML5 supplants XHTML

HTML5 supplants the XHTML specification. In HTML5, XHTML is redefined as a set of syntax rules and is no longer an independent markup specification. HTML5 can be expressed using either the strict syntax rules of XML or the looser syntax of HTML, which tolerates unclosed tags. This sensible change restores the unity of markup language functionality while allowing the mobile developer or designer the flexibility of choosing precise or lenient syntax. (Slackers, you can continue to slack off in HTML5.)

Motherhood, apple pie, and HTML5

Mobile pundits tout HTML5 as the antidote to practically every problem in mobile Web development. HTML5 is indeed a great leap forward in standardizing the advanced features of Web browsers. Its new elements and APIs unlock consistent implementations of rich Web application behavior. However, HTML5 will not lessen or extinguish several sins of mobile Web development, including the following:

- **Fragmentation:** Too many vendors implement mobile browsers, creating a fragmented marketplace and forcing developers to adapt Web content to play to browser strengths and avoid browser weaknesses.

- **Bugs:** As with any Web standard, HTML5 features may be incompletely or incorrectly implemented in some mobile browsers.

- **The rush to market:** Mobile browsers may support HTML5 too quickly, implementing features or syntax that end up changed in or cut from the final standard.

- **Lack of support for the mass market:** Many popular mobile Web sites use simple markup to quickly provide snackable chunks of relevant information to users. Upgrading these mobile Web sites to use HTML5, without implementing content adaptation to provide different versions of your site to different devices (covered in Chapter 6), could cut off access to millions of users with older, Web-accessible mobile browsers.

HTML5 on smartphones and dumbphones

The promise of HTML5 is realized only on mobile devices with modern, updatable Web browsers. As of this writing, iPhone, Droid, and Palm Pre smartphones implement portions of the HTML5 specification, as well as the latest version of CSS, *CSS3*. Smartphones provide an excellent platform for rolling out HTML5 applications to savvy mobile Web users. However, a large percentage of mobile subscribers still use non-smartphone devices, which have no capability for updating the browser or operating system.

Keeping up with the future

To find out more about the evolution of HTML5, visit the following Web sites:

- ✔ **www.w3.org/html/wg:** The Web site of the W3C HTML Working Group

- ✔ **www.whatwg.org:** The site for Web Hypertext Application Technology Working Group (WHATWG), founded by people working for major desktop Web browser vendors

- ✔ **www.w3.org/TR/html5:** The latest version of W3C's HTML5 Draft

Using Mobile-Specific Doctypes

The *doctype,* or Document Type Definition (DTD), is a declaration that should appear at the very top of any Web page, even before the open <html> tag. Essentially, the doctype tells the Web browser which markup language was used to write the page so that the browser knows how to render the page.

Web browsers struggle to provide support for all the different ways Web pages are written. If you leave off the doctype or use a doctype that doesn't match the code in your Web page, many browsers will resort to *Quirksmode* and take a best-guess approach to rendering your page. As you might imagine, the results are not very pretty sometimes. Don't let this happen to your pages, especially after you spend so much time making sure that your mobile pages were designed with the right markup language.

Following are some of the most common doctypes and what they tell a Web browser:

- ✔ By default, Dreamweaver adds the XHTML 1.0 Transitional doctype to its pages. Although you can change this setting in the preferences in Dreamweaver, by default, all pages are created using the XHMTL 1.0 transitional markup language. This doctype is a common choice for Web pages designed for the desktop Web. The following complies with the W3C recommendation:

```
<!DOCTYPE html PUBLIC "-//W3C//DTD XHTML 1.0
        Transitional//EN" "http://www.w3.org/TR/
        xhtml1/DTD/xhtml1-transitional.dtd">
```

- ✔ Three versions of XHTML MP are available: versions 1.0, 1.1, and 1.2. Most designers use version 1.1 or 1.2. The doctype for 1.1 is

```
<!DOCTYPE html PUBLIC "-//WAPFORUM//DTD XHTML Mobile
        1.1//EN" "http://www.openmobilealliance.org/
        tech/
        DTD/xhtml-mobile11.dtd">
```

✔ And the doctype for version 1.2 is

```
<!DOCTYPE html PUBLIC "-//WAPFORUM//DTD XHTML Mobile
        1.2//EN"

"http://www.openmobilealliance.org/tech/DTD/xhtml-
        mobile12.dtd">
```

✔ For pages designed with WML version 1.3, use the following:

```
<!DOCTYPE wml PUBLIC "-//WAPFORUM//DTD WML 1.3//
        EN""http://www.wapforum.org/DTD/wml13.dtd">
```

Chapter 6

Delivering Different Designs to Different Devices

In This Chapter

▶ Directing mobile devices

▶ Designing for particular mobile devices

▶ Planning a mobile site

*I*n the spacious kitchen of Spago Beverly Hills — the flagship restaurant of Chef Wolfgang Puck — each gourmet dish is carefully prepared to satisfy the supermodels and billionaires that dine there. The chefs are happy to accommodate their every wish.

In contrast, just a few miles away at the crowded take-out counter at the Wolfgang Puck Café at the Los Angeles County Airport, what you see in the little plastic lunch packages is what you get. The staff at this busy airport café work quickly and efficiently, but the goal is to help travelers get their food in a hurry — no one here has the time or resources to handle special requests.

As you consider the range of options for designing a mobile Web site for all the different mobile devices that may visit your pages, it may be helpful to use this culinary example for comparison. At the high end of the mobile Web design spectrum, companies such as Microsoft have implemented mobile design strategies akin to the fine dining experience at Spago. Developers put tremendous resources into creating a complex system that delivers different versions of the Microsoft Cloud Computing site (shown in Figure 6-1), optimized for each device that visits the site. At the low end of the list of mobile design options, other companies create just one alternate version of their desktop Web site, stripped down and streamlined to meet the basic needs of mobile devices, much like the prepackaged meals sold at the Wolfgang Puck Café.

In this chapter, we review what it takes to deliver different versions of your Web site to different mobile devices. In the first section, we describe a few key concepts and discuss how to develop such a system. In the second part of the chapter, we explore in detail how to plan and design a site that meets the needs of many different devices. To illustrate these concepts, we use the Microsoft Cloud Web site and include comments, interviews with designers, and screenshots of planning documents and designs. Figure 6-1 gives you an idea of what went into this complex mobile site.

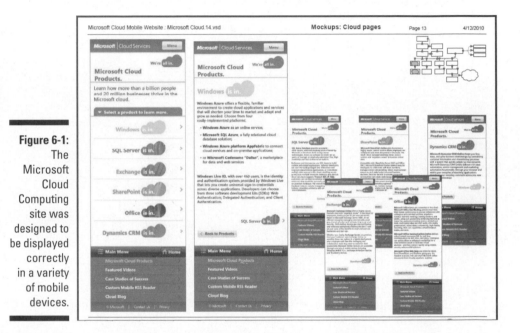

Figure 6-1: The Microsoft Cloud Computing site was designed to be displayed correctly in a variety of mobile devices.

Detecting and Directing Mobile Devices

Restaurants must get the right meal to the right table while the food is still hot, or they won't be in business long. To meet these goals, well-informed waitstaff must write the order correctly, and staff in a well-organized kitchen must prepare variations of the same meal quickly, without compromising quality.

Similarly, if you want to deliver tailored versions of your mobile Web site, you must properly detect what kind of device each visitor is using (device detection, which is like getting the order right), and then deliver the best version of your site for each device (content adaptation, which is like preparing each meal to order).

Before we delve into the details of device detection, let's begin with an overview. If you want to deliver different versions of a Web site to different devices, follow these general steps:

1. **Develop device profiles or parameters.**

   You first have to determine which devices you want to design your site to work well on. Since there are thousands of mobile phones and other devices available, it's generally best to categorize devices into a set of profiles or develop a set of parameters (such as image sizes) that you can mix and match, based on things like the screen size and multimedia support of each device.

2. **Develop (or acquire) a device database or a configuration file.**

   To deliver the right version of your site to the right device, you need a configuration file or database that contains detailed information about every device. Many private companies create their own device databases, but you can also use the open-source WURFL (Wireless Universal Resource File), described in the "Using open-source device detection scripts and services" section, later in this chapter.

3. **Write (or acquire) a program that can deliver the right version of your site to the right device.**

   The challenge here is to develop an application that can match the contents of the device database with the different design options (the device profiles, special URLs, or other parameters) that you've created for your site. Top mobile design firms create their own solutions, but you find information about open-source solutions, including Andy Moore's device detection solution (shown in Figure 6-2) in the "Using open-source device detection scripts and services" section.

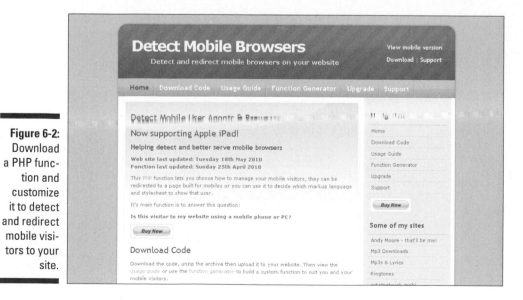

Figure 6-2: Download a PHP function and customize it to detect and redirect mobile visitors to your site.

4. **Develop a design that can be adapted to the needs of different devices on the fly, or create multiple designs, each optimized for a different device or device profile.**

   Each approach has tradeoffs, which we explore in the "Designing for Different Devices" section, later in this chapter. With either approach, expect to spend a significant amount of time creating a design (or designs) that will display well within the constraints of each device.

5. **Test, test, and test again, making adjustments as needed.**

   The many variations among devices and the sheer number of devices in use on the mobile Web make it almost impossible to deliver a perfectly optimized page to every device every time. Even if you do get your mobile design strategy right, the mobile Web is a moving target. Develop a strategy that best meets the needs of your site users today (and the limitations of your time and budget), and make refinements to keep your strategy up to date in the future.

Developing a device detection system

The basic concept of device detection is straightforward: A system identifies the visitor's device when it arrives at your site, and then directs the visitor to the best version of your Web site based on what the system knows about the device. (For a more technical explanation, see the upcoming sidebar "User agents and device detection.")

The challenge with device detection — and the subsequent redirection of visitors — is that approximately 8,000 devices are in use, with more being added all the time. Although the various categories of mobile phones have similarities, the specifics of what each device supports vary.

For example, you may think that all smartphones are similar, and that within that category, all BlackBerry phones are pretty much the same. However, BlackBerry phones vary dramatically. Many BlackBerry phones have screens that are 480 pixels wide, but some are limited to 160 pixels. The latest BlackBerry phones support JavaScript, XHTML MP, and CSS2 (covered in Chapter 5), but older models provide minimal or no support for CSS. In addition, you have the human factor: BlackBerry phones offer users many options, including the ability to turn JavaScript support on and off.

How you deliver the right version of your site to the right phone is the secret sauce of many high-end mobile Web design firms. Companies such as Ansible, which developed the Microsoft Cloud Computing site featured as a case study later in this chapter, have spent years developing a finely tuned device database and device detection applications.

User agents and device detection

When you open a Web page, your Web browser sends a user-agent string to the server that hosts the Web site. The *user-agent string* essentially introduces you to the server, describing what browser (and browser version) you're using, as well as other things about your computer or mobile device, such as the operating system. If you want to see how your browser introduces you, go to `http://whatsmyuseragent.com/`.

Device detection systems are designed to recognize user-agent strings and direct visitors based on the capabilities of each device. Because many Web sites use device detection to direct mobile visitors, you can't just open the mobile versions of some sites in a desktop browser on your computer. That's where

the User Agent Switcher comes in handy. This plug-in for Firefox (available at `https://addons.mozilla.org/en-US/firefox/addon/59/`) enables you to change the user agent of your Web browser, effectively tricking the server into thinking you're using an iPhone or any of the other user agents you can load into the plug-in.

Because the User Agent Switcher makes it possible to visit the mobile version of a Web site with a browser on a desktop computer, it also makes it possible to view the source code behind those pages. This is especially valuable because browsers on mobile devices do not offer an option to view the source code, which is standard in desktop browsers such as Firefox, Safari, Chrome, and Internet Explorer.

Essentially, you build up libraries of "ways of dealing with different stuff," explained Lee Andron, Director of Information Design and Strategy for Ansible. With every new mobile site that they develop, the company adds more processes to its object-oriented library. Thus, Ansible is constantly getting better at delivering video, audio, scripts, and other Web content to all the devices that visit their mobile sites.

You might not be able to compete with companies such as Ansible, but you can set up a similar system with far fewer resources. Like most things on the Web, open-source options are available, thanks to the generosity of programmers who share their work and offer applications for free (or for a donation). We cover a few of these options in the section that follows.

Using open-source device detection scripts and services

Although you can create your own configuration file or device database with the specifications of every mobile device you want to support and can write your own device detection scripts (if you're an experienced programmer), you're almost certainly better off starting with one of the open-source options included in this section. However, even with these great resources, you'll need some programming experience to get these solutions to work on your server.

WURFL

```
http://wurfl.sourceforge.net/
```

Used by a growing list of mobile Web developers, WURFL (Wireless Universal Resource File) is a freely available configuration file created by many contributors with the goal of providing a comprehensive list of all mobile devices in use today and what they can support in terms of Web design standards. Although no one claims that the list is flawless, it is regularly updated and well respected in the mobile development community.

Tera-WURFL

```
www.tera-wurfl.com
```

Built on WURFL (and linked to from the WURFL site), Tera-WURFL is an application created with PHP and MySQL. The Tera-WURFL application detects and matches mobile devices by first collecting user agent information from each site visitor and then passing that information to the Tera-WURFL library where it is evaluated and assigned to a UserAgentMatcher. Each UserAgentMatcher is designed to work with a device profile, made up of a group of devices with similar capabilities. Essentially, the Tera-WURFL gets you most of the way through the device detection and redirection process, but you still need to have a script that redirects visitors to the right version of your site based on the results.

Device Atlas

```
http://deviceatlas.com
```

If you want to create your own device database, or configuration file, a great place to start is Device Atlas. On the Device Atlas Web site you can look up the specific features supported by nearly any mobile phone, including what markup language, multimedia, and image formats each phone supports. Device Atlas also offers an API that you can use if you're developing your own device detection solution.

Andy Moore's solution detects and redirects visitors

```
http://detectmobilebrowsers.mobi
```

Andy Moore's solution is the simplest we've found for setting up an auto detection and redirection solution for your site. Note, however, that you still need at least basic PHP skills to set up and install the code.

Andy Moore's solution is a PHP function, which has eight parameters that you can easily define to handle common devices. As you see in Figure 6-3, you can use the drop-down menu options on his Web page to alter the settings for each option.

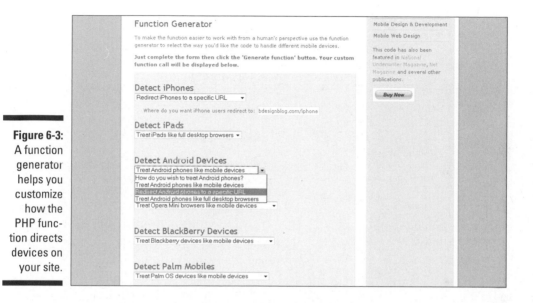

Figure 6-3:
A function generator helps you customize how the PHP function directs devices on your site.

Designing for Different Devices

You can design for different mobile devices using essentially two approaches. First, you can create two or more versions of your site and set each one up at a different URL. You can think of this as a small, medium, or large approach to mobile Web design.

The second option, content adaptation, could be likened to providing a custom suit for each frame or at least enough mix-and-match options to ensure a better fit than the first option.

You can also combine these two approaches, creating multiple page designs, matching them to a general device profile, and then tailoring each design a little further, based on screen size and other factors. However, few mobile designers we've spoken with go to this length to produce a usable mobile experience.

We prefer the content adaptation approach, although it is the more complicated option. Following is an overview of both design strategies and how mobile Web designers use them.

Creating mobile versions of a blog

Web blogs created with WordPress (or other blogging software) are a kind of dynamic Web site. All headlines, posts, and images are stored in a MySQL database, and pages are generated on the fly. Thus, creating a mobile-optimized version of a blog is relatively easy, and there is an ever-expanding list of blog themes available on the WordPress Web site to help you automate the process. Some mobile-optimized WordPress themes even take care of device detection, including the one featured in Chapter 9.

Designing for content adaptation

In the content adaptation approach, you create one Web site design and then adapt it to each device. Thus, the basic site structure is the same across all devices, but specific elements, such as image size or the appearance of videos, change based on what the device can support. For example, you can optimize your images in several sizes and then deliver the version of the image that best fits the screen size of each device.

This approach is possible only if you're working on a dynamic Web site, meaning the content of the site is stored in a database and the pages are created on the fly (as they are requested by a browser). Dynamic sites are generally built with technologies such as PHP, ASP.NET, or Java combined with a database like MySQL. An example of a dynamic Web site is Amazon, which creates a page that recommends books for you that are different from the ones it recommends for others, based on your previous visits to the site and books that you have purchased. A sophisticated dynamic site such as Amazon works by retrieving the images and descriptions of the books from a database and assembles them on a Web page as you access the site.

Many developers who follow the content adaptation approach also use caching. That means they can save, or *cache,* a version of the site optimized for a particular kind of phone. For example, if 40 percent of your traffic comes from iPhones, and all iPhones have the same specifications, you can save a lot of server power by creating the iPhone version once and then caching it so that you can serve that cached version rather than generate a new version for every iPhone that comes along.

The content adaptation approach is complicated and only suited to dynamic Web sites. If you're working on a static Web site, where each page of the site is a separate HTML file, your best option is to create a few different page designs and set each one up at its own URL, which is the approach covered in the next section.

Creating different versions of a site

Creating different versions of a Web site is easier to implement than the content adaptation approach, but you won't be able to match your designs to the unique specifications of every device as effectively. Still, creating different site versions is far superior to creating just one mobile version of your site (an approach covered in Chapter 3).

Because it's impractical (if not impossible) to create a different design for each of the thousands of devices that might visit your site, most developers start by creating two or more *device profiles* — categories of phones with similar features.

Here's an example of the two main profile categories you should consider, followed by a more detailed breakdown for low-end phones:

✔ **Profile 1:** A device profile for high-end touch-screen phones would include the iPhone, phones that run the Android operating system, those with the latest Palm OS, and the newest phones with the Microsoft Internet Explorer Web browser. With these as your target, you can design a version of your site optimized for a 320-pixel-wide screen, that includes JavaScript, video, and the latest markup language HTML5, as well as CSS3 (covered in Chapter 5). Because these high-end phones all use Web browsers that support this technology, you can do a lot with them.

✔ **Profile 2:** A device profile for low-end phones would include older BlackBerry and other smartphones, as well as all feature phones. In this profile, you would leave out JavaScript, which is not supported consistently (or at all) across these phones, limit or remove any video or audio files, and create the page markup with XHTML MP and CSS MP (covered in Chapter 5).

You can create as many profiles as you want and can base the profiles on any number of factors, but these two broad categories will cover most phones today. If you want to better serve the low-end phones, you could then create a second level of device profiles based on screen size.

If you create device profiles based on screen size, and you make them a subset of the first pair of profiles, you might define them as follows:

✔ **Profile 2A:** Tiny screens, those limited to 132 pixels or less

✔ **Profile 2B:** Small screens, between 132 and 240 pixels

✔ **Profile 2C:** Medium screens, those between 240 and 320 pixels

Top-down and bottom-up design

Whether you create multiple versions of your site design or use content adaptation, at some point you have to step back and think about what the site should look like. The two common approaches to site design follow:

✔ Design for the high end and strip down: In this approach, you come up with a great design that takes advantage of top-of-the-line features, and then you strip the design to a bare-bones version for low-end phones, while maintaining as much of the same look and feel as possible. In our unscientific survey of mobile Web design-

ers, we found that people with a design background tend to favor this approach.

✔ Design for the low end and build up: In the second approach, you determine the minimum of text, links, and images you want on your site, and then you add more design features, multimedia, and interactive content for devices that support it. In our many discussions with developers, we found that programmers and those who specialize in site architecture (covered in the last part of this chapter) prefer this approach.

As you create each mobile version of your Web site, consider how to take best advantage of the capabilities of the phones in each profile. For example, you may want to include video in the version you design for the Profile 1 phones, but not in the Profile 2 version you create for feature phones, which don't support video as well.

After you've built the different versions, you can publish each one at a special URL. For example, you could publish the site designed for Profile 1 at smartphones.yourdomainname.com and then publish the Profile 2 version at http:m.yourdomainname.com because it's more difficult to type on a feature phone. Also note that although you can use a domain name such as yourdomainname.com/mobile, instead, for a feature phone, it's best to use the m.domain example because it's difficult to add a forward slash on most feature phones. If you then go on to the second level of profiles, you could create three variations on that domain, one for each screen size.

With separate domains set up for each profile, you can then direct visitors to the best version using a simple detection script, like the one available on Andy Moore's Web site, covered previously (in the "Using open-source device detection scripts and services" section).

Planning a Mobile Web Project

Whether you will be creating multiple versions of a site or using content adaptation, it's wise to begin by thinking about what you want to include on the site and how to design the site so that it works on a wide range of devices.

To help you understand some of the best practices in planning a mobile Web site, this section focuses on a real-world mobile design success story from Ansible, Interpublic Group's full service mobile marketing agency.

The case study is based on a project that the Ansible team developed for Microsoft: transforming the desktop version of the Cloud Computing site, shown in Figure 6-4, into a mobile version that displays well on nearly every mobile device that might visit the site, including the Motorola RAZR, Apple iPhone, and BlackBerry Bold, also shown in Figure 6-4. Lee Andron, director of information design and strategy, and Sia Ea, senior creative manager, generously granted us a series of interviews. In addition, the Ansible team provided access to planning and design documents.

For the Cloud Computing site, Andron created the wireframe and the final Project Planning Document, Ea created the design, a team of programmers did the development work, and a project manager oversaw the entire process.

Figure 6-4:
The Microsoft Cloud Computing site as it appears in the Firefox Web browser on a desktop computer.

Creating wireframes

On larger projects such as the Cloud Computing site, Creative Director Andron explained, it's good practice to start by creating a *wireframe,* a skeletal model of a site not unlike a blueprint for a building. Wireframes are not unique to mobile design; most design firms that build big, complex Web sites create wireframes.

A good wireframe is like a diagram of a site that shows what happens when someone clicks on each page. Most developers who create wireframes agree that it's important to not add design elements at the initial stages — no color, no fancy fonts. The wireframe is a structural document designed to help you focus on how a site works without being distracted by design details, such as the color scheme. As the development process evolves, the initial wireframe document may grow to include design mockups and other details.

In the top-right corner of each wireframe document (such as the one in Figure 6-5), Andron included a miniature site map that shows where the page fits with the rest of the site.

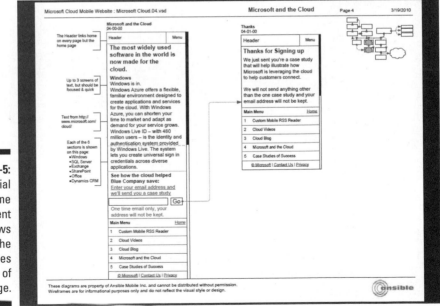

Figure 6-5: The initial wireframe document shows only the bare-bones structure of each page.

Although beginning by creating a wireframe may seem like it delays the start of development, most Web designers find that the project is more efficient in the long run because the design team can work out potential problems with navigation and functionality before adding the complexity of programming and design. And after the wireframe is approved, you can move forward with technology and design simultaneously because everyone is working from the same blueprint.

Dividing a project into manageable phases also makes it easier for clients to approve each stage of development; each phase can have a distinct focus, Andron said. Our client approves functionality, then design, and finally the text used on each page. Each approval is documented in the growing Project Design Document, which serves as a set of blueprints in the development process.

Resources and software for creating wireframes

You can create a wireframe document in almost any software program. Some designers use common applications, including Microsoft Word or PowerPoint, but there are a number of programs and online services designed specifically for creating wireframes. Here are a few:

Cacoo (www.cacoo.com): This online drawing program includes many icons and other features designed for creating wireframes, sitemaps, and charts. (Cost: free)

Balsamiq Mockups (www.balsamiq.com): This online drawing and collaboration tool offers more sophisticated features than Cacoo. (Cost: $79)

iPlotz (www.iplotz.com): An online tool you can use to create clickable and navigable wireframes and prototypes. (Cost: $15/mo)

Fairbuilder (www.flairbuilder.com): This online tool can be used to create complete interactive prototypes and wireframes. (Cost: $24/mo)

Microsoft Visio (www.microsoft.com/visio): A popular program among professionals who favor Microsoft products, Visio is only available for Windows computers. The program uses vector graphics and features a broad collection of templates and other sophisticated tools designed for developing complex projects. (Cost: $500+ for the professional version)

Omnigraffle (www.omnigroup.com): This program works on Macintosh computers and iPads and can be used to create diagrams, wireframes, and charts with many great design features built in. Omnigraffle can also import and export Visio documents. (Cost: $200 for the professional version)

Stepping through the development process

At Ansible, each new project begins with a Vision Document that defines the concept of what the site will accomplish. It helps the firm come to an agreement with the customer about the goals the site needs to achieve as well as the expected return on investment, or ROI. Andron is quick to admit that just because you can develop a different design for every mobile device, doesn't mean doing so is the best investment for all of his clients. As with any design project, you have to balance the options with the expected return on investment.

Even before Ansible signs a contract with a client, Andron often creates an initial site map. The initial site map often changes quite a bit by the time they get to the final version of the wireframe document (shown in Figure 6-6), but it serves as a guide that can help make sure the client and the development team are on the same page in terms of the scope of the project.

After a client signs off on the initial site map document, Andron and his team create a statement of work, where they define a budget and timeline.

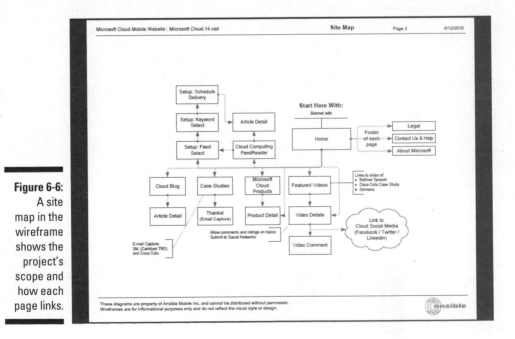

Figure 6-6:
A site map in the wireframe shows the project's scope and how each page links.

Once the client signs a contract, the team is ready to move full steam ahead. The entire development process goes something like this:

1. Create the detailed wireframe designs complete with site maps (refer to Figures 6-5 and 6-6) and discuss with the client to get approval.

2. The creative designer creates the initial page designs and presents them to the client for approval. For this project, the senior creative manager, Sia Ea, created designs for each of the main pages of the site, including the one shown in Figure 6-7.

Figure 6-7: As the wireframe document evolves into a more complete planning document, design elements are added.

3. Add the final copy — the text that will appear in the pages of the site, and get the client to sign off on all content.

The team at Ansible, like many designers, often uses "greeked" or placeholder text to show how copy will look on the initial page designs. However, Andron prefers to use real content from the site whenever possible because it can help clients more clearly visualize how the site will come together in the end. Screen designs are so small that text plays a fundamental roll in the design. He says, "If we include text in the site sourced from the campaign, we save time in the long run by suggesting what the copy of the site should say to achieve the goals of the project."

4. Combine all the elements (wireframe, design mockups, and content) into one complete Project Design Document, like the one shown in Figure 6-8.

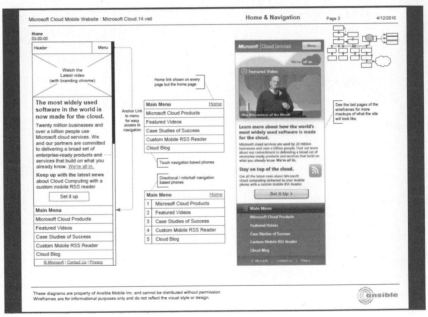

Figure 6-8: The middle of the page shows two kinds of navigation, one for touch-screen phones and one for keypads on a feature phone.

Creating a wireframe helps you work out complex navigational challenges before you get to the programming and development of a site. For example, the middle section of Figure 6-8 shows two kinds of navigation that will appear on the home page, one for devices with touch screens and a second for feature phones that are limited to numeric keypads. The need for dual navigation options makes mobile sites complex, but working out how to handle these differences before you start programming helps the development go more smoothly.

5. Notes are added to the document throughout the process

    At each stage of review with the client, Andron adds notes from the client to the Project Planning Document and includes those notes when the final document is passed on to the programmers. One of the challenges with creating a wireframe and other parts of the planning document, he explained, is that you're really serving two masters — one is the customer because the document must get their approval, and the other is the development team because, ultimately, the document has to be useful to the programmers and designers who create the site.

6. After the wireframes, creative designs, and copy deck are approved, the Project Design Document is complete and the programmers put the plan into action.

7. The final phases before the site goes live involve lots of testing.

    Andron said his team uses services like DeviceAnywhere to help with initial testing because it offers so many different devices on one site and the ability to test mobile services in other countries without having to physically go there. "The best way to test a mobile design, however, is to use real mobile devices," he said. In his office, Andron keeps several mobile phones on hand and uses them to view pages and test interactive features throughout the development process. (You find more about DeviceAnywhere and other testing options in Chapter 7.)

    After the site is built on a testing server and ready for final review, Andron demonstrates the site for the client on at least five phones running different operating systems and browsers (depending on the client's target audience).

    "Developing mobile Web design effectively requires a constant improvement process," Andron said, noting that at every stage, they are testing their assumptions and making changes as necessary to ensure that the final project will be successful.

The entire process of developing a Project Design Document with planning documents, such as the ones shown in Figures 6-5 through 6-8, may require more than a dozen revisions as new elements are added and changes are requested. The Ansible team created 14 versions of the Microsoft Cloud Computing site Project Design Document in the process of developing a site to reach the project goals. The final version consisted of an 18-page document, complete with a site map, navigation documents, real content, and design mockups plus the copy deck.

Andron saves a copy of the wireframe document with each significant revision so he can backtrack if things change significantly along the way, which is a common challenge with projects that include so many moving pieces. "We might have six or seven revisions before we even show the wireframe to a client," he said.

Considering the designer's perspective

The constraints that designers face when creating sites for the mobile Web would leave many artists feeling as though they were being asked to build three different model ships in one tiny bottle, while wearing a straightjacket. But Sia Ea, who was the design lead on the Ansible team for the Microsoft Cloud Computing site project, enjoys the challenge.

"Creating a Web design that looks good and works across a wide variety of mobile phones and other devices isn't easy," she said, "but it is satisfying." Ea likes to start by creating a version of the design that includes all of the most advanced features possible, and then stripping out the elements that won't work on low-end devices as she creates different versions.

Because the development process begins with a wireframe, her options are limited from the start by more than just the constraints of the mobile Web. "The wireframe is a map for the site, and includes many assumptions that also affect the design," she said. Although she had to base her design on the wireframe, she was able to negotiate some adjustments with Andron before they presented the design to the client.

Ea kept the colors already in use on the desktop version of the Cloud Computing site (refer to Figure 6-4), which consisted of bright colors on a white background. Fortunately, this color scheme makes text easy to read on a mobile device as well as on the desktop site. That said, Ea prefers to use darker backgrounds, with a light text color for navigation links because it helps them stand out on a small screen and makes it easier to identify where a user must click on a link (see the bottom of Figure 6-9 for an example).

Ea thinks anyone who has been designing for the desktop Web has a great background for mobile design because they already have experience designing for different computer platforms and browser differences. But they may still have to learn to deal with the fact that the differences among mobile devices are much greater because there are so many different devices and resolutions. In addition, browsers have different capabilities; for example, some can't render tables, and others don't render CSS or JavaScript. Knowing these limitations is critical when creating a design that will work across many devices.

Now the iPad is adding new challenges and opportunities in mobile design. In the past, the largest design Ea would create was 320 pixels wide, for an iPhone. As mobile screens got larger, she started making the largest images 480 pixels wide. Now she makes graphics that are 768 pixels wide so that they fill the screen on an iPad. In general, Ea creates the design with images in the largest size and then scales down the design for smaller devices.

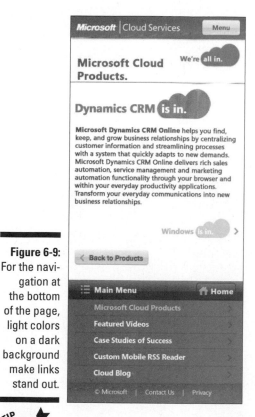

Figure 6-9:
For the navigation at the bottom of the page, light colors on a dark background make links stand out.

Following are some of Ea's tips for mobile Web design:

✔ Stick with fundamental design principles. An element's typography, composition, location, and scale are all important.

✔ Use grids for layout, and use colors that provide contrast. Use a white background and dark text when you have lots of copy, and use the reverse for site imagery. Keep links simple and easy to navigate.

✔ Don't make pages too long (no more than two or three screens). Keep copy short and ensure that the most important information appears at the top of the screen. "Having an iPhone will spoil you," she said, "because scrolling down a page on many devices requires tediously pressing a key, so limiting page length is extremely important."

✔ Keep users entertained and give them the capability of moving forward or backward.

Ea is quick to admit there are exceptions to any design rule. Although she generally recommends that you limit each page to no more than two screens of content, Figure 6-10 shows a page in the Cloud Computing site that is longer. The page shown in Figure 6-10 lists all the RSS feeds to which users of the Cloud Computing site can subscribe. "The desire to show the extensive list of articles users could choose from justified creating a longer page layout in this case," she said.

Figure 6-10: Page designs were limited to no more than two to three screens of content, except when show-casing a long list of RSS feeds.

Chapter 7

Testing and Publishing Mobile Web Sites

*Y*ou don't want your initial visitors to send you messages like, "Is it supposed to look like someone threw random pages of clip art into a blender?" That's why testing your site before you publish it live on the mobile Web is important.

The bad news is that just as designing for the mobile Web is more painstaking and demanding, so too is it tougher to reliably test your pages to make sure they look good on every possible mobile device, under every conceivable set of circumstances.

The good news is that mobile developers and designers have been aware of this problem for a long time and have gradually chipped away at the problem. At least four levels of mobile testing are available right now, and this chapter explains the testing methods you can choose from, ranging from free and open source on the low end, to an expensive and complex *device farm* (an array of mobile devices, all activated with data plans and connections to the mobile Web) on the high end. You find an introduction to the online testing tools, including the ones provided by the World Wide Web Consortium (WC3) for testing your site's code (which tests how the code works under the hood rather than how the page looks in different devices). You find steps that walk you through checking links with Dreamweaver. And when you complete all the rigors of testing, you also find steps for publishing your site using Dreamweaver's built-in File Transfer Protocol (FTP) tools as well as an introduction to other popular FTP options.

Understanding user agents and user agent switchers

You see a couple terms a lot in this chapter: *user agent, user agent switcher,* and *HTTP request header.* Most of mobile Web testing involves interpreting or manipulating these snippets of computer code. Why are user agents and headers important in mobile Web design? Because they tell the Web server what kind of device, operating system, and browser you are using when you visit a Web site.

If you've ever seen one of those movies about upper-crust Victorian England in which polite guests requesting to be admitted into a mansion place their business cards on a silver tray that a silent, obsequious butler then carries and presents to the master of the house, well, user agents aren't quite that stuffy, but the basic principle is the same.

When you type a Web address into a Web browser, or click a link to navigate to a Web page, a series of functions happen invisibly and with lightning speed. Your browser sends an HTTP request header, which includes a user agent, to the Web server. The *user agent* includes information about what kind of phone or mobile device is accessing a Web site. Many mobile Web developers install scripts on the server which use the information submitted by user agents to determine which version of the Web site to deliver to each visitor based on what mobile device the user agent identifies. You learn more about how to set up systems like this in Chapter 6. What's important to understand when you're testing mobile Web sites is that if a Web site is set up to deliver a particular version of a site based on the user agent, you may not be able to see the mobile version of a site if you're using an emulator or simulator on a desktop computer, unless you find a way to "trick" the server into believing you're using a mobile device. That's where user agent switchers come in and why the user agent switcher add-ons, available for the Firefox and Safari Web browsers, and so useful when you're developing or testing mobile Web sites.

Comparing Mobile Testing Solutions

The most important principle to understand when testing your mobile Web site can be summed up in one well-worn aphorism: "In theory, there is no difference between theory and practice — but in practice, there is." Just so is it with the mobile Web. Although the simulators and emulators we include in this chapter approximate how various devices will display a Web page, in the real world of mobile devices and carriers lurk all sorts of variables, quirks, and oddities you can't replicate with even the best mobile simulators on your desktop computer.

No matter how accurate the emulators or browser add ons you use to make the computer on your desktop act like a mobile phone, they can't factor in all the variables of local wireless carriers. Wireless carriers have a lot of power and they can cause real problems by, for example, deciding that video gobbles up too much bandwidth and putting a cap on usage. No matter how much work you've put into optimizing your mobile video Web site, the ultimate performance of your pages will depend on the wireless connection and any number of things a carrier might do to your pages before they get to a user's mobile device (including blocking large video files).

For example, in September 2007, Vodaphone UK (one of the big mobile carriers in the United Kingdom) decided to start stripping out the user agent from the HTML headers coming in from mobile devices (find more on user agents in the nearby sidebar "Understanding user agents and user agent switchers"). Overnight, mobile sites all over England stopped working properly because the detection scripts on Web servers could no longer recognize whether visitors to sites were using mobile devices or desktop computers, which meant they couldn't direct mobile visitors to the mobile version of a Web site (more on how detection scripts work in Chapter 6). Usually, when a Web site isn't working properly for your audience, you look for problems on either end of the chain — that is, either the site on the server is poorly designed or the implementation on the device in the user's hand is breaking down. But in this case, the problem occurred somewhere in the middle, in a place completely outside the view or control of mobile Web designers. Fortunately the company reversed its decision and things are working well again in England, but it's a good example of how even the best mobile simulators aren't perfect because you can't test all of the variables in mobile design unless you factor in wireless carriers.

This is why — in practice — there simply is no substitute for pulling out a mobile device, firing up the browser, and loading the Web page you've just designed on real devices, on each of the carriers your visitors are likely to be using. However, before you go out on a crazed shopping spree to amass your own collection of the 8,000 (and growing!) mobile devices that can access the Web, there are some easier and far cheaper means by which to test your site that will give you a good idea of how your pages will work on mobile devices.

Here are the three main methods for testing mobile Web designs:

✔ Browser add-ons or plug-ins

✔ Mobile emulators and simulators

✔ The actual device(s)

We examine each one of these in detail in the following sections.

Installing Mobile Add-Ons for Firefox

The quickest (and cheapest) way to see whether your mobile Web designs are at all functional is to use add-ons in Firefox to impersonate a mobile device requesting a page. One of the most useful add-ons for mobile Web designers is the User Agent Switcher described in detail in this section. This add-on makes it possible for you to control the HTTP request header and user agent that

Firefox sends to a Web server, tricking the server into identifying your computer as a mobile device so that sites that use device detection will send back the mobile version of a Web page rather than the desktop version.

Combining the User Agent Switcher with other add-ons that cause Firefox to render Web pages in a narrow window can give you a rough approximation of how mobile Web pages will display. Most Firefox add-ons are free, although some developers ask that you donate money if you like how they work. We encourage you to support their efforts.

Although these add-ons are constantly improving, there are some very basic ways in which a desktop browser, no matter how it's configured, will never match the behavior of a mobile device. Because processor speed, memory, storage, and connection reliability are so much better in the desktop environment, any emulator you use on your computer can give you a false sense of confidence.

Although there are add-ons for Safari and Internet Explorer, they're nowhere near as extensive and up to date as the stuff created by the vibrant open-source community that develops for Firefox. If you want to browse through the entire list of add-ons for the Firefox browser, go to the Firefox add-on home page at `https://addons.mozilla.org/en-US/firefox`.

To install any Firefox add-ons, including the ones that we describe specifically in the following sections, follow these steps:

1. **Using the Firefox Web browser, navigate to the page on the Firefox site that features the add-on you want to add to your browser.**

   One of our top recommendations is the User Agent Switcher, described in more detail in the following section. You can find that add-on at `https://addons.mozilla.org/en-US/firefox/addon/59` or you can search for the title of the add-on using the search box on the Firefox add-on home page.

2. **Click the Add to Firefox button.**

   A window pops up, asking whether you're certain that you want to install this add-on and warning you to install add-ons only from developers you trust.

   Meanwhile, a little countdown timer runs while the add-on loads, until finally the Install button is no longer grayed out.

3. **Click the Install button.**

   Another window opens, and a progress bar shows that the add-on is installed. After the add-on is installed into Firefox, you're prompted to restart Firefox.

4. **Restart Firefox after each add-on.**

   Alternatively, you can install a bunch of add-ons at once and then restart to activate them all.

The following sections highlight some of our favorite add-ons for doing mobile Web testing using your desktop computer.

User Agent Switcher

The User Agent Switcher is one of the most useful add-ons we've found for basic mobile testing. As you might suspect from the name, the *User Agent Switcher* (https://addons.mozilla.org/en-US/firefox/addon/59) allows you to change the identifying string of code that your browser sends to a server to introduce you (for more on user agents, read the sidebar, "Understanding user agents and user agent switchers" earlier in this chapter).

Without the User Agent Switcher, Firefox sends its default user agent code in the HTTP request header, and you will have a hard time viewing many mobile-optimized Web pages because many sites automatically redirect visitors to the mobile version of a site based on the information in the request header. The User Agent Switcher (see Figure 7-1) comes with an eclectic mix of about a dozen browsers and devices that you can set your Firefox browser to impersonate. After you install the add-on, you can add more user agents, so you can test your Web site designs across a broader spectrum of devices.

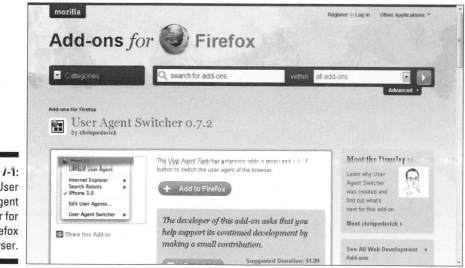

Figure 7-1:
The User Agent Switcher for the Firefox browser.

To activate the User Agent Switcher, in Firefox, choose Tools⇨Default User Agent⇨*Browser You Want to Emulate.* Then reload the page in Firefox to see the new version.

To install more user agents:

1. **After you install the User Agent Switcher, covered in the previous section, open the Firefox Web browser and navigate to `http://mobiforge.com/developing/blog/user-agent-switcher-config-file`.**

   At the end of the blog post is a link to a text file containing user agents for a wider variety of phones and mobile browsers.

2. **Right-click (⌘-click on a Mac) the useragentswitcher.xml_.txt link and choose Save Link As.**

   The Enter Name of File to Save To dialog box opens.

3. **Navigate to the folder on your local hard drive where you want to save the file.**

4. **In the File Name field of the Enter Name of File to Save To dialog box, you need to change the name of this file by deleting the _ `.txt` from the end of the filename.**

   This is a little clumsy, we know — but the file must end with `.xml` not `.txt` for it to be recognized by the User Agent Switcher when you import it in the steps that follow. Fortunately, the solution is easy. Just delete the _ `.txt` off the end so that the filename is shortened to `useragentswitcher.xml`. (If you prefer, you can delete the `.txt` extension from the filename after you save the file; just make sure you do it before you move on to Step 6.)

5. **Click the Save button.**

6. **Choose Tools⇨Default User Agent⇨User Agent Switcher⇨Options.**

   The User Agent Switcher Options dialog box opens to allow you to import other user agents.

7. **Click the Import button.**

   The Import User Agents dialog box opens.

8. **Navigate to where you saved the `useragentswitcher.xml` file, click the file to select it, and then click the Open button.**

   The Import User Agent dialog box closes and returns you to the User Agent Switcher Options dialog box, which now displays a longer list of browsers and devices because it includes all of the user agents from the `.xml` file (as shown in Figure 7-2).

9. **To activate any of these new user agents, choose Tools⇨Default User Agent and select the user agent you want to emulate.**

   If you want to add more devices to the list, do a Google search for *user agent .xml files* and repeat the steps in this section.

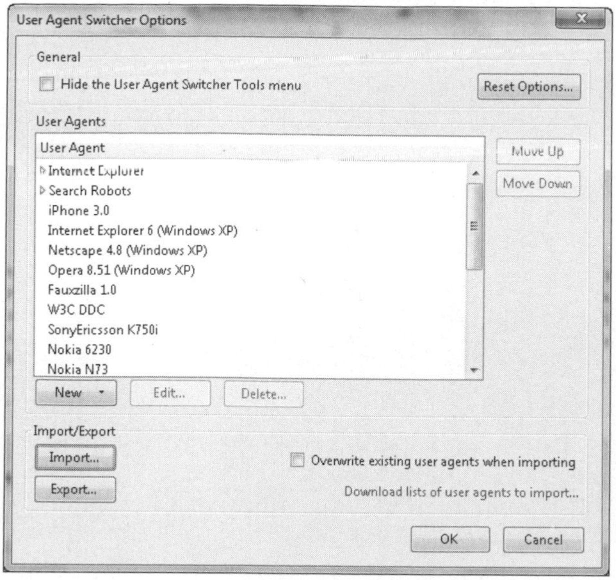

Figure 7-2:
With the
User Agent
Switcher
add-on,
Firefox can
impersonate
a variety
of Web
browsers
and mobile
devices,
including
the iPhone.

Small Screen Renderer

The Small Screen Renderer add-on (https://addons.mozilla.org/
en-US/firefox/addon/526) displays Web pages in a very narrow columnar format in Firefox. Used in conjunction with the User Agent Switcher add-
on, this can give you a pretty good visual approximation of what a Web page
might look like on the small screen of a mobile device.

To activate the Small Screen Renderer, choose View➪Small Screen
Rendering. You can use the Small Screen Renderer without the User Agent
Switcher. However, if you don't have the User Agent Switcher activated and
set to a mobile device, all the Small Screen Renderer will do is display the
desktop version of a Web site in a very narrow columnar format. We encourage you to use these two add-ons together for best results.

For example, ESPN devotes significant resources to making their Web presence as mobile-friendly as possible, but you won't be able to see the mobile
versions of the site by entering www.espn.com into a Web browser on a
desktop computer unless you use the User Agent Switcher (covered in the
previous section). Combine the User Agent Switcher add-on with the Small
Screen Renderer, and you can get a pretty good idea of how a site like ESPN
will look in a variety of different mobile devices. Figure 7-3 shows the ESPN
site as it appears in Internet Explorer 8 on a desktop computer. Compare that
to Figure 7-4, which shows how the ESPN site displays in Firefox on a desktop computer, when the Small Screen Renderer add-on is used with the User
Agent Switcher set to impersonate a Nokia N70 mobile phone.

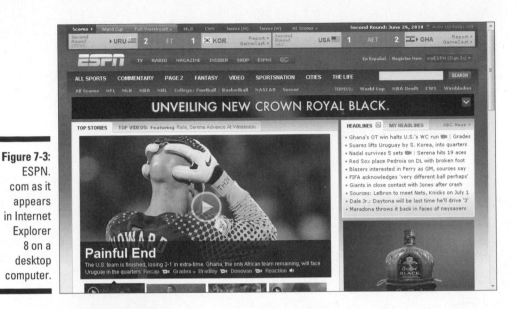

Figure 7-3:
ESPN.
com as it
appears
in Internet
Explorer
8 on a
desktop
computer.

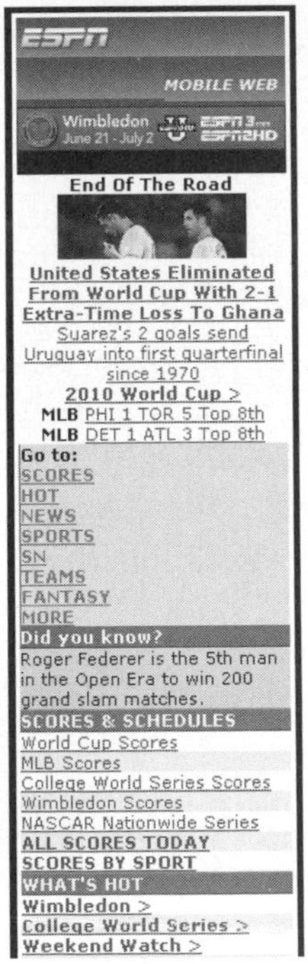

Figure 7-4:
ESPN.com
displayed
in Firefox
using the
User Agent
Switcher
and Small
Screen
Renderer
add-ons.

XHTML Mobile Profile

The XHTML Mobile Profile add-on (`https://addons.mozilla.org/en-US/firefox/addon/1345`) allows Firefox to display XHTML MP Web pages more effectively. You learn more about designing pages for mobile devices using the XHTML Mobile Profile in Chapters 3 and 6.

wmlbrowser

The wmlbrowser (`https://addons.mozilla.org/en-US/firefox/addon/62`) runs in the background to allow Firefox to display mobile Web pages designed in Wireless Markup Language (WML). Most Mobile Web designers don't use WML anymore, but there are still many old Web pages on the Internet that were created this way. For more on WML, see Chapter 5.

Using Mobile Emulators

You can preview mobile designs and get a pretty good idea of how they will look on many different mobile devices by using mobile emulators (also called simulators). We offer more detailed descriptions in the section that follows, but here are three general categories of mobile testing options that simulate mobile Web browsers, operating systems, and the limitations of mobile devices:

- **Mobile emulators that work within a desktop Web browser:** You'll find many Web sites that offer mobile emulators. These are the simplest but most limited options for testing how Web sites will appear on mobile devices.

- **Emulators you download and install on your computer:** Many device manufacturers offer emulators of their devices, as well as more complete SDKs (software development kits) that can be downloaded and installed on your computer.

- **More advanced options:** It's difficult to categorize all of the testing options in the ever-changing world of mobile Web design, so we're lumping several high-end services (including our favorites) into this category.

Testing with online mobile emulators in a Web browser

Although they offer the simplest option for testing mobile Web designs, most emulators that work within a Web browser suffer from two big limitations. First, they are running on your computer, which almost certainly has a much faster processor and many other capabilities you won't find on mobile phones, and second, unless you're using the User Agent Switcher described in the "Installing Mobile Add-Ons for Firefox" section earlier in this chapter, all you're doing is opening the desktop version of a site in a small window within a Web browser.

iPhone

Although you may be tempted to test your pages in the online emulators at `www.iphonetester.com` or `www.testiphone.com`, beware that they can be very misleading if your goal is to see what your site will look like on an actual iPhone. For example, we tested both of these online tools by entering the URL of a site we know includes files created with Adobe Flash. If you know much about the limitations of the iPhone, you know that the iPhone doesn't support Flash. But, despite that well-known limitation, both of these iPhone emulators displayed the Flash files perfectly. We consider that rather misleading and have to give them low marks as a result. Like many online emulators that work within a Web browser, these services do little more than show you how your pages will look within the limited screen size of a mobile phone.

Opera Mini

If you want to see how your mobile Web page looks on some of the most limited, low-end mobile devices on the market, you can test with the Opera Mini demo site (`www.opera.com/mini/demo`), which does a pretty good job of showing how a page will display within the limited functionality of the Opera mini Web browser. This emulator is especially useful if you are targeting the vast international market that is more likely to use the Opera browser than most mobile phone users in the United States. *Tip:* For best results, use this emulator in combination with the User Agent Switcher described in the "Installing Mobile Add-Ons for Firefox" section earlier in this chapter.

dotMobi

The dotMobi site features an emulator at `http://mtld.mobi/emulator.php`, which simulates how Web sites look on some of the most basic mobile devices, including the Sony K750 and the Nokia N70 (see Figure 7-5). Although the selection is very limited, and like other options in this category it works best when used with the User Agent Switcher described in the "Installing Mobile Add-Ons for Firefox" section earlier in this chapter, the service can give you an idea of what your mobile site may look like in some of the most limited phones still in use today.

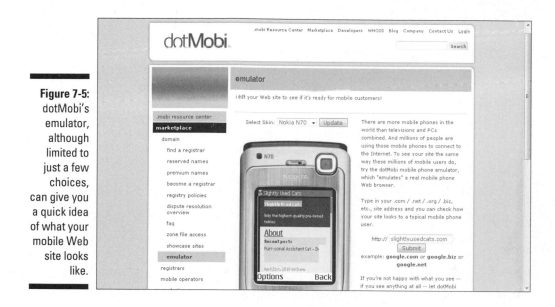

Figure 7-5:
dotMobi's
emulator,
although
limited to
just a few
choices,
can give you
a quick idea
of what your
mobile Web
site looks
like.

The dotMobi site also includes a code-testing engine similar to the testing services on the W3C Web site (see the "Testing Your Site Code with the W3C Tools" section, later in this chapter). The dotMobi code-testing engine checks your mobile code for conflicts or errors that might have slipped past you. To use this service, navigate to `http://ready.mobi/index.html` and enter the URL of any site that you want to test.

Downloading mobile emulators and SDKs

Although it takes more time and effort to download, install, and use Mobile emulators and SDKs, these tools generally do a better job of simulating how a mobile device will work on a desktop computer than most of the emulators you'll find on the Web. These tools are most often used by programmers creating applications for mobile devices, but they can also be useful to mobile Web designers.

Phones that run Android

The Google Android operating system is being used in an ever-growing list of mobile devices. You can download the Android SDK, which includes a mobile device emulator, by visiting `http://developer.android.com/guide/developing/tools/emulator.html`.

The Android emulator, as shown in Figure 7-6, is a little tricky to manipulate using a desktop computer. Be careful when clicking on the screen to use the directional buttons (also known as a "D-Pad") when you move around pages because they can cause the screen to keep moving long after you stop.

BlackBerry

The profusion of BlackBerry devices, which come in many different screen sizes and with different versions of the browser and operating system, make designing for BlackBerry phones especially demanding. To help manage these variations, you can download emulators for a wide range of BlackBerry devices at `www.blackberry.com/developers/downloads/simulators/`. You must sign up for an account with BlackBerry before you can download the emulators, but they are available for free.

As you can see from the menu shown in Figure 7-7, BlackBerry offers emulators for dozens of BlackBerry phones, used on a variety of carriers. Once you have decided which BlackBerry emulator you want to download, double-click the name of the device, and follow the instructions on the BlackBerry Web site to install the emulator on your computer.

Figure 7-6:
The Android
Emulator.

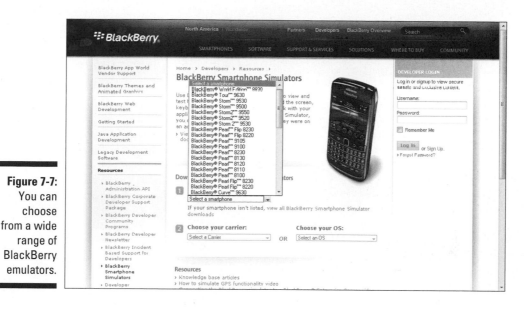

Figure 7-7:
You can
choose
from a wide
range of
BlackBerry
emulators.

iPhone

Apple offers an extensive developer program, but you have to pay $99 to participate and gain access to Apple's SDKs, simulators, and other support services.

Testing with more sophisticated services

If you have the money and you work on a project in which it's critical that your mobile Web site be tested across a wide variety of devices, the high-end services may be worth the cost.

DeviceAnywhere

Our favorite option for testing mobile designs on a wide variety of devices using a desktop computer, DeviceAnywhere (www.deviceanywhere.com) allows you to access more than 1,500 handsets and test them as they would perform on carriers in the United States, Canada, England, Spain, Germany, France, and Brazil.

The electronic innards of all the devices are wired into long racks connected to the Internet; when you sign up for the service, you can choose a device (see Figure 7-8 for an idea of the line-up of available devices) and then use your computer mouse and keyboard to manipulate it. For example, you can type a URL into a browser on any phone directly to see how it will display in that phone's Web browser, on its operating system, as it should be delivered by the carrier you selected. You can also click a simulated keypad to send a Short Message Service (SMS, or "text") message, and even connect a microphone and speaker to your computer to test audio-related features, such as listening to music or using the microphone to leave a short voice message.

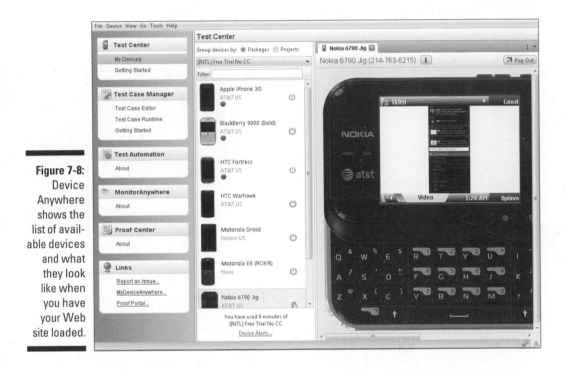

Figure 7-8: Device Anywhere shows the list of available devices and what they look like when you have your Web site loaded.

To use DeviceAnywhere, you first sign up for an account and then download and install their special software on your hard drive. After you launch their program, you access the DeviceAnywhere service using their program over the Internet where you can access a wide variety of mobile devices.

After you open the DeviceAnywhere service, you scroll through a list of available phones, as shown in Figure 7-8. Sometimes devices are busy or out of commission, but after extensive testing, we found the service to be remarkably reliable. When you find a device you want to use, right-click (⌘-click on the Mac) to select and open the device.

After a device opens on your screen, you can use your mouse to click the buttons on the image of the phone to interact as if you were pressing the keys on the phone's keypad. It can take a little trial and error to figure out how to use some devices, especially limited feature phones that you may never have used before, but DeviceAnywhere includes a few special tools to help you enter URLs and interact with each phone.

The first three hours of testing are free (albeit limited to eight of the most popular devices), but after that, the testing packages can get expensive. The time spent testing the devices is measured in 6-minute (1/10 of an hour) increments, and the devices have a built-in fail-safe mechanism that shuts them down and disconnects you if you forget and leave one running in the background for 30 minutes. Additional testing hours cost about $16/hour, with package deals reducing the cost.

The quickest way to run through your minutes is to get carried away with the cornucopia of devices that are available to play with at DeviceAnywhere. Always right-click (on a Mac, ⌘-click) to disconnect the device as soon as you're done testing.

Keynote

Keynote (www.keynote.com) offers a high-end service that includes testing your mobile Web sites, applications, and other services for you. Keynote serves big companies and is a premium (by that, we mean not cheap) service that provides testing and monitoring using real devices on a broad range of mobile carriers all over the world.

Services from device manufacturers

Some device manufacturers provide support services for designers and developers of mobile Web sites and applications, although you may have to pay hefty fees for such special help. For example, Research in Motion (RIM), the maker of the BlackBerry line of smartphones, might set up a server and custom-built emulator to help a large bank test its mobile banking site across a variety of BlackBerry phones. Check with device manufacturers for more information on their custom services if you need this kind of high-level support.

Testing with Adobe's Device Central

If you use Adobe Dreamweaver, bundled along with it is the Device Central application that makes it possible for you to see your designs on some mobile devices. The initial selection is quite limited, but you can add new phone profiles. The functionality of the devices is still somewhat less accurate than in high-end emulators like DeviceAnywhere, but if you use Dreamweaver, this is a quick way to at least get an idea of how your site will display on a variety of devices. While much of Device Central focuses on empowering you to test Flash Lite applications on mobile devices, you can test any Web page on your hard drive using this program.

Follow these steps to preview your pages with Device Central:

1. **Open a Web page that you want to preview in Dreamweaver, choose File⇨Preview in Browser, and select Device Central from the list of options.**

The page opens in Device Central, which displays the page in one of the many mobile emulators installed in the program.

2. **In the Test Center panel on the left, choose My Devices. Then in the panel in the middle, select any device.**

   The page you're previewing displays in that device. You can choose any of the available options (indicated by a green circle) in the list of devices in the center panel to view the page in different devices.

3. **Study the page carefully and test all the links, rollovers, and any other special effects to make sure that the page appears the way you want it to on this mobile device.**

   You navigate around a Web page using these devices, much like you would if you had the real phone. For example, use your mouse to click the navigation arrows just above the keypad to scroll up, down, left, and right.

4. **Close Device Central and return to Dreamweaver to make any necessary changes to the page.**

You can add more devices to Adobe Device Central on a Windows computer by choosing Devices⇨Download Device Profile, but your computer must be connected to the Internet for this feature to work. On a Mac, choose Devices⇨Add to Test Devices.

Testing with the Actual Devices

Every mobile designer worth his salt admits that you can only do so much with tools on a desktop computer to simulate what users do in the real world with your carefully crafted mobile Web pages. For instance, the following are just some of the problems that could arise when you view your Web designs the way mobile phone users see them:

- ✔ Your color scheme is unreadable under harsh daylight conditions.
- ✔ Your multimedia files are too large to work on the limited processor of a mobile device.
- ✔ Clicking on your navigation links is frustrating, or even impossible, given the limited interface options of a mobile device.
- ✔ Scrolling through long pages of data is exceptionally tedious.
- ✔ Having your page open for 15 minutes completely drains the battery.

You can't know these things sitting in a comfy chair in a safe, air-conditioned office with all of the power of your desktop computer and the interface options of a mouse and keyboard.

True mobile gurus say the best option is to have shelves, drawers, or closets overflowing with mobile testing units, but most settle for a representative sampling of the 3 to 10 most common devices. If you don't have the resources to keep multiple mobile phones on hand for testing, consider these options:

- Use *the friends and family plan.* That is, reach out to all your friends and family members, ask them what kinds of phones they use, and then enlist them as testers for your site(s).

- As your needs grow, you may find that you need to add more handsets to your roster of supported testing platforms (after all, you can't expect your friends to rush out and buy the latest, greatest mobile gizmo just because you need to see how your images resize). The next stage in assembling an ad-hoc mobile testing network is to start reaching out to people through social-networking sites, such as Facebook, Twitter, MySpace, or LinkedIn. Simply ask via these networks whether people can check out your mobile site and leave you a note about what they think and what device they used to access the site.

- Join professional associations, such as Mobile Monday (www.mobile monday.net), or any group of Web designers, and attend (or organize) gatherings where you get together and test each other's sites.

- Make frequent trips to electronics and cellphone stores (rotating the stores so that the clerks don't get sick of your incessant questions), and even stop people on the street or in shopping malls to ask them whether they can help.

Testing Your Site Code with the W3C Tools

Before you take that last fateful step and hit the button to make your mobile Web site finally go live, do one last check (dubbed *an idiot check*) to make sure that you haven't missed something obvious.

Testing your Web designs with the W3C validation tools has always been a good idea, but it's even more important for mobile Web design. Desktop Web browsers, including Internet Explorer, Firefox, and Chrome, are surprisingly forgiving of common errors in XHTML code. Mobile Web browsers are not. That's because mobile Web browsers are much smaller applications than their desktop counterparts and don't have the capacity to handle even the most common mistakes in coding.

The W3C, long revered for its work on developing and encouraging the use of standards on the Web, has a new mobileOK Checker (see Figure 7-9) that checks for known issues on mobile phones (http://validator.w3.org/

mobile). The tester runs through your site, checking your code for known conflicts and errors, and then returns a report on what you need to do to clean up things.

While you're at it, test the markup language on your site at http:// validator.w3.org/ and then test the CSS (Cascading Style Sheets) on your site at http://jigsaw.w3.org/css-validator/.

REMEMBER

Your pages work better in Web browsers when they're error-free, and search engines will like them better, too.

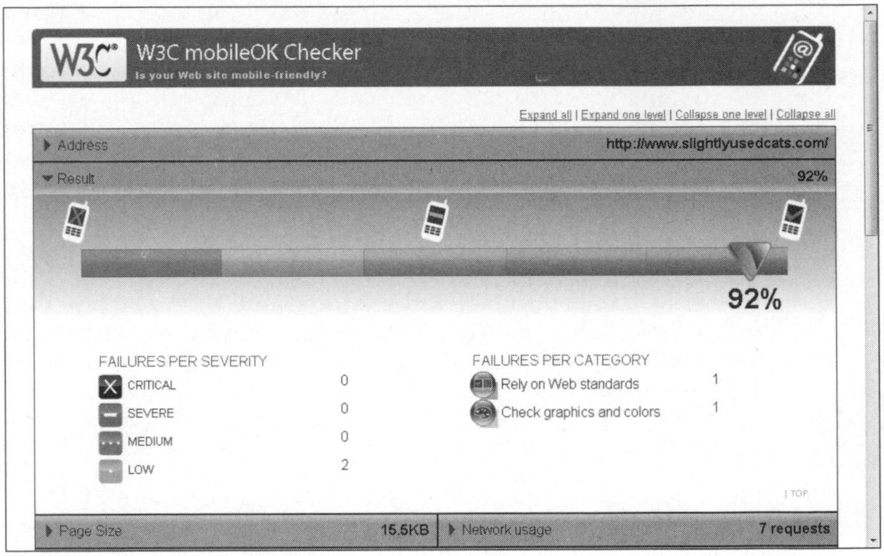

Figure 7-9: The W3C mobileOK Checker can be a bit of an ego-deflator, but it gives you all the stats you need to make any last-minute fixes on glaring errors.

Choosing a Mobile Domain

You can upload your mobile Web page files to your Web server using FTP, just as you would upload the files of any desktop Web site (as you learn in the section that follows). The real challenge is deciding where to put your mobile version. At least eight (at last count) domain variations are commonly in use for mobile Web sites. Some mobile Web designers publish their mobile sites to a new domain with the .mobi domain ending. Many other designers are using *subdomains,* a version of a regular domain that shares the same basic address.

Table 7-1 demonstrates some common subdomains and shows some examples of what the full URL would look like.

Table 7-1	Common Mobile Subdomains
Subdomain Prefix	*Example*
`iphone`	`iphone.slightlyusedcats.com`
`m`	`m.slightlyusedcats.com`
`mobile`	`mobile.slightlyusedcats.com`
`pda`	`pda.slightlyusedcats.com`
`xhtml`	`xhtml.digitalfamily.com`
`wap`	`wap.artesianmedia.com`
`wml`	`wml.hardnewsinc.com`
`wireless`	`wireless.sipsfromthefirehose.com`

Some mobile designers prefer to use folder names to add a mobile address. In this case, you simply upload the mobile version of your site to a special folder with a name such as `/m`, `/mobile`, `/i` or `/iphone`, `/gmm`, `/portable`, or `/wireless`. If you set this folder up at the main root directory level of your site, and name the home page of your mobile site index.html, the URL would look something like this: `www.digitalfamily.com/m/`.

Our testing has shown that on low-end feature phones, it is often difficult to enter the "/" character. If you are designing a site for such basic devices, you might want to consider setting up a subdomain that uses a prefix, such as those included in the Table 7-1, rather than a folder name.

After you set up your mobile site (or sites) at one or more special URLs, you can link directly to those addresses and promote the addresses in your advertising. If you want to route the traffic from mobile sites directly to these addresses, you have to use some kind of mobile detection and redirection system. For more on this subject, please see Chapter 6.

Publishing Your Mobile Web Site

After you create and test your Web site so that it's ready to publish on the Web, you can use Dreamweaver's publishing tools to upload your site to your Web server. Which features you use depends on the kind of Web server you use. If you use a commercial service provider, you most likely need Dreamweaver's FTP features, which we cover in detail in the following section. (If you prefer to use your own FTP program, see the nearby sidebar, "Using a dedicated FTP program.")

Using a dedicated FTP program

If you prefer to use a dedicated FTP program instead of Dreamweaver's built-in features, you can download FTP programs for the Mac and PC at the following Web addresses:

✔ `http://fireftp.mozdev.org`: FireFTP is a nifty little FTP program that's an add-on to Firefox and a great alternative to Dreamweaver's FTP features. Ideal for fixing things when you're on the road and don't have Dreamweaver handy or when you just want to view the files on your server without using Dreamweaver, this program can be added to any version of Firefox (for free).

✔ `http://filezilla-project.org`: FileZilla is a popular open-source option that works on computers running Windows, Mac, and Linux operating systems.

✔ `www.ipswitch.com`: A popular FTP program for the PC, WS_FTP is such a sophisticated FTP program that many Web designers will pay for the cost of this program, which offers a free trial version.

✔ `www.cuteftp.com`: A popular Windows program, CuteFTP, can be downloaded from the Web site.

✔ `www.fetchsoftworks.com` and `www.panic.com/transmit`: If you use a Macintosh computer, popular options are Fetch, available for download at the former Web address, and Transmit, available for download at the latter address.

✔ `http://cyberduck.ch`: Web designers working on the Mac platform are singling out the freeware program Cyberduck for praise because it works not just with FTP programs, but also for managing Amazon S3 cloud-based sites.

You need the following information from your Web hosting service before you can configure Dreamweaver's FTP features. Most service providers send this information in an e-mail message when you sign up for an account. If you don't have this information, you need to contact your service provider for it because it's unique to your account on your Web hosting service. Here's what you need:

✔ **The FTP hostname:** A hostname is basically a human-readable nickname used by the Internet to locate a particular server. For example: `ftp.domainname.com`.

✔ The **path to the Web directory (optional but highly recommended):** The path looks similar to `/web/htdocs/slightlyusedcats`.

✔ **Your FTP login or username:** This is your personal username, which you created or was assigned to you when you established your Web hosting account.

✔ **Your FTP password**

✔ **Any special instructions from your server:** For example, you may need to use Passive FTP or any of the other advanced settings covered in the section that follows. This varies from server to server, so you need to ask your Web hosting service. (If you're having trouble connecting and you're not sure about these options, you can always experiment by selecting and deselecting these options to see whether a setting enables you to connect.)

Setting up Dreamweaver's FTP features

After you gather all your FTP information, you're ready to set up Dreamweaver's FTP publishing features. This process can seem daunting and often takes a few tries to get right, but the good news is that you have to do it only once. (Dreamweaver saves these settings for you so you don't have to set them up every time you want to upload new pages to your site.)

Follow these steps to set up Dreamweaver's FTP features and publish files to a Web server:

1. **Open Dreamweaver and choose Site⇨Manage Sites.**

    The Manage Sites dialog box opens.

2. **In the list of defined sites, select the site you want to publish and then click the Edit button.**

    The Site Setup dialog box opens. If your site isn't listed in this dialog box, you haven't set up your site.

3. **Select Servers from the categories listed in the left panel of the Site Setup dialog box.**

    The server list appears. If you haven't set up any Web servers in Dreamweaver, this list is blank, as shown in Figure 7-10. Any servers you have set up properly are listed in this dialog box.

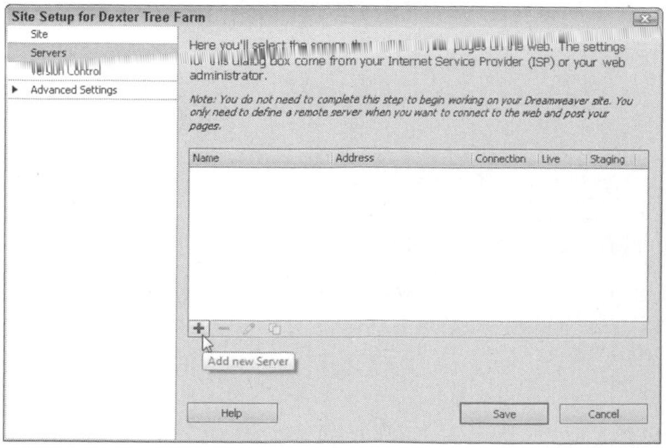

Figure 7-10: Click the small plus sign at the bottom of the Site Setup dialog box to open the Basic server configuration window where you can enter your FTP information.

4. Click the small plus sign at the bottom left of the server list area, as shown in Figure 7-10.

The Basic tab opens in the Servers dialog box and FTP is selected automatically, as shown in Figure 7-11. (If you need to use an option other than FTP, look ahead to the list at the end of these steps.)

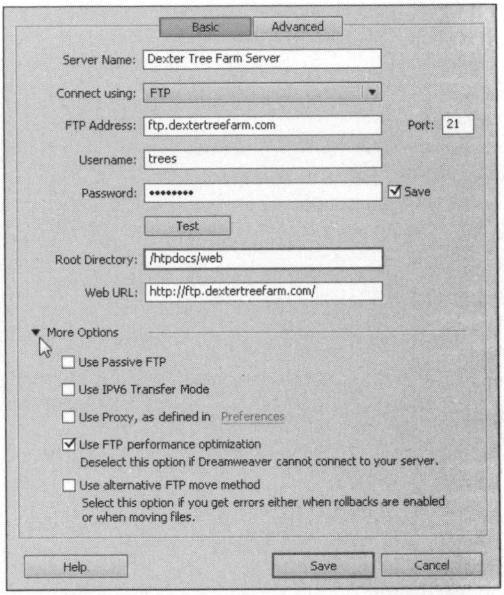

Figure 7-11:
Enter all the
information
from your
Web hosting
company,
including
your name
and pass-
word, in
the Basic
Server
Setup dialog
box.

Basic	Advanced

Server Name: Dexter Tree Farm Server

Connect using: FTP

FTP Address: ftp.dextertreefarm.com   Port: 21

Username: trees

Password: ••••••••   ☑ Save

Test

Root Directory: /htpdocs/web

Web URL: http://ftp.dextertreefarm.com/

▼ More Options

☐ Use Passive FTP

☐ Use IPV6 Transfer Mode

☐ Use Proxy, as defined in Preferences

☑ Use FTP performance optimization
Deselect this option if Dreamweaver cannot connect to your server.

☐ Use alternative FTP move method
Select this option if you get errors either when rollbacks are enabled
or when moving files.

Help   Save   Cancel

5. Enter a name in the Server Name field.

You can name your server anything you like. Choose a name that lets you easily choose among the servers you've set up. (If you only use one Web server to host your site, this doesn't matter as much as if you host your site on multiple sites, which is generally done only by very large or international sites.)

6. Enter the FTP address for your Web server account.

Again this information depends on how your Web server is set up, but most use one of the following: ftp.*servername*.com, ftp.*your domainname*.com, or simply *yourdomain*.com without anything at the beginning of the domain.

7. In the Username and Password fields, type your username (or login name) and password, respectively.

Again, this information is unique to your account on your Web server.

8. **Select the Save check box to the right of the Password field if you want Dreamweaver to store your access information.**

   This is handy because you can then automatically connect to the server anytime you want to upload or download pages. However, selecting the Save check box could enable anyone with access to your computer to gain access to your Web server.

9. **Click the Test button to make sure you've entered everything correctly.**

   Making a mistake is so easy, so the ability to test the connection and make any needed adjustments before you close this dialog box is helpful. If you connect without any problems, Dreamweaver responds with a box saying `Dreamweaver connected to your Web server successfully`. (*Note:* You must save the password to use the test feature, but you can deselect the Save box after you test if you prefer not to save the password in the program.)

   If you have trouble connecting to your site, skip ahead to Step 11 for a few advanced options that may help.

10. **In the Root Directory (also known as the local site folder) field, type the directory name of the remote site in which documents visible to the public are stored.**

    The root directory usually looks something like `public_html/` or `www/ htdocs/`. Again, this depends on your server.

    If you upload your files to the wrong directory on your server, they aren't visible when you view your site through a browser.

11. **Click the small arrow to the left of More Options.**

    You may not need to change any of these settings, but if you have trouble connecting to your server and are sure you've entered your username, password, and FTP address correctly, adjusting these settings may enable you to connect.

    Select and deselect each of these options and then click the Test button after each change to see whether any of these adjustments make the difference and enable you to connect to your server.

    A little experimentation with settings before waiting on hold with tech support is usually worth the effort. But if you're really having trouble establishing a connection with your server, call or e-mail the tech support staff at your Web server. The only people who can help you are those who run your Web server because the settings are specific to your service provider and can vary dramatically from one hosting company to another. We've done our best to give you the most common options here, and with a little trial and error, the suggestions here should help you connect to most Web hosting companies. If you're really stuck though, ask for more help from the people who run your server.

12. **After you fill in everything, click the Test button; if you successfully connect to your server, click the Save button to save your settings.**

    Dreamweaver saves all your FTP settings (assuming you opted to save the password). The beauty is that you never have to enter these settings again after they work properly, and you can access your Web server from the Files panel in Dreamweaver, as you can read about in the next section.

Dreamweaver provides five access options. If you work at a large company or university, you're likely to use one of the following options rather than FTP. The options available from the Connect Using drop-down list (see Figure 7-11) are as follows:

- ✔ **FTP:** Provides basic File Transfer Protocol connection and transfer features.

- ✔ **SFTP:** Provides a more secure FTP connection. If you can use a secure connection, it's definitely the preferred choice, and it's required by some Web servers to maintain higher levels of security.

- ✔ **Local/Network:** Select this option if you're using a Web server on a local network, such as your company's or university's server. For specific settings and requirements, check with your system administrator.

- ✔ **WebDAV:** Select this option if you're using a server with the WebDAV (Web-based Distributed Authoring and Versioning) protocol, such as Microsoft IIS.

- ✔ **RDS:** Select the RDS (Rapid Development Services) option if you're using ColdFusion on a remote server.

Publishing files to a Web server with FTP

You can upload pages to your server and download pages from your server using the built-in FTP capabilities of Dreamweaver.

To transfer files between your hard drive and a remote server (after you've successfully set up the FTP features we cover in the preceding section of this chapter), follow these steps:

1. **Make sure the site you want to work on is selected in the Files panel in Dreamweaver.**

2. **In the top left of the Files panel, click the Connects to Remote Host button (which looks like a blue electrical cable plugging into itself).**

   If you're not already connected to the Internet, the Connects to Remote Host button starts your Internet connection. If you have trouble connecting this way, establish your Internet connection as you usually do to check e-mail or surf the Web, and then return to Dreamweaver and click the Connects to Remote Host button after you're connected. When your computer is online, Dreamweaver should have no trouble automatically establishing an FTP connection with your host server.

If you still have trouble establishing a connection to your Web server, refer to the preceding section, "Setting up Dreamweaver's FTP features," and make sure that you specified the server information correctly.

3. **After you establish a connection between your computer and your Web server, click the Expand/Collapse button (which looks like stacked horizontal lines at the far right of the top of the Files panel).**

When you click this button, Dreamweaver displays both the local folder with your site on your hard drive and the remote folder with the site on your server. We prefer this dual view because seeing both folders side by side makes moving files from one place to another easier. This dual view also helps us visualize the structure of the site on the server.

You can also view your local site folder by choosing Local View from the drop-down list at the top right (see Figure 7-12). Or choose Remote View to see only the files on the server.

Figure 7-12:
The row
of buttons
across
the top
control FTP
functions,
making it
easy to con-
nect to your
Web server
and upload/
download
files.

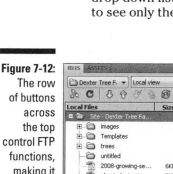

4. **To *upload* (or transfer from your hard drive to your Web server) a file, select the file from the Local View panel (which displays the files on your hard drive) and click the Put Files button (the up arrow) in the Files panel.**

The files are copied automatically to your server when you transfer them. You can select multiple files or folders to be transferred simultaneously.

After you upload files to you server, test your work by using a Web browser to view them online. Sometimes things that look and work fine on your computer (such as links) don't work on the server.

5. **To *download* (or transfer from your Web server to your hard drive) files or folders, select the files or folders from the Remote View panel (which displays the files on your server) and click the Get Files button (the down arrow) in the Files panel.**

   The files are copied automatically to your hard drive when you transfer them.

   When you copy files to or from your server, the files you transfer overwrite the files already at the destination. Dreamweaver notifies you about the overwriting if it notices you're replacing a newer file with an older one, but it can't always correctly assess the proper time differences. Take note of these warnings but keep in mind that you can get warnings that aren't always accurate when they're based on the age of a file, especially if you use more than one computer to work on your Web site.

   When the transfer is complete, you can open the files on your hard drive.

6. **To close this dual-panel dialog box and return to Dreamweaver's main workspace, simply click the Expand/Collapse button again.**

Finding and Fixing Broken Links

If you're trying to rein in a chaotic Web site or if you just want to check a site for broken links, you'll be pleased to discover Dreamweaver's Link Checker. You can use this feature to verify the links in a single file or an entire Web site, and Link Checker can automatically fix all the referring links at once if a link is broken.

For example, assume that someone on your team (because you would never do such a thing yourself) changed the name of a file from new.htm to old. htm without using the Files panel or any of Dreamweaver's automatic link update features. Maybe this person changed the name using another program or simply renamed it in Explorer (Windows) or Finder (Mac). Changing the filename was easy, but what this person may not have realized is that if he didn't change the links to the file when the file was renamed, the links are now broken.

If only one page links to the file that your clueless teammate changed, fixing the broken link isn't such a big deal. As long as you remember which file the page links from, you can simply open that page and use the Property inspector to reset the link the same way you created the link in the first place.

But many times, a single page in a Web site is linked to many other pages. When that's the case, fixing all the link references can be time-consuming, and forgetting some of them is all too easy. That's why Link Checker is so helpful.

If you're working on a dynamic, database-driven site or if your site was altered with programming that was performed outside Dreamweaver, Link Checker may not work properly. Link Checker works best for sites with static HTML pages and sites created using DWT Dreamweaver templates.

You must have the entire site on your hard drive and you must have completed the site setup process for Link Checker to work properly.

Checking for broken links

To check a site for broken links, follow these steps:

1. **In the drop-down list on the left at the top of the Files panel, select the site you want to work on.**

   If you already have the site open in Dreamweaver, you can skip this step.

2. **Choose Site⇨Check Links Sitewide.**

   The Link Checker tab opens in the Results panel at the bottom of the page, just under the Property inspector, as shown in Figure 7-13. The tab displays a list of internal and external links as well as any pages, images, or other items not linked from any other page in the site — dubbed *orphans.* Unused images can waste space on your server, so this list is handy if you want to clean up old images or other elements you no longer use on the site.

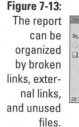

   Most service providers limit the amount of space on your server and charge extra if you exceed that limit. You can save valuable server space by deleting unused files, especially if they're image or multi-media files. But just because you delete them from your hard drive doesn't mean they're deleted from the server. Make sure you remove them from the Remote Site window in the Files panel as well as the Local Site panel.

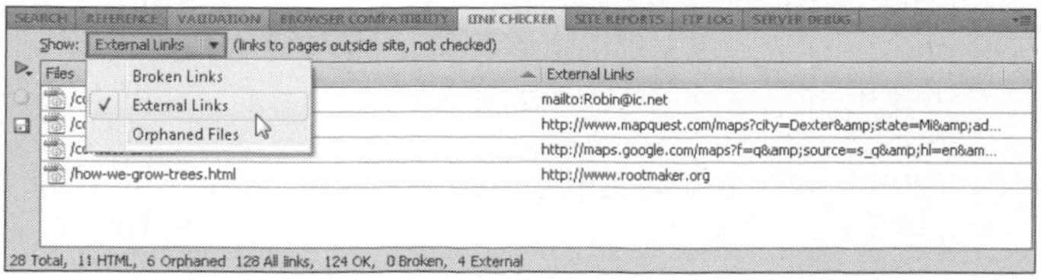

Figure 7-13:
The report can be organized by broken links, exter-nal links, and unused files.

Fixing broken links and missing images

Broken links are one of the worst problems you can have on a Web site. After you identify a broken link in a site, fix it as soon as possible. Nothing turns off visitors faster than clicking a link and getting a `File Not Found` error page, especially if they're looking for information fast on a mobile device. Fortunately, Dreamweaver makes it simple to fix broken links or detect when images are missing by providing quick access to files with broken links and automating the process of fixing multiple links to the same file.

After using the Link Checker tab described in the preceding section to identify broken links or missing images, follow these steps to fix them by using the Results panel:

1. **With the Results panel open at the bottom of the page, double-click a filename that Dreamweaver identifies as a broken link or missing image.**

   The page and its corresponding Property inspector open. The Results panel remains visible.

2. **Select the broken link or missing image on the open page.**

3. **In the Property inspector, click the Browse button (which looks like a folder) to the right of the Src text box to fix an *image*. To fix a *link*, click the Browse button next to the Link text box.**

   If you're fixing an image, the Select Image Source dialog box appears, where you can select the image file you need. However, if you're fixing a link, you see a slightly different dialog box, where you need to browse for the file in your site folder.

4. **Click to select the file you need and then click OK.**

   If you replace an image, the image file reappears on the page. The link automatically changes to reflect the new filename and location.

If the link that you correct appears in multiple pages and you fix the link using the broken link's Results panel, Dreamweaver prompts you with a dialog box asking whether you want to fix the remaining broken link references to the file. Click the Yes button to automatically correct all other references. Click the No button to leave the other links unchanged.

Testing Your Work with Dreamweaver's Site Reporting Feature

If you've used Dreamweaver to build your mobile Web site, you can check your work using the Dreamweaver Site Reporting feature. This feature allows you to create a variety of reports and even customize them to identify problems with external links, redundant and empty tags, untitled documents, and missing alternate text. You can easily miss things — especially when you work on a tight deadline — and common problems in Web design are magnified on the mobile platform.

Follow these steps to produce a site report of your entire Web site:

1. **In the drop-down list at the top left of the Files panel, select the site you want to work on.**

   If you already have the site you want to test open in Dreamweaver, you can skip this step. *Note:* Your site appears in the Files panel list only if you've completed the site setup process. See "Setting up Dreamweaver's FTP features," earlier in this chapter, for more on this.

2. **Make sure any documents you have open in Dreamweaver's work-space are saved by choosing File⇨Save All.**

3. **Choose Site⇨Reports.**

   The Reports dialog box appears (see Figure 7-14).

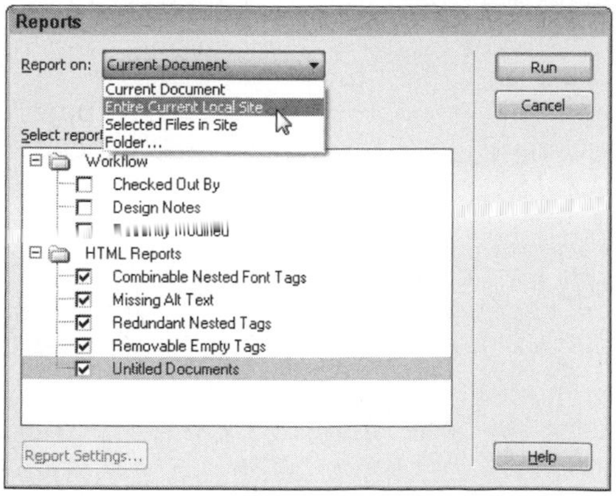

Figure 7-14:
In the Reports dialog box, you can select any and all options, and run reports on a single page or the entire site.

4. In the Report On drop-down list, choose Entire Current Local Site.

We most commonly use this feature to test an entire site just before publishing it to the Web, but you can choose to check only a single page by opening the page in Dreamweaver and then choosing Current Document in the Report On drop-down list. You can also run a report on selected files or on a particular folder. If you choose Selected Files in Site, you must first click to select the pages you want to check in the Files panel.

5. In the Select Reports section, select the check boxes for the reports you want.

You can select as many reports as you want. Table 7-2 demonstrates some of the reports that you can generate.

6. Click the Run button to create the report(s).

If you haven't already done so, you may be prompted to save your file, set up your site, or select a folder.

The Results panel appears, as shown in Figure 7-15, displaying a list of problems found on the site. To sort the list by category (such as filename, line number, or description), click the corresponding column heading.

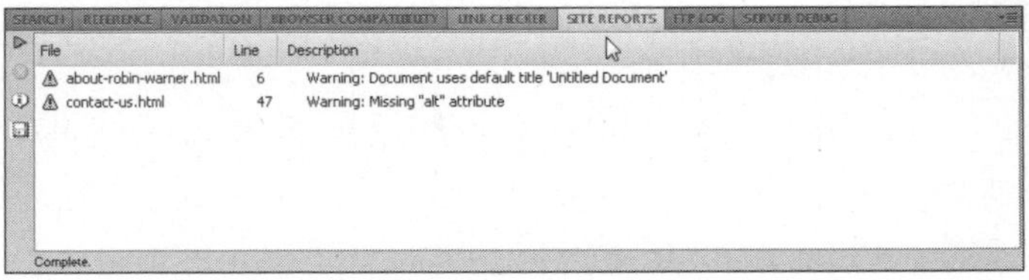

Figure 7-15: The Results panel displays a list of problems on your site.

	File	Line	Description
⚠	about-robin-warner.html	6	Warning: Document uses default title 'Untitled Document'
⚠	contact-us.html	47	Warning: Missing "alt" attribute

Complete.

7. Double-click any item in the Results panel to open the corresponding file in the document window.

The file opens, and the error is highlighted in the workspace.

You can also right-click (Windows) or Control-click (Mac) any line of the report and choose More Info to find additional details about the specific error or condition.

8. Use the Property inspector or another Dreamweaver feature to correct the identified problem and then save the file.

For more on how to maintain a site and fix problems in the design, please consult a book on Web design, such as *Dreamweaver CS5 For Dummies*.

Table 7-2	Site Report Options
Report Name	**What It Does**
Checked Out By	Lists files checked out of the site and identifies the person who checked them out. This feature is used only if you've set up the site to also work with Adobe Contribute.
Design Notes	Lists design notes used in the site.
Recently Modified	Lists files that have been edited within a specified time period. You can set the time period for the report by selecting the Recently Modified check box and then clicking the Report Settings button at the bottom of the dialog box.
Combinable Nested Font Tags	Lists all instances where you can combine nested tags. For example, `<font color="#000000"><font size="2">Great Web Sites You Should Visit</font></font>` is listed because you can simplify the code by combining the two font tags into `<font color="#000000" size="2">Great Web Sites You Should Visit</font>`.
Missing Alt Text	Lists all the image tags that don't include alt text. *Alt text* is a text description for an image tag included in the HTML code as an alternative if the image isn't displayed. Alt text is important to anyone who uses a special browser that reads Web pages.
Redundant Nested Tags	Lists all places where you have redundant nested tags. For example, `<h1>Good headlines <h1>are harder to write</h1>` than you might `think</h1>` is listed because you can simplify the code by removing the second `<h1>` tag to make the code look like this: `<h1>Good headlines are harder to write than you might think</h1>`.
Removable Empty Tags	Lists the empty tags on your site. Empty tags can occur when you delete an image, text section, or other element without deleting all the tags applied to the element.
Untitled Documents	Lists filenames that don't have a title. The `title` tag is easy to forget because it doesn't appear in the body of the page. The `title` tag specifies the text that appears at the very top of the browser window and also the text that appears in the Favorites list when someone bookmarks a page. You can enter a title for any page by entering text in the Title field just above the work area or in the Title field in the Page Properties dialog box.

Part III
Multimedia, Marketing, and E-Commerce

The 5th Wave   By Rich Tennant

"You ever notice how much more streaming media there is than there used to be?"

In this part . . .

Many of the popular video and multimedia formats that work well on the Web don't display at all on mobile devices, but that doesn't mean you can't use video. You just have to find the right format, which is what we help you do in this part.

E-commerce offers similar challenges, but we give you some great ways to sell even over mobile, and with the right technology, you can reach the growing mobile audience with e-commerce tools that work even on mobile devices.

And don't forget that you need to promote your mobile Web site, which is why you need the social media and marketing tips we include in this part.

Chapter 8

Using Images and Multimedia in Mobile Designs

*J*ust two decades ago, the predominant way that pictures and phones interacted was when an unruly 4 year old used a crayon to draw on the handset; as for video, the involvement was pretty much limited to chucking the device at the TV, hoping to hit the Off button when your legs fell asleep on the couch.

How times have changed.

According to Nielsen's "Three Screen Report," nearly 50 percent of mobile phone users have watched video on their handsets, with teenagers leading the way at about seven hours a month spent staring at tiny screens with headphones crammed in their ears, immersed in what researchers dub *cocooning media.*

Meanwhile, the widespread inclusion of increasingly higher-resolution cameras onto mobile devices has resulted in forests of hands upraised at just about any noteworthy public event as the crowds of people use their mobile phones to take pictures or record video.

People use their mobile devices to record, play, and share the significant experiences in their lives, the way that an earlier generation used Polaroid pictures or scrapbooks to capture moments in time. The challenge for designers is that in the last decade, everyone has taken it for granted that we can put all manner of media onto Web sites, as increasing broadband penetration, disk storage, and display resolution have made the browsing experience almost as quick and rewarding as changing channels on an HDTV. It's almost commonplace for movies and TV shows to use audio, video, and wild animated "splash" pages that load in Flash before the rest of the site is displayed.

If you're old enough to remember the early days of the Internet, just seeing a photo-realistic image appear on a full-color monitor was a thrill. We aren't saying that the mobile Web has to go back to those days (even though many experts say that a good way to think of designing for mobile is to pretend it's 1996, the era of 56K dialup modems).

Although the multimedia that spices up Web sites can be problematic on the mobile platform, that doesn't mean you can't use multimedia at all. In this chapter, we explain the best strategies to make your mobile Web sites dazzle, despite the constraints.

Understanding Screen Resolution and Color Depth

Before we talk about putting visual elements onto mobile device screens, we need to take a moment to define some of the essential terminology. If you're new to creating multimedia for the Web, understanding these basic concepts can help you when you optimize photos, videos, and more for your mobile site design. If you have a good grasp of display technology, consider this a review. If you're anxious to get into the meat of this chapter, skip to the section "Optimizing Images for the Mobile Web," later in this chapter.

This chapter explains basic concepts and options that work well in mobile Web designs. For steps that explain how to set these options by using a graphics editor, such as Photoshop or Photoshop Elements, flip to Appendix B.

Color depth

Color depth refers to the number of colors a screen can display, generally referred to by the number of *bits*. Each pixel on a display has a numerical value; for example, 1-bit color means that the pixel could be either black or white. That pixel would either be *on* (white) or *off* (black). The color depth then increases in *binary* (computer language) code. For example, 8-bit color is 2^8, or 256 colors.

You can choose or change an image's color depth in a graphics editor. Here's what you need to know about color depth when you design for different phones:

✔ **Feature phones:** Many low-end feature phones still display in 8 bit color, which gives images a vaguely cartoony look.

✔ **Smartphones:** Most smartphones use the same standard as desktop and laptop computers, and display in 24-bit color, which translates into 16,777,216 possible colors.

Some very high-end graphics cards support 40- and 64-bit color (281.5 trillion possible colors), which most sane people would argue is overkill for a device that might be viewed in bright sunlight or under sickly fluorescent lamps.

Web designers have worked for years to master the art of compressing JPEG images or reducing the number of colors in GIF and PNG files to make them download faster. On the mobile Web, optimizing images so they download quickly is even more important. The more you can restrict your color palette, the smaller the file sizes of your images and the faster the page loads.

Screen resolution

Hand in hand with color depth, screen resolution is the other factor that affects how crisp and lifelike the images appear. You're probably more familiar with the calculations and proportions relating to screen resolution because they're the type of thing that monitor manufacturers like to tout when marketing their products.

As you might expect, the screen resolutions on mobile devices are nowhere near as large as on desktop or laptop computers. A good, new, LCD monitor or laptop display probably clocks in at around 1920-x-1080-pixel resolution.

The highest-resolution mobile devices as of this writing are 960 pixels wide, and many mobile phone displays are restricted to 120 pixels wide.

Aspect ratios and orientations

The problem with mobile displays is that not only are they in different resolutions, but they're also in different aspect ratios, which can be affected by the way you hold the device. First, look at aspect ratios: A standard TV displays video in 4:3 aspect ratio (or 1:1.33). This is the almost-square format that generations of boob-tube addicts know and love. Basically, for every 4 pixels across, 3 pixels are down. So the standard-definition TV signal is 640 x 480. Recently, with HDTV, there's been a move to 16:9 aspect ratio (or 1:1.85). This ratio is also dubbed *widescreen,* and a common resolution is 1280 x 720.

The fun starts when you design mobile Web sites, which display on screens with different aspect ratios:

✔ **Feature phone aspect ratios:** These vary. For instance, the Motorola RAZR, in which the display is built into a clamshell-style unit, is tall and skinny with a resolution of 176-x-220 pixels, which breaks down into the unwieldy resolution ratio of 49:55. Many Nokia models have screens that are 176 x 144 in resolution. These narrow and tall feature phone screens are still massively popular in emerging markets, and designing for them is one of the more challenging tasks you can face.

✔ **Smartphone aspect ratios:** Fortunately, the trend is that new smartphones come out in more standard resolutions, such as 320 x 240. Astute mathematicians may note that this is exactly half the resolution of standard-definition TV. Online video addicts may note that this is the resolution used by YouTube for most of its early existence — hardly a coincidence given the increased demand by users to watch at least some rudimentary video on their handsets.

Further complicating the situation is the increasing use of accelerometers in handsets that detect when the phone is held upright (portrait mode) or tilted sideways (landscape), and the soon-to-be-common touch-screen phones with ultra-high display resolutions of 960 x 640.

For a sample of all the possible permutations of display capabilities, check out the list of more than 8,000 devices maintained at DeviceAtlas (`http://deviceatlas.com/user/10138`).

Optimizing Images for the Mobile Web

Just as there is a world of difference between the images for print designs and the images used on the desktop Web, so is there a difference between images on the desktop Web and the mobile Web. In both cases, moving to the newer platform means having to adjust images to have the best quality while taking up the smallest possible file size. In this section, we'll guide you through the process of taking images meant for the desktop Web and processing them so that they still look decent on mobile devices.

Sizing images for small screens

Cramming your 360-degree panorama photos onto a tiny feature phone's screen makes no sense. Not only would the photos not display correctly, but that files alone would probably eat up the user's entire monthly data plan allowance (and take a day to download). Your designs need to honor the constraints your users labor under and give them the option to click through to higher-resolution images only if they want to see them, rather than forcing visitors to download large images on the home page of your mobile site.

If you plan to put images on your mobile Web site, the design process goes more smoothly if you have a strategy to handle the different screen resolutions and aspect ratios on mobile devices. If you're designing just one version of your Web site for the mobile Web (as described in Chapter 3), you can get away with optimizing just one small version of each image that will work on most screen sizes. If you have the resources to develop more than one mobile version of your site, as we cover in Chapter 6, your best option is to create several versions of each image, optimized for different screen sizes, and then deliver the best version of the image to each device. The following sections explain strategies for sizing your image files, depending on the design strategy you choose.

Sizing one image to fit most screens

A practical and timesaving way to create images optimized to work on a particular handset and operating system is to create one simple Web-optimized image that displays on the majority of phones. You rely on the browser rendering engine on the phone to perform the resizing tasks. Although this isn't a foolproof method, most mobile browser creators know the browser needs to access a wide variety of sites and content, and they build rendering engines that *transcode* (or transform) that content so it displays more or less correctly onscreen. (For an introduction to how transcoding works, see Chapter 2.)

Using multiple image sizes

If you have the resources and time, the best solution is to tailor a site to each handset's capabilities. With this approach, you create multiple versions of each image in different sizes, from 120-pixels wide to 640 pixels, and then deliver the size that best fits the device with some kind of device detection script, as we describe in Chapter 6.

This is obviously much easier said than done, particularly if you're trying to keep a dynamic site such as the Huffington Post or ESPN updated with fresh content on a daily (or even hourly) basis.

If you design a portfolio site — where the whole point is to empower your client to show off images of his work anywhere, anytime — you may have a legitimate need to include higher-resolution images with larger file sizes. The best way to handle this situation is to link to the larger images from thumbnails or short text descriptions on the home page, or in the main portfolio section of your site. That way, your most important pages load quickly with small versions of your images that can be viewed by all your visitors, and those who are interested in (and have devices capable of handling) high-resolution images can choose to download them.

If you have a lot of images that need to be resized (for example, if you have a fashion portfolio in which the clothing designs are updated each season), you can automate the process of resizing and optimizing images using the Actions panel in Photoshop (for detailed instructions about setting up actions to resize many images at once, see Appendix B).

Choosing an image format

If you work with photos or other images with millions of colors, the JPEG format is your best choice for the mobile Web, just as it is for the desktop Web. With JPEGs, you can make the file size smaller by applying compression. The more compression, the smaller the image, but if you compress the image too much, the image can look like it was sandblasted and left out in the sun. For more about the differences among the various image formats and tips on how to best convert an image to a mobile-friendly format, see Appendix B.

For images with limited colors, such as line art, logos, and cartoons, the best format for mobile devices and Web pages is PNG. Some designers will tell you that the GIF format is the safer choice for very old mobile devices and some low-end feature phones, but the vast majority of phones surfing the mobile Web today support the PNG format, and this format does a better job at maintaining image quality and small file sizes than GIFs. With both GIF and PNG files, you optimize (or reduce the file size) by reducing the number of colors. You find detailed instructions for optimizing GIF, PNG, and JPEG files using the Save for Web and Devices dialog box, discussed in Appendix B.

Fancy image effects, such as transparent GIFs and PNGs, that are precisely laid out with text wrapped around them are extremely iffy on low-end feature phones and older mobile devices. Mobile browser rendering engines are likely to display the image and text on top of each other, to break apart the words letter by letter, to show the text in narrow vertical lines, or to just have a nervous breakdown and display nothing at all. You're better off simplifying the design for the mobile site, choosing a design that doesn't require transparency, or both.

Keeping file sizes small

After you know how to optimize PNGs and JPEGs and appreciate the goal of making them as small as possible, you may ask, "How small is small enough?"

Mobile Web designers obsess over ways to make their page sizes smaller, without crossing the invisible line between "loads too slow" and "looks junky." Although this is a mostly subjective judgment call, the following points are good to remember:

- ✔ **The larger your graphics files, the longer people have to wait for them to download before they can see them.** You may have the most beautiful picture of Mount Fuji on the front page of your Web site, but if it takes forever to download, most people aren't patient enough to wait to see it.

- ✔ **When you build pages with multiple graphics, you have to consider the cumulative download time of all the graphics on the page.** Even if each image is a small file size, they can add up. Unlike most other things in life, smaller is definitely better on the mobile Web.

- ✔ **Limit a mobile Web page to about 25K, although you can get away with larger sizes if you design for smartphones on a 3G or 4G network.** In contrast, most Web pros consider anything from about 75K to 150K a good maximum *cumulative* size for all the elements on a page designed for the desktop Web. Without getting too technical, the most basic 2G data connections range from about 80 to 100 Kbps, meaning that a 150K desktop page in this size range takes up to 20 seconds to transmit (and possibly a few seconds longer for the mobile device's CPU to process and render). Most mobile users get frustrated and abandon a page that takes that long. The 3G and 4G networks promise data speeds that range from 14 Mbps to 1 Gbps, although the actual speeds delivered to customers is the subject of some rather fierce debate.

Dreamweaver makes it easy to determine the total file size and download time of your page:

- ✔ **A page's total file size** appears in the status bar at the bottom of the document window, as shown in Figure 8-1. In the small text at the bottom of a Web page, the status bar shows the total size of all the images, text, and code on the page. In the figure, at more than 100K, this page is far too large to download efficiently over most mobile connections.

- ✔ **The download time,** based upon a particular connection speed, also appears in the status bar. You can change the connection speed by choosing Edit➪Preferences➪Status Bar➪Connection Speed. On a Mac, choose Dreamweaver➪Preferences➪Status Bar➪Connection Speed.

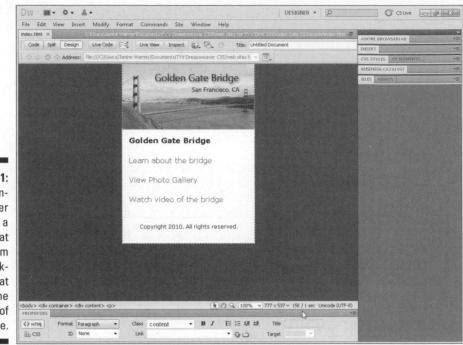

Figure 8-1:
Dream-
weaver
includes a
feature at
the bottom
of the work-
space that
displays the
total size of
the page.

Resizing images in WordPress

If you use the WordPress blogging tool, depending on how large the image you are embedding in your blog is, you can specify up to three sizes for images. When you upload an image to the media manager, WordPress auto-matically resizes the image to small, medium, and large sizes. You can specify the dimensions of those three options in the WordPress Dashboard adminis-trative tools. (*Note:* If the image you upload is already smaller than the speci-fied option, the blogging software pretty much doesn't bother with it. If the image is larger than the largest size, the original size is preserved as a fourth option.) If you are designing your blog for the mobile Web, one approach to managing image size is to take advantage of this automatic resizing function by setting the small photo size to the dimensions for a low-end phone (240 pixels is a good choice), the medium to the dimensions for a high-end phone (320 pixels is a good choice), and the large size to best fit the desktop version of your site (the best size will depend on the design of your site).

You can change the specified sizes on the Media Settings page in WordPress Dashboard. To find these options (as shown in Figure 8-2), open the Dashboard and then choose Settings⇨Media. Many of the plug-ins we cover in Chapter 9 take care of image resizing, but setting the default images sizes to what you want to use on the different pages of your blog is a good practice and a great way to automate the delivery of differently sized images to different devices.

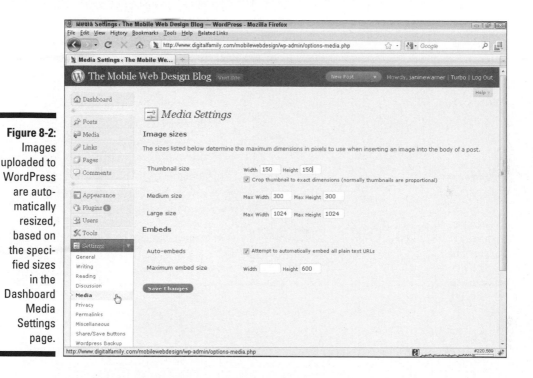

Figure 8-2: Images uploaded to WordPress are automatically resized, based on the specified sizes in the Dashboard Media Settings page.

Automating image resizing in Adobe Photoshop

Optimizing images for the Web is time-consuming enough (you find detailed instructions in Appendix B), but if you need to optimize multiple versions in multiple sizes, you can waste hours on this task if you try to resize each one manually.

Luckily, Photoshop, the most popular image-editing program, makes it possible to resize images automatically by creating Actions (macro scripts that automate a series of steps; see Figure 8-3). In Photoshop, you can create Actions with the Actions panel. Creating Actions takes some concentrated attention, but after you set them up, you can save lots of time when you create multiple versions of images. You find detailed instructions for creating Actions to automate the process of resizing and optimizing images in Appendix B.

Figure 8-3:
Photoshop
macros can
automate
the resizing
of images.

Inserting Images into Mobile Page Designs

You can insert images into pages designed for mobile devices just as you would insert them into any other Web page, using the HTML image tag. The HTML image tag is supported by nearly all mobile devices, making it relatively easy to include images in the display area of nearly any mobile phone.

The following is a well-crafted image tag that will insert a photograph that is 280 pixels by 55 pixels in size and saved as a JPEG:

```
<img src="GoldenGateBridge.jpg" alt="Golden Gate Bridge"
          height="55" width="280" />
```

Here are a few best practices when inserting images into any Web page. These are especially important when you're designing for the mobile Web:

✔ **Use ALT text.** Make sure to include Alternative text to describe the image. Because many mobile phones include the option to turn images off, the Alt text may be all that your visitors see. If you insert a logo or other image with text, make sure to include the text in the Alt field of the image tag (as shown in the image tag code example above).

✔ **Limit the size of images.** It's best to use a relatively narrow width, 280 pixels or smaller, to fit within the limited space of most mobile screens. When designing for the smallest mobile devices, you can specify the width using a percentage so that the image automatically adjusts to the screen size. For example, if you set the size attribute in the image tag to width=95%, the image will fill 95 percent of the width of the display area. If you use a percentage for width, you don't need to specify a height.

✔ **Specify a height and width for each image.** Using the height and width attributes, as shown in the image tag code example above, helps Web browsers load pages more quickly because they don't have to download each image to determine the height and width.

✔ **Use supported image formats.** Most devices display GIF and JPEG images. Increasingly, mobile devices also support images in the PNG format, and some even support animated GIFs.

Creating Mobile-Friendly Galleries and Slide Shows

Many desktop Web sites feature galleries and slide shows. Unfortunately, many of these implementations rely on Flash to work, and as you might be aware of by now, many mobile devices don't support Flash. Slide shows usually differ from galleries in the following ways:

✔ Once you click on the "Play" button on a slide show, the images cycle through in the order that the creator of the slide show set up, and as rapidly (or slowly) as that person decided was optimal. Good slide shows have buttons that you can push to advance to the next picture, to pause, or to skip backwards. Bad ones replicate the experience of being trapped in some boring relative's basement, forced to watch hours of bland vacation photos.

✔ Slide shows often incorporate some kind of accompanying sound that goes with the photos; this can be a voiceover, explaining what the photos are about, or a musical track. Adding sound to the photos means that the photos have to be synced to appear and disappear to the cues in the soundtrack, which can be tricky.

✔ Galleries tend to be more passive. Usually, there's an array of thumbnail shots of the photos, and when users click on them, the photo selected expands to fill most of the page. Some galleries do use Flash or Microsoft's Silverlight technology to animate the transitions from one image to the next.

One of the best options for smartphones and touch-screen phones is to create slide shows or galleries with JavaScript. Although not all phones support JavaScript — and even some that do (BlackBerry phones, for example) aren't consistent about their support and allow users to turn off JavaScript if they prefer — most of the recent generation of Web-enabled phones can handle galleries and slide shows designed with JavaScript.

If you know enough about JavaScript, you can create your own scripts, but many programs can help. The following sections introduce a few options for galleries and slide shows, as well as a cool way for you to create a photo gallery using your mobile phone camera, where the photos you take are shown with little markers on an online map.

Make sure the photos you add to any gallery you create are optimized for the mobile Web, as we explain earlier in the section, "Optimizing Images for the Mobile Web."

Finding a gallery plug-in or service

Here are a few programs, plug-ins, and online photo services that you can use to spruce up your mobile site with slide shows and galleries:

- ✔ **Flickr:** (www.flickr.com) One of the most popular photo-sharing sites, Flickr makes it easy to upload photos to its server and to display them on any site in a variety of ways. Flickr does a great job on many high-end mobile devices, such as the iPhone, shown in Figure 8-4, but doesn't always take best advantage of the display space, even on high-end phones, such as the Motorola Droid, shown in landscape view in Figure 8-5. To embed a slide show of Flickr images in any Web page, navigate to the Flickr photostream you want to add to your site, click on the Slideshow link, and then click on Share. On the share page, click on the Customize This HTML link to open a page where you can specify the dimensions for the slide show. After you adjust the settings, you simply copy the HTML code from Flickr in your Web page.

- ✔ **SmugMug:** (www.smugmug.com) This photo-sharing site offers some very cool tools to customize the way your galleries display on your site. You can choose whether first time visitors to your site see a banner prompting them to switch to the lightweight mobile version. You can also password-protect the photos in your galleries, and SmugMug has an integrated shopping cart to allow you to sell your photos as well.

- ✔ **Jaipho:** (www.jaipho.com) This JavaScript gallery is designed for the iPhone and makes it easy to create a gallery that mimics the look and feel of the original iPhone Photo application. You can quickly scroll through photos, both vertically and horizontally. Just tap a photo to enlarge it and then tap again to return to browsing. Jaipho includes a companion application — *Pipho* (www.jaipho.com/content/pipho-php-image-gallery-iphone) — which is installed on the server to make it easy for users to add images to galleries by uploading them.

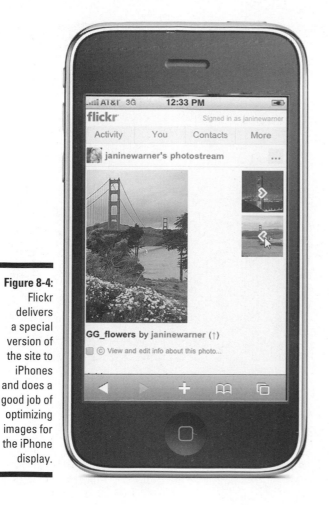

Figure 8-4:
Flickr
delivers
a special
version of
the site to
iPhones
and does a
good job of
optimizing
images for
the iPhone
display.

✔ **Dreamweaver extensions:** (www.adobe.com/exchange) As we write this book, none of the extensions on the Adobe site are designed specifically to create JQuery or AJAX features for mobile devices, but if you design pages for high-end phones, most of these extensions create code that displays on iPhones and other touch-screen phones or smartphones. Extensions are little plug-ins or widgets that you can add to Dreamweaver to empower it to do things that weren't included in the original program.

✔ **Shadowbox:** (www.shadowbox-js.com) If you use a WordPress blog, Shadowbox is one of the most popular and flexible plug-ins. Shadowbox handles images and video (although if your video is in a format incompatible with the device, it won't solve this conflict). With Shadowbox, you can easily scroll through a gallery of images. The JavaScript displays well on most high-end phones, but the results vary, depending on how the device handles JavaScript.

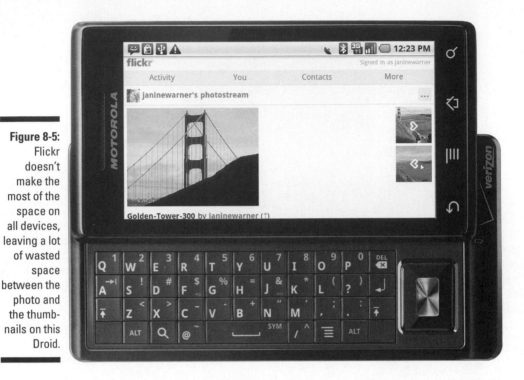

Figure 8-5:
Flickr doesn't make the most of the space on all devices, leaving a lot of wasted space between the photo and the thumbnails on this Droid.

In Figure 8-6, you see how a photo in Shadowbox displays on an HTC touch-screen phone. In this example, the image isn't scaled properly, so you see a very small image on this relatively high-resolution screen.

- **Visual LightBox:** (http://visuallightbox.com) This free plug-in is similar to Shadowbox, but it works on sites that don't have WordPress installed. You can also set Visual LightBox to import images from Flickr.

Creating mobile slide shows in the 3GP format

3GP is the name for files encoded with specifications developed by the 3rd Generation Partnership Project (3GPP). The video codec used is pretty much the same as MPEG-4; it's a media container that's playable on 3G phones, although some 2G and 4G phones also play it. Files in this format have the .3gp file extension. A version of 3GP exists for CDMA-based phones, dubbed *3GPP2;* files encoded with this standard have the extension .3g2.

Figure 8-6:
Shadowbox
plug-ins
work well
on some
devices but
have trouble
scaling on
others, such
as the HTC
Touch.

When you create slide shows for the mobile platform, use the image-optimization measures we explain in the earlier section, "Optimizing Images for the Mobile Web," to create folders of photos appropriate for the devices you target. Additionally, follow the guidelines in the following section, "Optimizing Audio for the Mobile Web," to encode your audio files so they play smoothly on mobile devices. Here are some programs and sites where you can create a slide show that plays on anything but the most basic feature phones:

✔ **Animoto:** (http://animoto.com) This online service allows you to upload photos, choose from themes and fancy transitions, and add music from its library. You're limited to slide shows of only 30 seconds in duration unless you pay $30 a year to upgrade to Animoto's professional level.

✔ **Adobe Premiere Elements:** (www.adobe.com/products/premiereel)
This is the simplest video-editing program that exports to the 3GP format.
If you're new to video editing, Premiere Elements has an Instant Movie
feature that automatically takes your images and adds fancy transitions
and effects to the presentation. Adobe Premiere Elements costs about
$80 (although you may find promotions and deals, sometimes packaging
Premiere and Photoshop Elements together). *Adobe Premiere Elements
8 For Dummies,* by Keith Underdahl, can guide you through the basics of
editing and exporting video in this program.

✔ **DVD-Photo-Slideshow.com:** (www.dvd-photo-slideshow.com)
This program allows you to easily create slide shows and export them
to a variety of platforms, including 3GP. This program is specifically
designed to help you easily create fancy slide shows for a variety of
distribution platforms, and it includes many transitions and effects,
although many of them are aimed more toward the family market. A free
trial is available on the Web site, and the program costs about $60.

✔ **Adobe After Effects:** (www.adobe.com/products/aftereffects)
This is a rather high-end solution, and many professional media companies that give presentations use After Effects to make their slide shows
have that stunning, television-commercial look and feel. After Effects
exports in 3GP, MP4, and just about any other video format you can
think of, although the learning curve for this program can be kind of
steep. The current version of After Effects costs about $999.

Mapping a photo gallery

A fun way to get users more engaged and take advantage of the unique
powers of the mobile Web is to create a photo gallery in which pictures taken
with a mobile phone can be uploaded and displayed on a Google map that
automatically places the photos where they were taken.

You could build all this functionality by hand-coding scripts that take the GPS
data encoded in the latest digital photos, but Google has already built sites
and scripts that do this for you for free, so why reinvent the map?

Many mobile sites benefit from including maps, because location is so
important to mobile users. You can make your maps even more interactive
and useful by combining them with photos. Whether you're looking for an
easy way for you to add photos to your own maps, or you want to open up
the maps on your site to your online community, combining the power of
Google's free Picasa photo-sharing service (see Figure 8-7) with Google Maps
(as shown in Figure 8-8) is a powerful, easy, and cost-effective option. (Did we
mention it's free? All you have to do is sign up for a free Google account.)

Adding photos to maps is a great way to improve the directions on your
Web site. For example, if you're creating a site for a restaurant that's down

some tricky side streets, with a blind entrance from the parking lot, just use this process to create a map that potential customers can follow along with on their mobile device to show not only where the restaurant is located on the map, but also a picture (or a series of pictures) that shows the street-level view of where customers should park, how best to enter, and any other useful details.

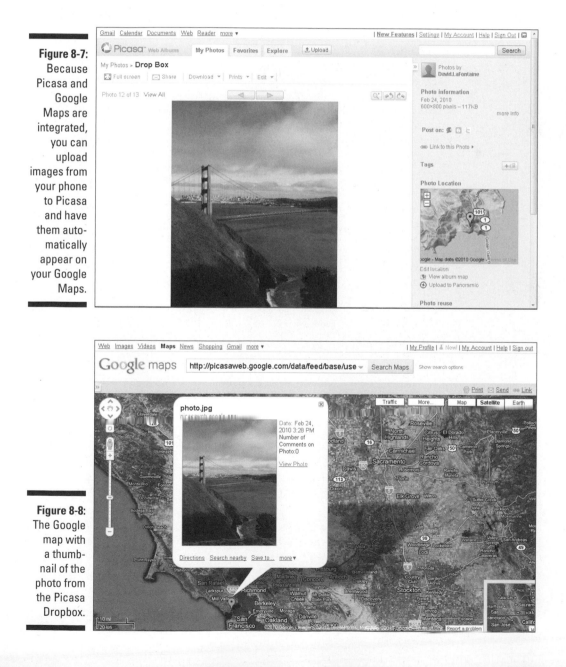

Figure 8-7: Because Picasa and Google Maps are integrated, you can upload images from your phone to Picasa and have them automatically appear on your Google Maps.

Figure 8-8: The Google map with a thumbnail of the photo from the Picasa Dropbox.

If your Web site serves a community, such as a travel club, marathon racers, or any other group that likes to share photos, the nifty features at Picasa make it easy for anyone to upload photos from a cellphone and automatically create photo galleries. If the phone includes geo data (most smartphones do), you can add photos automatically to a Google map. Then when your travel club members are taking photos out the window on their next road trip, everyone on your site can see the photos in real time and track where the club members go by following the photos across a map.

If you already have a Gmail account, you're already signed up for Picasa and Google Maps. If you don't have a Gmail account, sign up for one at `http://picasaweb.google.com` before following these steps.

To set up Picasa so that you (and anyone you share your account with) can automatically upload photos from a phone, follow these steps. (To then add your photos to a map, continue with the instructions in the next section.)

1. **Log in to your Picasa account with your Google user ID and password and then click the Settings link in the upper-right corner.**

   The User Settings page opens.

2. **Click the General tab and specify the options you want.**

   You can set your nickname, upload a profile picture, and change the URL for your photo gallery.

3. **Select the Allow Me check box to upload photos by e-mail.**

   You must select this check box if you want to send photos directly from your phone.

4. **In the Enter a Secret Word field, type a secret word.**

   This secret word is used as part of the e-mail address for you or your users to send photos to Picasa. The secret word must be 6–15 characters, and it looks like this when you use it as an e-mail: *YourName*.*Secretword*@picasaweb.com. You can see the address appear below the secret word box while you type it in.

   Any photos sent to this e-mail address are published automatically in your or your client's Picasa photo feed. This opens the possibility that some prankster could upload objectionable photos, so be careful to use a secret word that's hard to guess and only give this address to people you trust.

5. **Click the Save Changes button and then e-mail a photo from your mobile device to the address you generated from Picasa that includes the secret word.**

   The subject line for your e-mail is the headline. Just attach the photo or image to the e-mail as you normally would from your mobile phone.

If your phone has a newer digital camera with a GPS sensor In It, you can add your photos to a Google map by continuing the Picasa setup process with these steps:

1. **Click the My Photos tab in Picasa.**

   The page with your photo albums opens.

2. **Click the Drop Box album and then choose Edit⇨Album Properties.**

   The Edit Album Information window opens. You can edit the title and fill in a description of the gallery.

3. **In the Share drop-down list, choose Public and then click the Save Changes button.**

4. **On the right side of the screen, right-click the RSS link and choose Copy Link Location.**

5. **Open a new tab in your browser and navigate to `http://maps.google.com`.**

   The Google Maps page opens.

6. **Press Ctrl+C (on a Mac, Command+C) to paste the RSS link into the Search Maps field.**

   This causes little pins to appear on the Google map, and the pins correspond to the places where you took the photos. See Figure 8-8 for an idea of how this will display on the map. Clicking a thumbnail brings up a larger version of the image, along with the latitude and longitude, the title of the photo, and the option to view the photo at full size.

7. **In the top-right corner of your Google map, click the Link link.**

   The Link dialog box opens.

8. **Do either of the following with the code:**

   - *Send the link to this map to your friends via e-mail.*

   - *Embed code that allows you to add this live map of all the places you take photos of to any blog or Web site.*

Optimizing Audio for the Mobile Web

Getting sound to come out of your phone seems like a no-brainer, right? After all, phones were pretty much designed to play sounds — if they didn't, everyone would walk around shouting into these plastic rectangles for no real reason. The key here is that increasingly, phones come with decent-quality headsets (or *earbuds*) that allow users to listen to songs and podcasts in stereo. Although the iPhone has definitely accelerated this trend, other mobile devices played music long before Apple's game-changing device hit the market.

Most enlightened Web designers know that users get annoyed when you set up Web pages to automatically play cheesy 8-bit MIDI songs that sound like the soundtrack to an '80s vintage video game. But there are valid reasons to include audio on your mobile Web site. If you haven't already added audio content to the mix on your Web site, here are some possible innovative uses for audio that mobile users might want to have at their fingertips — for convenience, to pass the time productively, to better answer a question, or to solve a crisis situation while they're away from the home or office:

✔ Nature sites could include examples of birdcalls or wild animal noises, so birdwatchers can identify birds (or grouchy mama bears) by sound when they're out in the field.

✔ A bed-and-breakfast could have a site that provides instructions for motorists who are driving, who can't (and shouldn't) take their eyes off windy country roads to constantly check the small print on a mobile screen.

✔ A religious site that wants members of the congregation to hear the latest sermon, hymns, or meditation.

✔ Health sites may want to demonstrate exactly what a dangerous whooping cough sounds like as opposed to just the flu.

✔ Musicians can provide short teaser clips of their works to incentivize fans to click to download a higher-quality version.

✔ A health and fitness site in which a personal trainer talks users through a special workout program that they can follow along with at the gym.

In the following sections, you discover the basics you need to know if you want to add audio to your mobile site.

Figuring out formats, file size, and more

As with any other multimedia, the biggest challenge comes from the fact that the capabilities, bandwidth, memory, and wireless connection speed are uneven and unpredictable across different devices. The good news is that unlike so many other multimedia elements, there is one format for audio that nearly every device is equipped to play: MP3.

MP3 doesn't provide the best compression *codec* (the mathematical formula that takes an audio file and reduces its size). In fact, music engineers groan and rub their temples when forced to listen to what highly compressed MP3s played through tiny speakers sound like. But MP3 is pretty much a universal standard just because so many people have used it for so long. Thus, the main choice is how much to compress your MP3 to make sure that a mobile user can play it?

HE-ACC: Improving on MP3?

Competing audio compression formats, such as HE-AAC (High-Efficiency Advanced Audio Coding), are emerging. They claim to offer the same quality as MP3 at half the file size. However, the performance of this standard is unpredictable, even on the latest smartphones, because to uncompress the audio file, you need an extremely fast (for mobile, at least) CPU operating at full load capacity.

If you're absolutely committed to providing the best possible audio experience at the lowest possible file size, you can experiment with common audio-ripping software, such as Nero (www.nero.com), to encode some of your audio files into HE-AAC and then test to see whether your targeted mobile devices play them under real-world conditions (many manufacturers' claims of compatibility turn out to be somewhat, shall we say, overly optimistic). Just be aware that the quest for perfect audio fidelity can be a bottomless rabbit hole down which many good Web developers have disappeared.

Essentially, you compress an audio file in an audio editor by setting the bitrate for the file. *Bitrate* — a measure of the file's audio quality — is the number of bits of digital information per second that is decoded and turned into a sound. In much the same way that reducing color depth in images (which we describe earlier in this chapter) represents a tradeoff between quality and file size, so too does bitrate work for audio files. Bigger is usually better, up to a point. The following explains the differences in bitrate for the desktop and mobile Web:

- **On the regular desktop Web, bitrates range from 96 to 320 kbps.** Professionals consider 96 *kbps* (kilobits per second, sometimes referred to as *kbit/s*, or even abbreviated to just the capital "K") adequate for a file that contains human speech, such as an interview or monologue. Until recently, 128 kbps was considered standard for music, and the vast majority of songs sold on iTunes were at this bitrate; however, sites like MOG (www.mog.com) are making a name for themselves by offering music at 320 kbps or higher for true audiophiles.

- **For the mobile Web, aim for 64 kbps or lower.** The giant music-streaming service Pandora has found that 64 kbps is the highest practical bitrate due to bandwidth and dropout constraints.

Streaming audio versus downloads versus podcasts

You can enable your mobile user to access your audio files in a few ways:

✔ **Streaming audio** refers to a process whereby the audio files are transferred continuously, bit by bit, to the mobile device while the user listens. The file isn't saved on the device but is sent to the user every time she requests it. This option is the best for low-end feature phones that have very little (or no) memory to store files for playback. However, to stream audio, you need to clear complicated technical hurdles (which we explain in the next section) to ensure that the audio files play as promised.

✔ **Downloadable audio** is a file that, not surprisingly, you download and then play on your mobile device without being connected to the wireless Web.

✔ **Podcasts** are downloadable audio files with a Really Simple Syndication (RSS) tag that allows users to subscribe to the podcast so that every episode of the podcast series downloads automatically. Creating podcasts is beyond the scope of this book, but you can find free videos and tips for creating podcasts at `www.dummies.com`. For a more in-depth look at podcasting, check out *Podcasting For Dummies,* 2nd Edition, by Tee Morris, Chuck Tomasi, Evo Terra, and Kreg Steppe.

Linking to audio files

Providing a link so your visitors can download an audio file is the simplest option, especially compared to streaming audio. We recommend linking to audio files rather than using the `<object>` tag, which is more common on the desktop Web. Even some of the best designed mobile sites that feature audio, including National Public Radio, link to audio files rather than inserting them directly into a Web page.

Linking to audio from a mobile site works the same way it does on a desktop Web site: You upload the audio file to a folder on your Web server (or to the content-delivery network or *CDN* that you use). Then you simply insert a link to the audio file in any Web page in your site. A link to an audio file looks like this:

```
<a href="http://www.YourSite.com/audio/YourSong.mp3">
        Click to play my song!</a><Tip>
```

The long-awaited HTML5 standard promises to simplify the process of adding audio and video to Web pages. Unfortunately, until the HTML5 standard is adopted by the majority of mobile devices, we recommend sticking with the simplest options for maximum compatibility. If you use device detection and content adaptation (see Chapter 6) to direct the users of the latest smartphones, then HTML5 is a great option for smartphones, including the iPhone, Droid, and a growing list of other devices that support HTML5.

We strongly discourage any use of the `<bgsound>` command to play background music for a mobile Web page. Similarly, using the `<object>` or `<embed>` tag with the `autostart=true` command to automatically play an audio file upon page load is a real no-no. These commands either cause an error or force the mobile user to download the entire audio file to see the contents of your page.

Playing downloadable audio

How audio plays over the mobile Web depends on the device that tries to play it. Here's a quick review of the often uneven results you can expect when someone tries to play an MP3 by clicking a link to a song on a mobile phone:

- ✔ The iPhone exits the browser and launches its QuickTime app to play the song.

- ✔ Some BlackBerry phones launch BerryTunes or another app or widget that handles multimedia. Other BlackBerry phones (including many issued by big corporations or government agencies that have imposed strict security controls) return an error message.

- ✔ The most recent releases of the Motorola RAZR on the AT&T network download the song to the phone and bring up a media player. The original Motorola V3 versions on Sprint try to add the song to the ringtone library.

- ✔ Depending on the version of Android and the user settings, the phone plays the song in a browser, exits to a widget, or prompts the user to enable Flash 10.1 to handle multimedia content.

Streaming your audio

If audio is a significant element of your site, you may want to invest in the resources to set up your own streaming audio server. Before you start down this path, we should warn you this is a technically complex and often expensive option. Here's what you need to know to get started:

- ✔ **Choosing a streaming format:** Almost every device plays MP3s, but many devices require streaming audio to be delivered in 3GP or MP4 format. Additionally, field testing has shown that using the audio/3GPP format is problematic, and some devices will only play audio that is contained in the video/3GPP format. We recommend that you consult DeviceAtlas to see if the devices you are targeting support the format you want. If you are unsure, you can use the video/3GPP format for maximum compatibility, even though the resulting file sizes are somewhat larger.

- ✔ **Setting up a streaming server:** If you want to consistently stream large quantities of audio to your users, you have to set up or have access to a streaming media server, such as Darwin Streaming Server (`http://dss.macosforge.org`).

If you want to get serious about streaming audio to your users, having the audio stored on your own server can make a difference in the amount of time it takes before the audio loads because the mobile device doesn't have to access two servers — your Web site's server and the server where the audio is hosted. If you can deliver the audio from the same server that your Web site is hosted from, it almost always plays faster (unless you have a very slow server).

✔ **Following streaming protocols:** You then have to make your files compliant with Real Time Streaming Protocol (RTSP), which means you have to include a *hint* track with the file during the encoding process to tell your server how to package the data so that it flows across the wireless connection to the mobile user as seamlessly as possible. You can add the hint track when you are encoding with most recording software, or even with Apple's QuickTime Pro.

E-mailing audio files to get around mobile problems and restrictions

Before you throw up your hands in frustration and resort to just buying a really loud boombox and driving through the streets blasting your audio files at top volume to make sure people hear them, we have a simple and elegant workaround that not only allows you to deliver audio to users on both their desktop and almost any mobile device but also encourages them to register and give up some valuable data in exchange.

First, we credit Jonathan Thaler (www.whenimmobile.com) for allowing us to share this neat trick with you. Jonathan works with a number of musicians and knows that one of the most important things for a musician is to share her latest singles. Here's how he solved the problem of making it easy for anyone with a mobile device to hear the music of his client, singer Tori Sparks (www.torisparks.com).

Tori has offered music on her desktop Web site, shown in Figure 8-9, for some time, but she wanted to make it easy for fans at her concerts and other events to easily get her music — and not have to remember to go visit her Web site later.

Because Jonathan designed multiple versions of Tori's site, optimized for different types of mobile devices, you find more options on some phones than others. All the mobile versions of the site include the ability to e-mail a sound file. High-end phones, such as the iPhone, also include images and video files you can play within the pages of the site (more on how to do that in the next section).

You can see the mobile version of Tori's site shown on a BlackBerry phone in Figure 8-10. And In Figure 8-11, you see the iPhone version, which has more images and video clips hosted by YouTube.

Figure 8-9:
Tori Sparks'
desktop
Web site.

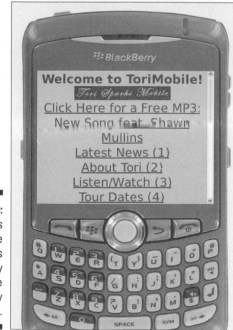

Figure 8-10:
Tori's
mobile site
displays
mostly
text on the
BlackBerry
Curve.

Figure 8-11:
Tori's site
displays
photos and
video on the
iPhone.

Fans can download an audio file from any of the versions of Tori Sparks' Web site because of the innovative use of an e-mail form on a mobile site. Rather than wrestling with all the conflicting standards to make sure that none of her fans felt left out, Jonathan worked out an e-mail solution that automatically sends an MP3 file to almost any mobile device when a user enters an e-mail address into a form. Here's how it works:

1. He set up a simple HTML form with a field for an e-mail address and a submit button and connected it to an automated e-mail script on his server.

   Because HTML form tags are widely supported on mobile devices, fans can fill in the form with their e-mail addresses using almost any Web-enabled mobile phone.

2. Fans who enter an e-mail address are sent a message with the music file as an attachment.

   Sending the MP3 as an attachment to an e-mail message means the song isn't subject to the vagaries of the many mobile browsers. Any phone capable of browsing the mobile Web can also send and receive e-mail.

3. When the message comes in, the users can save the attachment to the device.

4. To play the file, fans can then exit the e-mail program and use whatever MP3 player was installed in the device to play the song.

   Again, because MP3s are so popular, every device built in the last five years supports them.

   Better still, when they get back to their home or office, most of Tori's fans find a copy of the same message waiting in their e-mail inbox, so they can also add it to iTunes, Winamp, Windows Media Player, or any other audio player they may have on their computer. And, of course, the e-mail also contains links so the user can buy more of Tori's music.

This elegant solution not only makes it easy for Tori to share her music with almost anyone who has a mobile phone, it's also a great excuse to collect e-mail addresses, which she uses to promote upcoming shows and merchandise in her store.

To set up a system like the one on Tori's site — that e-mails a sound file when a user enters an e-mail address — do the following:

✔ **Optimize the audio file so that it downloads quickly.** Make sure that you abide by the bitrate encoding suggestions in the section "Figuring out formats, file size, and more" earlier in this chapter; MP3 files quickly reach the multi-megabyte size, and a large download may be blocked by the user's e-mail service.

✔ **Set up an e-mail form and script that works on your server.** Creating an HTML form where a user can enter an e-mail address is easy: Use the standard HTML form tag, a simple form text field, and a submit button. If you're not familiar with setting up scripts to handle e-mail forms on your Web server, you may need to consult with your Web hosting service to set up an e-mail form script. Many hosting services include an e-mail form script as part of the service, but on some servers you may need to install and configure script yourself. Any standard form mail script that allows attachments should work; however, beware that most hosting services have strict rules about how scripts can be set up on their systems to prevent malicious users from sending obscene content or spam.

Adding Video to Your Mobile Web Site

Ever since the days of the first portable TVs, video addicts have dreamed of ways to watch their favorite shows, no matter where they were. Early attempts at this ranged from suitcase-sized monstrosities that weighed as much as a small child, to the Sony Watchman with its rabbit-ear antenna that required viewers to wrap tinfoil around it and stand in awkward yoga-like positions to get good reception.

The advent of so-called "TV anywhere" always seems a few years down the road, but the rollout of the high-speed wireless data networks may finally bring the dream to reality.

As you might have figured out, video brings together all the most difficult challenges of designing for the mobile Web: the plethora of screen resolutions to display the picture on and the large file sizes burdening the digital distribution networks. Video professionals who are trying to make the transition to the mobile space mutter darkly about dense technical specifications and toss around phrases like *backhaul* and *data packet prioritization* (words so obscure we don't even bother to define them here). And, not to be repetitive, but one of the biggest challenges is that the most popular video format on the Web (Flash) isn't supported on the vast majority of mobile devices.

If we shovel out the reams of data specifications and intricate formatting requirements you need to become an expert in creating your custom mobile video site, we'd take up the remainder of this book (and probably a couple others). Unless you're part of a dedicated, well-funded team working for a large media company, this would probably only confuse the issues and, worse yet, would get you no closer to actually delivering video clips to visitors of your Web sites. Therefore, we suggest that (at least to start out) you leave the deeply technical issues to people who have already spent years working on this problem and concentrate instead on how best to take advantage of the fruits of their labors. In Figure 8-12, you see how the programmers at YouTube design video to display on an iPhone. Hosting video on YouTube makes it easy because you can simply add a link to the video and YouTube delivers the best version for the detected device.

In the following sections, we introduce you to your video-hosting options, namely content delivery networks (CDNs) and video-sharing sites. We then explain the basics of embedding a video hosted on the video-sharing site YouTube into your mobile Web site. And finally, we include a sample of the code you can use to embed video directly on your pages if you host the video on your own Web server.

Comparing CDNs with video-sharing sites

When you look for a third party to deliver your video content to your mobile users, a dedicated *content delivery network (CDN)* provides high-end services for a price. A video-sharing site, such as YouTube, Vimeo, or Viddler, offers free or low-cost services.

Figure 8-12: Tori Sparks' music videos on YouTube as they appear on the iPhone.

The essential trade-off between a CDN and a video-sharing site is cost versus control. The more you pay, the more you can control the kind of experience that your mobile users get. The less you pay (and free is about as less as you can get), the more you're at the mercy of someone else's decisions. You have to weigh the trade-offs, and we encourage you to do your research. To help you get started, the following sections provide a comparison of the advantages and disadvantages of each.

Checking out CDNs

Dedicated CDNs offer many advantages:

- ✔ **Provide tools for you to customize the player** with your own logo or messages.
- ✔ **Allow you to insert your own advertising,** and in some cases, they maintain their own ad server so you can customize which ads appear depending on the user, time of day, location of user, and so on.

✔ **Maintain their own performance metrics system,** so you can track who watches your videos, when and where they watch, and all sorts of other data useful to you (and advertisers).

✔ **Provide better customer support;** after all, if you're paying for their services, there better be someone there to help if you need it.

✔ **Allow for batch uploading** so that you can publish a collection of videos all at once, rather than having to do so one at a time.

✔ **Offer better copyright protection of your content.**

✔ **Make it possible to restrict which geographic regions or domains are allowed to access your videos.**

✔ **Allow you to post videos of any length (within reason).**

✔ **Deliver video in higher quality** because CDNs spend more time tinkering with compression algorithms.

Some of the disadvantages of dedicated CDNs:

✔ **Can be very costly** — hosting packages start in the hundreds of dollars for 200 gigabytes of videos served per month (about 50 full-length DVDs) and rise sharply after that.

Did we mention that CDNs are expensive? If you get a hit viral video, your hosting bills can quickly skyrocket into the thousands (or tens of thousands) of dollars. That may be fine if you've worked out a great advertising model or charge for your videos, but if you don't, this probably isn't your best option.

✔ **Require you to manage social-media aspects of your videos,** such as sharing, commenting, embedding, and so on.

Hundreds of CDNs are on the market. Some of the most popular are

✔ **Akamai:** www.akamai.com

✔ **Delve Networks:** www.delvenetworks.com

✔ **Ooyala:** www.ooyala.com

✔ **EdgeCast Networks:** www.edgecast.com

✔ **Limelight Networks:** www.limelightnetworks.com

✔ **Mobile CDN:** http://mobilecdn.com

Exploring video-sharing sites

Video-sharing sites offer many advantages:

✓ **Free or at least very cheap when compared with CDNs.**

✓ **Easy to use.** If they weren't, millions of teenagers around the world couldn't share their deeply held convictions that homework is, like, totally unfair.

✓ **Bandwidth costs and concerns are someone else's problem.**

✓ **Easy to share the content** — your users can embed your videos on their sites, e-mail friends, leave comments, post to Facebook, and so on.

✓ **Traffic already comes to these sites, so you don't have to go out of your way to do lots of search engine optimization (SEO) to get your video to appear in search engines.**

Some of the disadvantages of video-sharing sites:

✓ **Videos may be delivered with poor quality.** Because video-sharing sites process many thousands of videos per day, they really can't pay attention to all the details of making your little project look its best.

✓ **Their ads may appear on your content.** If you try to put in your own ads or if your video is blatantly commercial, many sites yank it.

✓ **Your content can be banned or taken down at anytime, for any reason, solely at their discretion.**

✓ **After you upload your content to their site, you may no longer be the sole owner of the rights to control where, when, and how your video is displayed, packaged, advertised, or sold.** Read the End User Licensing Agreements fully; don't just agree to it.

✓ **The length of the videos is limited to what the video-sharing site dictates (usually ten minutes or less).**

✓ **Analytics are limited.** You probably don't get much data to gauge user engagement, or to see which sections of a video are the most popular, where the audience fast-forwarded, and so on.

✓ **Because the videos are hosted on someone else's server, the value of the traffic that comes from your site goes to the video-sharing site, not yours.** Traffic can cost you money because of hosting and bandwidth fees, but it can also contribute to higher search engine rankings and advertising opportunities.

Among the most popular video-sharing sites:

✓ **YouTube:** www.youtube.com

✓ **Vimeo:** www.vimeo.com

✓ **Viddler:** www.viddler.com

✔ **Dailymotion:** www.dailymotion.com

✔ **Revver:** www.revver.com

✔ **Babelgum:** http://babelgum.com/mobile

Hosting mobile video on YouTube

For designers who don't want to struggle too much to figure out whole new lexicons of technical specifications, the simplest option is to let YouTube do all the work of hosting and delivering video.

Upload a video to this popular Web site, set a link to it on your mobile Web page, and you're all set. YouTube is smart enough to detect your users' devices and deliver videos optimized for their platform. For example, even with the mighty iPhone, users with the 3G version get higher-quality videos than iPhone 1.0 users because YouTube knows that the first-generation iPhones download video much more slowly, and even the most beautiful video in the world does no good if the user yanks out his hair while all the data tries to fit through a 2G pipe.

Inserting a YouTube video directly into a mobile Web page

If you want to take the YouTube video solution to the next level, here's another great tip from Jonathan Thaler. Instead of just linking to YouTube, peel out the actual reference to the video from the YouTube page and add your own code to insert the video directly into your mobile page. The advantage of this approach is that you don't have to send users to the YouTube site. Although the video is still hosted on YouTube, you can make a video play within your mobile page. See Figure 8-13 for an example of videos hosted on YouTube that are inserted into a mobile Web page; Figure 8-12 shows those videos as they appear if you link to them on the YouTube page. Inserting videos into your pages works best when designing pages for high-end mobile devices, such as the iPhone and Droid phones.

To insert a YouTube video directly into your mobile Web page, you need the User Agent add-on for Firefox (covered in Chapter 7). The User Agent add-on is important because you need to visit the correct page on YouTube — the one that's optimized for your mobile device. The Firefox User Agent tricks YouTube into identifying the Firefox Web browser as a mobile device (even when you use it on a computer), which makes it possible to view the code you need for each type of mobile phone. To find the code you need on YouTube, follow these steps:

Figure 8-13:
You can
embed vid-
eos hosted
on YouTube
on mobile-
optimized
Web pages.

1. Launch Firefox with the User Agent add-on installed.

2. **Choose Tools⇨Default User Agent and then select the device you want Firefox to mimic, such as the iPhone.**

   In Chapter 7, you find instructions for adding user agents for many different devices to the User Agent add-on.

3. **Open the YouTube page with the video you want to add to your page.**

   With the user agent activated, YouTube displays a version of the video optimized for the device you have selected from the user agent options.

4. **Right-click (Command-click on a Mac) and chose Properties.**

5. **Copy the last string of code, just after the equal (=) sign, from the Address field in the Element Properties window, shown in Figure 8-14.**

   This code corresponds directly to the version of the video that is being displayed in your browser. It should look something like this: `0NesG6e74Jw`. (This is the code for a video we took of the Golden Gate Bridge. You're welcome to use it to test this trick yourself.)

6. **In a Web page editor, such as Dreamweaver, paste the code you copied in Step 5 into your Web page using the code we provide in Listing 8-1.**

If you want to reach the broadest audience, stick with XHTML and use the `<object>`, `<param>`, and `<embed>` tags, as we show in Listing 8-1. (If you prefer not to type this code, you can copy it from our Web site at `www.DigitalFamily.com/mobile`.)

Listing 8-1 shows the code you need in order to insert mobile-optimized video from YouTube so that it will play within a mobile Web page.

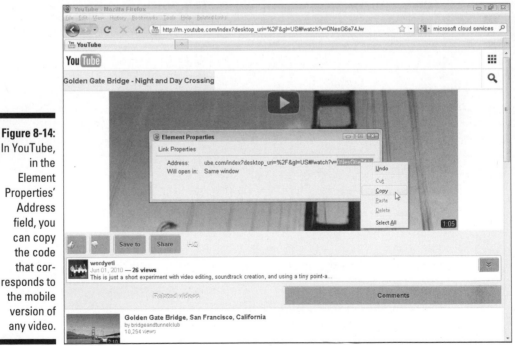

Figure 8-14: In YouTube, in the Element Properties' Address field, you can copy the code that corresponds to the mobile version of any video.

Listing 8-1   Inserting a YouTube video into a mobile Web page

```
<OBJECT width="140" height="105">
<param name="movie" value="http://www.youtube.com/v/
        YOURVIDEOCODEHERE"></param>
<param name="wmode" value="transparent"></param>
<embed src="http://www.youtube.com/v/YOURVIDEOCODEHERE"
        type="application/x-shockwave-flash"
        wmode="transparent" width="140" height="105"></
        embed>
</OBJECT>
```

Inserting video hosted on your server into a mobile Web page

If you host your videos on your own Web server, you can insert them into a Mobile Web page just as you would insert them into any other Web page using the <object>, <param>, and <embed> tags. The trick is to make sure you deliver your video in a format that works well on mobile devices, and, ideally, you should deliver different versions of each video to different devices based on the capabilities of each device. Because getting the video into the best format and hosting it on your own server are relatively complicated tasks, we recommend that you consider using a CDN or a video service like YouTube. However, if you want to host your own video and need instructions for inserting video into a Web page using Dreamweaver, you will find detailed instructions in *Dreamweaver CS5 For Dummies*. You can also find tutorials on inserting video in the Dreamweaver section at www. DigitalFamily.com.

Designing your mobile site so users watch your video

One of the most common mistakes made by designers jumping into the mobile Web is to assume that because designing Web pages that work on mobile devices is so different from designing for the desktop Web, the people who use these devices must be starting from scratch, too.

If you're in that camp, picture us clearing our throats, holding up a bullhorn and then shouting "WRONG!"

Your users arrive at the mobile Web with a lot of baggage. Anyone who has spent time surfing the desktop Web has assumptions and expectations about how things work and burned fingers from all the bad experiences they've had. If you're old enough, you may remember the awful experience common to Web surfers in the late '90s (at least until Microsoft plugged the security hole in IE) when unexpected problems frequently arose, such as an unending stream of pop-up windows mouse-trapped in your browser, no matter how desperately you clicked to close them.

So with video on your mobile Web site, realize that this isn't the first time around the block for your users. They've probably watched online videos before. They know how the video's supposed to work; more importantly, they know how it's not supposed to work and what can go wrong. Things that are annoying on the desktop Web can become major roadblocks on the mobile platform.

Remember, your mobile users are likely to be in a hurry, going in and out of cell coverage, or paying by the byte for the data you send them. You need to give visitors the confidence that you aren't going to abuse their trust by sending them something massively long, horridly inappropriate, or worse. (If you've ever had the experience of being *Rickrolled* — clicking a seemingly relevant link that actually takes you to the Rick Astley's "Never Gonna Give You Up" video — you can appreciate why many Web surfers have become cautious about clicking video links.)

When you add video to your mobile site, abide by these simple guidelines:

- ✔ **Use descriptive text.** Make sure that you tell your users what they're going to get if they choose to invest their time and attention in your video. On mobile, even a modest length video can take a long time to load and play. If your users feel deceived, they aren't likely to click other videos on your site or perhaps come back at all.

- ✔ **Make the video easy to play.** Clicking an image or title of a video needs to make it play. Moving the cursor on tiny mobile screens is hard enough; don't make your users hunt to find the link or control to make your video play.

- ✔ **Show video length and file size.** Related to descriptive text, but important enough to warrant its own mention. Be upfront about your content; tell your users how long the video runs and how big the file is. Better to have them bookmark your page to look at later on a desktop than to frustrate them with a sluggish download or infuriate them by eating their allowed data transmission for the month.

Chapter 9

Making Your Blog Mobile-Friendly

*B*efore we get to the technical details, it's necessary to take a minute and think conceptually about the *why* before we get all tangled up in the *how*. Specifically. . . .

   ✔ Why would someone want to read your blog on their mobile device, and under what circumstances?

   ✔ Why would you want to update your blog using the rudimentary (by comparison) keyboard, camera, screen, and data connection of a mobile device?

The answer to both questions is the same: because you can do it away from the home, office, or home office.

Of course, the next consideration becomes the circumstances that compel that kind of interaction versus the more established means of accessing the Web. If people are looking at your blog on their phone, fancy design flourishes are obviously not what they're after. Therefore, the simple plug-ins we demonstrate in this chapter will allow you to serve up a stripped-down version of your blog specifically for mobile.

Streamlining the blog-reading experience to adapt to the mobile platform is balanced by immediacy, which is what mobile contributes to blog creation. Writing from anywhere, at any time — even live-streaming audio and video on some of the new services — means you can share your experiences with a global audience in real time. It's comparable to being the star of your very own *Truman Show*.

We begin this chapter by explaining how to install the dotMobi WordPress plug-in. Certainly many other options are available, each specific to the particular blogging software you use, but because WordPress is the preeminent blogging platform, we feature it here.

Additionally, this chapter shows off some of the exciting new tools that allow bloggers to break out of the "blogging in your pajamas" stereotype and take creating blog posts away from the desktop and into the world. If you like, though, you can still wear your pajamas.

Prioritizing Your Blog Features

A hard and fast design rule is "All emphasis is no emphasis." If you have a page full of huge bold type and exclamation points, and everything is flashing and jumping around, what are you really telling your readers? Not much, actually, because most sane humans will quickly click away from that kind of monstrosity.

When it comes to re-conceptualizing what your blog should look like on the mobile platform, you have to apply the rules of mobile Web design with ruthless efficiency. Most bloggers, as they grow comfortable with their blogs, start collecting widgets, plug-ins, and features that they like.

Bloggers are, by their very nature, like technology magpies. We see some new, shiny thing and want to drag it into the nest and play with it for a while. Before you know it, the blog's sidebars are overflowing with code snippets that show off the top books you've read lately, the countries your blog visitors are from, the tune you're listening to, and the number of cows you milked in the Facebook game Farmville.

On a desktop, this means your readers have to scroll down a bit more to find your older posts, or they have a momentary giggle while contemplating the dancing bears next to the podcast player.

But on the mobile platform, those sidebar widgets slow down page loads, create conflicts with operating systems or handset capabilities, and generally just gum up the works.

Similarly, the complex multi-box layouts of some of the more sophisticated blogs — the ones that make a blog front page look like the front page of *The New York Times* or ESPN — just don't translate well to a 2-inch, 128-pixel-wide screen — or even to a 4-inch, 320-pixel-wide screen.

We recommend that you take a few minutes to think strategically about your blog and what you really want people to see when they access it from a mobile device. Table 9-1 offers suggestions, based on some of the most common blog subjects.

Table 9-1	Migrating Blog Features to a Mobile Site	
Blog Feature	*Can You Migrate This to the Mobile Web?*	*Then You Should*
Slide shows and other image-intensive content	Yes; but Flash-based galleries or slide shows (that are common on photo sites) won't work on most mobile devices.	Create photo galleries that will work — see Chapter 8.
Video	Yes, but it's very tricky.	Either use a hosting service, such as YouTube or Vimeo, or if you have proprietary video, post multiple versions for the various handsets and operating systems. See Chapter 8.
Long posts	Yes	Partition the pages into bite-sized pieces that won't overwhelm mobile devices. See Chapter 6 for details on content adaptation and prioritization.
Lists people may need to search while on the go (Many organizations, such as Little League, churches, and non-profits, have schedules of events, contact information, and maps that fit this category.)	Yes	Put crucial information in widgets in the sidebar, and then choose which ones you want to make visible on the home page. See Chapter 6 for details on content adaptation and prioritization.

continued

Table 9-1 *(continued)*

Blog Feature	Can You Migrate This to the Mobile Web?	Then You Should
Contact information	Yes	Create a "Text" widget containing this information, and use the theme to make sure it appears on the home page.
Large images	Possible, but not advisable.	Make sure the Shrink Large Images option is chosen. See Chapter 8 for an image-resizing tutorial.
Flash-based layout or banners	No	Convert to JavaScript or Ajax

Adding the dotMobi Plug-in to Your WordPress Blog

Obviously, designing a plug-in that functions with every blog's style and configuration is impossible. There are just too many variations on the basic themes of WordPress for any one-size solution to fit all.

However, the dotMobi plug-in transforms most standard blogs in the following ways:

✔ **Simplifies the banner and color scheme.** Large images or rich media content in banners slows down page loading.

✔ **Stacks headlines in a long row.** Mobile users like to zip up and down through easy-to-grasp headlines, rather than the traditional blog format, where posts can make pages scroll through six or seven screen-lengths.

✔ **Moves sidebars to the bottom of the page.** Because most mobile screens are still narrow, having content appear on the sides means either things get squeezed and unreadable, or the users have to scroll side-to-side as well.

After you install the dotMobi plug-in, you can adjust several settings so that your blog and its contents display as logically and attractively as possible.

Although we cannot anticipate every situation or need, the following sections should get you started on "mobilizing" your blog so that you can test and refine the settings on your own.

In Figure 9-1 you see how the dotMobi plug-in alters the appearance of the Slightly Used Cats blog across a collection of different mobile devices. Figure 9-1 shows how the blog displays in Firefox on a desktop computer. It also shows the blog on a Droid phone, a BlackBerry, and a Motorola RAZR.

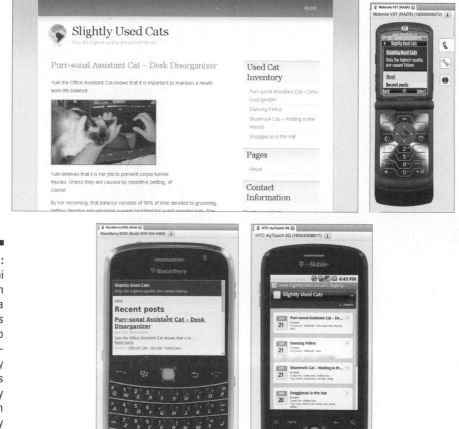

Figure 9-1: The dotMobi plug-in transforms a WordPress blog into mobile-friendly versions that display well on a variety of mobile devices.

What's a plug-in?

A plug-in is a software package that you add to your blog so your blog can do things beyond the capabilities in the basic installation. Plug-ins allow your blog to have long comment threads and fight off spammers, or let your users give five-star ratings to your blog posts and then share them on Twitter, Digg, Reddit, or Facebook.

Thousands of WordPress plug-ins can be found at `http://wordpress.org/extend/plugins`. You can spend hours browsing the myriad ways that programmers around the world have tried to customize the functions of your blog; if you have any PHP programming skills, you might even come up with some new ways on your own.

Installing the dotMobi plug-in

The steps in this section walk you through the process of installing the dot-Mobi plug-in on your WordPress blog.

One risk of installing complex plug-ins, including the dotMobi pack, is that when WordPress periodically updates its software, the update sometimes conflicts with your plug-ins. If this happens, you may have to deactivate or uninstall the plug-in until it is updated as well.

Now that you know what the gotchas are, you're prepared to look out for them and are ready to install the plug-in as follows:

1. **Open a new tab in your browser and navigate to `http://wordpress.org/extend/plugins/wordpress-mobile-pack`.**

   The WordPress Mobile Pack page appears, as shown in Figure 9-2.

Figure 9-2: WordPress Mobile Pack page in the Plugin Directory of WordPress.org.

2. **Click the Download button on the right of the WordPress Mobile Pack page (not the Download button in the WordPress.org header at the very top right).**

3. **In the window that appears, choose where you want to save the Zip file containing the WordPress Mobile Pack plug-in. Click Save to download the file.**

4. **Log in to your WordPress blog, and click Plugins on the sidebar on the left of the page.**

5. **On the drop-down menu that appears, choose Add New.**

   The Install Plugins page appears, as shown in Figure 9-3. This page is very useful for WordPress bloggers; you can use it to browse all kinds of plug-ins. The tag cloud in the center of the page gives you a snapshot of the most popular plug-ins that bloggers are searching for and using. This page is also where you upload plug-ins you want to add to your blog.

Figure 9-3:
The Install Plugins page allows you to upload the plug-in you just downloaded and find others that might lead you in entirely new directions with your blog.

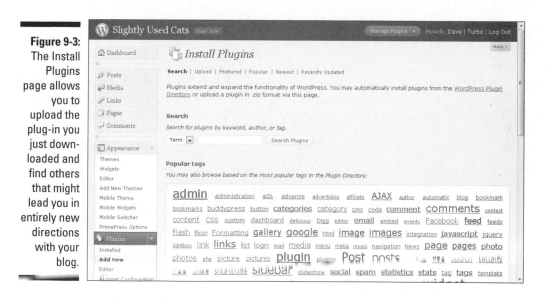

6. **Click the Upload link near the top of the page.**

   The Upload page opens and allows you to easily upload the Zip file containing your plug-in to your blog database without having to use an FTP program.

   The Featured, Popular, Newest, and Recently Updated links can keep you up to date on the latest plug-ins bloggers are using.

7. **Click the Browse button.**

   A window opens and lists your default directory.

8. **Navigate to where you just saved the WordPress Mobile Pack Zip file. Select it and then click the Open button.**

9. **Click the Install Now button.**

   Your computer automatically uploads the plug-in to the proper directory in your WordPress blog and unzips the contents of the file.

10. **Click the Return to Plugins Page link.**

    The Manage Plugins page opens.

11. **Click the Activate link under WordPress Mobile Pack.**

    Your blog activates the plug-in and *Plugin Activated* appears at the top of the page. If there is a conflict between this plug-in and one of your other plug-ins, or with your blog's theme, you receive an error message. If this happens, you have to troubleshoot by systematically deactivating and reactivating the conflicting plug-ins or features of your blog.

You can shortcut this process by navigating to the plug-in directory of WordPress and searching for the Mobile Pack plug-in there. Unfortunately, whenever a plug-in gets popular, there are always spammers and scammers who try to piggyback on the plug-in's success by putting out copycat versions that can damage your blog — or worse. These copycat versions are often variations on the spelling or word order of the original plug-in, and they can be hard to spot. If you do choose to install the Mobile Pack using the one-click method, be sure that you have researched this thoroughly, and that you're getting what you expect.

At this point, you can sit back and let the automatically selected settings take over and determine how your blog will look on mobile devices, or you can dig a little deeper into the various settings to try to customize the look. We lead you through some of the options in the upcoming sections. You don't have to know any real computer programming to adjust these options, although you have to invest some time and effort in testing the various settings.

If you have some PHP and CSS skills, you can really take matters into your own hands and edit the various files to totally customize how this plug-in makes your blog look.

Tweaking the mobile switcher

With the dotMobi plug-in installed, the first thing that a mobile browser encounters when it tries to access your blog is the mobile switcher. Before we get into customizing how this nifty bit of code works, here's a brief explanation: The mobile switching agent tells the mobile browser to ignore all the files on how to format the blog's content for the desktop environment and to use the coding in the WordPress Mobile Plugin pack to filter the content. For more on mobile switchers, see Chapter 2. Here's how to adjust the settings:

1. **Open a browser and navigate to your WordPress blog's Dashboard.**

2. **Click Plugins on the left sidebar.**

   The Manage Plugins page appears.

3. **Scroll to the WordPress Mobile Pack plug-in and click the Switcher link.**

   Alternatively, you can access the Mobile Switcher by selecting it from the Appearance tab, as shown in Figure 9-4.

   The Mobile Switcher page opens, as shown in Figure 9-4. This page contains various drop-down menus you can use to adjust the settings.

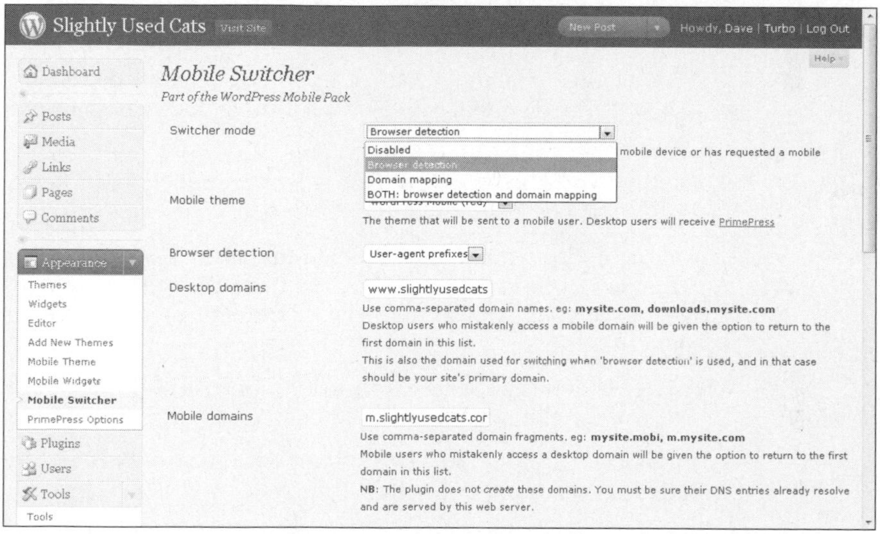

Figure 9-4:
The Mobile
Switcher
page
allows you
to control
what mobile
users see
on your site.

4. **On the Switcher Mode drop-down menu, choose from the following options:**

   • *Disabled:* Choose this when you want there to be no switching, perhaps because you have a site that is designed to be seen only on mobile devices.

   • *Browser Detection:* When users access your blog, their browser sends a little information to your server, telling it what kind of browser and operating system is making the request. Think of it like a polite guest knocking on your door and announcing who they are. This mode is pretty effective, although very new or non-standard browsers may not be recognized; therefore, the users would be sent to your desktop site. (To guard against that kind of error, see Step 9).

- *Domain Mapping:* This identifies whether the visitor to your blog is trying to access a mobile domain (say `m.slightlyusedcats.com`, `slightlyusedcats.com/m/`, or `slightlyusedcats.mobi`) or just the regular desktop site. This is quite effective if your users are typing in the complete address. However, it requires that you create a completely separate mobile site at that address.

- *Both Browser Detection and Domain Mapping:* The advantage of using this setting is that it covers almost all possible mobile user access scenarios and flashes a warning message when your user tries to access the mobile site through a desktop browser or vice-versa.

5. **On the Mobile Theme drop-down, choose which theme you want your mobile users to see.**

   The defaults are limited to the base color scheme, as well as blue, green, or red. If you customize and save a mobile theme of your own, it appears here, too.

6. **On the Browser Detection drop-down menu, choose User-Agent Prefixes if you like.**

   This drop-down menu is available only when you choose Browser Detection or Both Browser Detection and Domain Mapping in Step 4, because if you're not using Browser Detection, the choices here will not be available.

   As we write this book, the only option here is User-Agent Prefixes. However, updates to this mobile pack may provide more options.

7. **In the Desktop Domains box, change the text only if you have a complicated or custom-built site.**

   The default is your primary Web address where users hitting your site from traditional desktop or laptop computers are sent. If you don't know what you're doing here, leave it alone.

8. **In the Mobile Domains box, enter the names of any custom mobile domains you've created.**

   As we mention in Step 4, you can create a completely different site at an `m.`*whatever*`.com` or *whatever*`.mobi` domain. However, just filling in a variation of your existing domain address does not magically create this site. Creating subdomains like these requires a fair amount of specialized knowledge and access to server-level functions that not all Web hosts offer.

9. **(Optional) Select the Footer Links check box to allow your users to override the mobile switcher.**

   This places a link on the bottom of the page that allows users to defeat the switcher in case it sends a desktop user to a mobile page, or vice-versa. If you're confident in the switcher and want to save space on your page, don't include the link, but most people choose to just in case.

Allow your users to choose which version of your blog they want to see; maybe a desktop user is on a particularly slow connection and just wants to access the simplest version of your site.

10. **Click the Save Changes button when you are done.**

Customizing your mobile theme

Although you can choose the basic color scheme of the existing mobile themes when you configure the mobile switcher (see the preceding section), the Mobile Theme page allows you to further customize what your mobile users see when they access your blog.

1. **Open a browser and navigate to your WordPress blog's Dashboard.**

2. **Click Plugins on the left sidebar.**

   The Manage Plugins page appears.

3. **Scroll to the WordPress Mobile Pack plug-in and click the Themes link.**

   Alternatively, you can click on the Mobile Theme link under the Appearance tab, as shown in Figure 9-5.

   The Mobile Theme page opens, as shown in Figure 9-5. This page contains various drop-down menus you can use to adjust the settings.

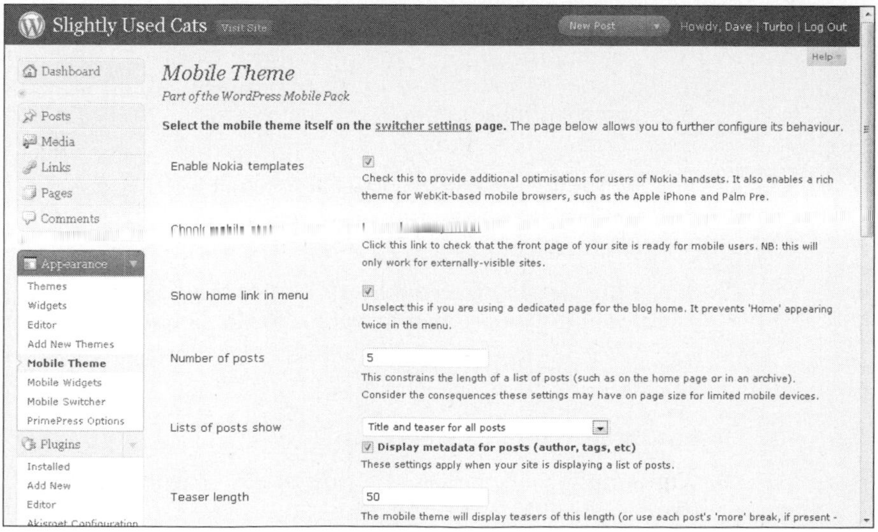

Figure 9-5:
The Mobile Theme page allows you to customize the switcher settings further.

4. **Ensure the Enable Nokia Templates option is selected (checked).**

Despite all the hype about smartphones, such as the iPhone or Droid, Nokia handsets are still the most popular in the world, especially in developing nations.

5. **If you have a dedicated page, deselect the Show Home Link in Menu check box.**

If you have a dedicated home page for your blog (such as a big picture, a video, or an animation), you want to deselect this check box. Otherwise the plug-in places two Home links on your mobile page. If you do not have a dedicated home page, leave this check box selected.

6. **Choose the number of posts to display on your home page or archive page.**

The default is five. If you want your blog to load quicker, type a smaller number. If you want your readers to see more items and aren't worried about load times (or believe that your readers mostly have fast phones or a lot of patience), then increase the number. Experiment with this setting until you are happy with how your blog downloads and displays in a browser.

7. **On the Lists of Posts Show drop-down menu, choose one of the following options:**

   a. *Title Only* causes the mobile version of your blog to display only the title of your blog posts. Again, this is a tradeoff between detail and loading speed.

   b. *Title and Teaser for the First Post, Title for the Rest* is a good compromise setting. Your readers see the title of your most recent post and the first few words of the post; after that, readers just see the headlines.

   c. *Title and Teaser for All Posts* displays as much information as possible to get your readers to click through to the full posts. Of course, having this setting selected means that the pages load slower. Your readers may get frustrated and abandon your blog.

8. **Select the Display Metadata for Posts option if you want to display additional information about your posts.**

If you choose this, each post also shows the name of the author and any tags you've chosen.

9. **Choose the teaser length (if any).**

The default is 50 characters. If you want a longer teaser, type a larger number. Again, this is something you should experiment with.

10. **Type the number of widget items you want to display.**

The default is five. Your widgets will not display in a sidebar on your mobile blog; instead, they appear in a bar at the bottom of the page. If your widget has a lot of information in it, only a short teaser and a link to the full list will appear.

11. **Select the Remove Media option if you want remove all rich media content from on your blog.**

Depending on what you blog about, this can be one of the most crucial decisions you make. If you use a lot of multimedia in your blog posts, then removing all your audio, video, or Flash files may leave you with little content to offer mobile visitors. However, if you mostly post text and photos on your site and occasionally have audio, video, or Flash, removing these elements may be in your best interest. Rich media elements are usually large in size; users may not want to wait around — or burn up their limited data plans — waiting for your home page to download. When you choose to remove media, the plug-in removes the object, embed, marquee, script, frame, and iframe HTML tags and their content.

12. **Select the Partition Large Pages option to break up your content into bite-size pieces.**

If you tend to write long posts (if your post requires the user to scroll through more than four screens of content, it's long), you might want to give your audience a break with this option. If, however, you want people to load only one page at a time and avoid clicking repeatedly to load page after page, then leave this check box deselected.

13. **Select the Shrink Images option to resize your pictures to fit on mobile screens.**

Shrinking images might not be a good idea in some circumstances. If you are a photographer and are afraid that the resizing engine in this plug-in might add noise or distortion to your photos, or you prefer to handle the resizing yourself, leave Shrink Images unchecked. Otherwise, it doesn't make much sense to have a poster-resolution image on a postage-stamp-size screen.

14. **Select the Clear Cache Now option if you want to ensure that the resized images are the ones that appear for mobile users.**

Sometimes, WordPress caches images locally so that it doesn't have to keep going into the database to retrieve them. If you chose to resize images, but haven't cleared the cache, your blog could continue to deliver the large image files.

15. **Select the Simplify Styling option.**

This removes any little flourishes that have crept into your posts and pages, such as having ornate initial capital letters or having unique styles as frames around pictures. On the mobile Web, these kinds of elements are referred to as "drag," as in "All the fancy typography and design on that blog are dragging it down like an anchor thrown into bottomless quicksand."

16. **Click Save Changes when you are done customizing your settings.**

    Call up your blog on your mobile device to see what your changes have done to your blog's appearance.

Choosing which widgets to display

If you're a blogger, you've probably added a widget or two (or ten). When you set up your WordPress blog for the mobile Web using the dotMobi plug-in, here's how to display widgets for your readers:

1. **Open a browser and navigate to your WordPress blog's Dashboard.**

2. **Click Plugins on the left sidebar.**

    The Manage Plugins page appears.

3. **Scroll to the WordPress Mobile Pack plug-in and click the Mobile Widgets link.**

    The Mobile Widgets page appears, as shown in Figure 9-6. This page contains various check boxes that allow you to winnow your widgets to just the ones that are absolutely essential to your blog. You can enable your widgets on the regular Widgets page, where you can drag and drop the elements to add, subtract, or re-order the content.

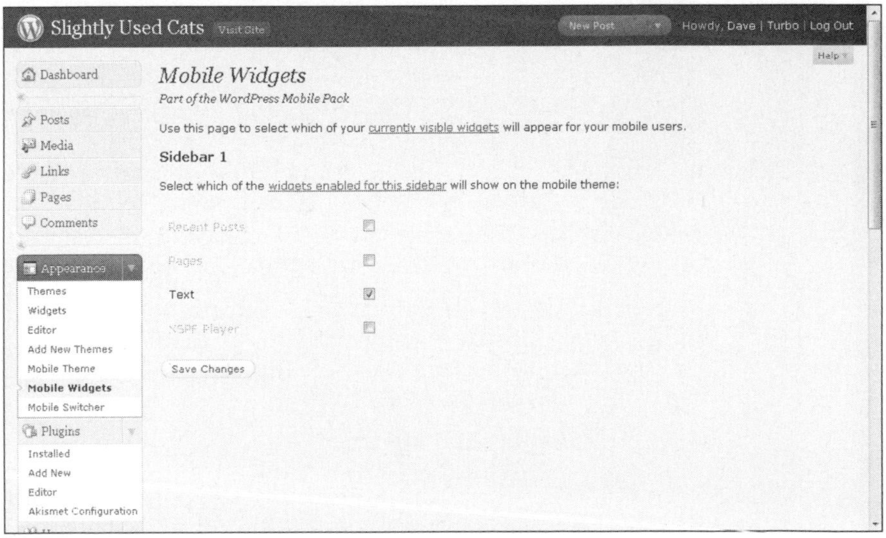

Figure 9-6:
The Mobile Widgets page.

   4. Select which widgets you want to appear on the mobile version of your blog.

   Accepted wisdom is that no more than three widgets should load when you hit a mobile page. (Purists say anything more than three is pushing it.) Consider carefully what information absolutely, positively has to be on your mobile blog. Widgets for stock tickers, Twitter feeds, Flickr slide shows, or MP3 players can severely clog page load times. Keep widgets to things like your About page or Recent Posts.

   5. Click the Save Changes button.

Blogging from a Mobile Device

   As mobile devices increasingly include full alphanumeric ("QWERTY," for the letters on the top row) keypads, users are taking advantage. Before, typing a post with a telephone keypad, where you had to push the 9 key four times to enter a Z, was something only die-hard bloggers with fast and muscular thumbs dared to try.

   You have dozens of ways to post to your blog from mobile devices; the various App Stores are overflowing with custom-built tools to empower bloggers to capture every waking second of their lives in words, pictures, and video. We encourage you to check these apps out (if your mobile device supports downloaded apps) and see whether any of them suit your needs.

   However, if you don't want to tie your blogging future to the whims of an App developer, some free and easy tools enable you to add and update posts using the most basic skills and setup — namely mobile blogging via e-mail.

   In only 20 years, e-mail has become so ubiquitous; it seems that every life form on the evolutionary scale higher than an amoeba has a Gmail account. One of the strengths of blogging is that refreshing a Web page is (almost) as easy as typing an e-mail message and attaching a file. Well, that last step has been bridged by updates to blogging software that allow blogs to take incoming e-mails and turn them into blog posts. Admittedly, sending an e-mail does not allow you to format the post with precision or to preview it to see how it looks — but it gets the content into your blog immediately from any device that is capable of sending an e-mail.

   In the sections that follow, we explain how you set up a WordPress blog to accept blog posts via e-mail. If you use a blogging platform other than WordPress (such as Blogger or TypePad), the specific steps you follow will vary but the basic idea is the same.

With the addition of audio recording, cameras that take up to 8 megapixel images, and even video recording, bloggers now have a cornucopia of tools at their disposal. If you want to use photo-sharing services, such as Picasa, to construct geotagged maps showing the exact locations of the pictures you take, or use live streaming sites, such as Ustream or Kyte, to be your own broadcast network, flip to Chapter 8. This section focuses only on text posts.

Creating a secret e-mail address

Before you start blogging via e-mail, you have to create a unique e-mail address to send your blog posts to. The creation process will vary depending on the way your Web hosting service or e-mail is set up. Essentially, you can use any e-mail address, but there are significant risks to doing this with a Gmail, Hotmail, or Yahoo! account because so many spammers and noxious advertisers randomly blanket every possible address with messages that would then wind up as content on your blog.

Don't use your regular e-mail address. All the e-mail you get in your Inbox daily (including secret love notes or chain letters from your crazy uncle) posts automatically and immediately to your blog. WordPress recommends you create a really obscure e-mail address (see the examples below) and keep this e-mail address as secret as possible. If it gets out in the open, spammers can then hijack your blog by sending whatever noxious material they want to that Inbox, and your blog will automatically post it.

So before you start down this path, make sure that you have a safe and secure e-mail address that is dedicated only to receiving e-mails that will then be converted into blog posts. You can share this e-mail address with (very) trusted friends, say a group on a vacation or at a big concert, so they can post their impressions to your blog as quickly and easily as possible.

To make your special blogging e-mail address safe and secure, WordPress prompts you to use semi-random strings of letters and numbers, such as 4lrp59qs@yourmail.com. Since nobody sane has a name like 4lrp59qs, the automated programs that spammers use to guess common names won't hit upon this combination for their unwanted messages.

Converting e-mails into WordPress posts

Here's how to set up your WordPress blog to accept your e-mails and turn them into content:

1. **Open a browser and navigate to your WordPress blog's Dashboard.**
2. **Click Settings on the left sidebar.**

Depending on how you have set up your own blog, your Settings tab may be in a different location, such as at the bottom of the sidebar.

3. Click the Writing link.

The Writing Settings page opens, as shown in Figure 9-7. This page enables you to adjust many of the settings for creating new posts. Skip the first two sections because they have nothing to do with creating posts via e-mail; make changes to them only if you know what you are doing.

Under the Post via E-Mail heading is a paragraph containing three suggested "random strings," which look like this: 23anir8r2c. These are for you to use as usernames to send your blog posts to. That is, you send your e-mails to 23anir8r2c@*yourdomain*.com and they automatically publish.

4. Enter the mail server for your e-mail account.

If you have your own self-hosted WordPress blog, the mail server will probably look similar to mail.*yourblogname*.com.

5. Enter the secret e-mail address in the Login Name box.

6. Enter the password you established for this e-mail account.

7. Choose a category from the Default Mail Category drop-down menu.

If you want the posts from your mobile device to go into a special category (such as Out and About), you would choose that here.

8. Click Save Changes.

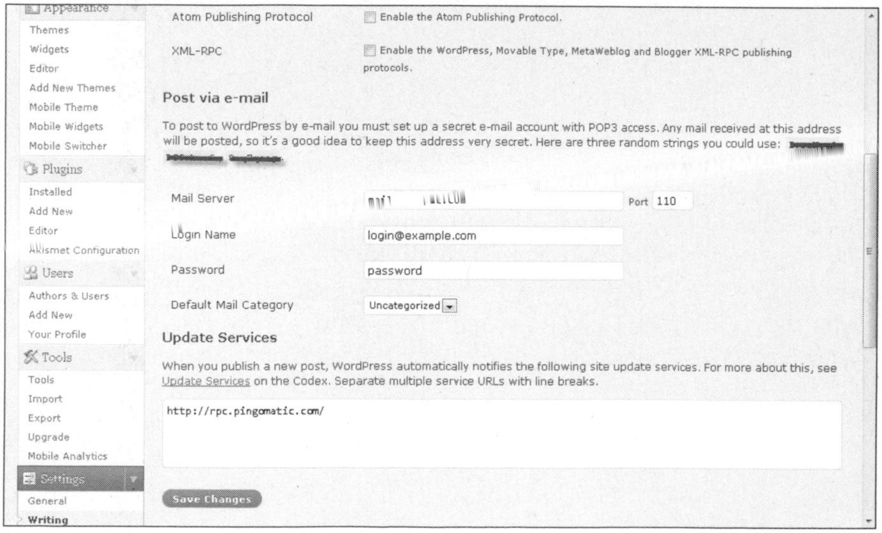

Figure 9-7:
The Writing Settings page opens your blog to publishing content sent via e-mail.

Blogging on the mobile Web: An interview with Doc Searls

Doc Searls — alpha blogger and co-author of "The Cluetrain Manifesto" — is one of the guys who was around when the Internet was created, and who had a real hand in shaping and giving voice to its emerging culture. He is a firm believer in the righteousness of open-source technology, the wisdom of the crowd, the promise of many-to-many communication, and taking pictures out of airplane windows.

Searls has made it his life's work to study the implications of the many-to-many information flow that blogging makes possible (see his blog shown in the figure). His long-term insights on where blogging is headed, now that it can be created and consumer anywhere, are essential to any blogger hoping to make the transition to the mobile platform.

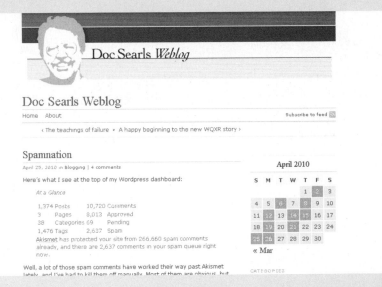

Q: Migrating blogs to function on the mobile platform seems to run headlong into a whole bunch of conflicting considerations; are any of the following guidelines (culled from "expert" advice) accurate, and if so, to what extent?

Before we go there, it's important to note that WordPress, Drupal, and other popular authoring systems are not yet optimized for mobile [*Ed. Note: Besides the plug-in demonstrated in this chapter, which helps optimize the theme for a blog*]. This is bound to change, but soon isn't fast enough. I think the presence of the iPad in the world will help. Authors will soon be writing, consciously, for three sizes of screens: desktop/laptop, tablet, and smartphone.

Meanwhile, the best format for mobile is plain HTML. This is what Dave Winer does with his news rivers. I keep a bookmark for http://nytimesriver.com in my iPhone browser because it loads instantly, and looks great — if what you're trying to do is actually *read*.

Sometimes simpler is better. This is especially the case when space and processing power are limited, as they are with mobile devices. The same goes for streaming. The streaming equivalent of a 50,000-watt radio station is a 24 Kbps stream: the lowest useful bit rate. That's because you can receive it with GPRS (Edge) and not just 3G and Wi-Fi.

The problem at the moment is that designers want to fancy things up, which is only natural. They want pretty Web sites, sparkling audio, and high-resolution video because those things flatter their work and align with their ideals. But, in the real world, those ideals are often at odds with actual use. In the long run, this conflict sorts out because we get both the pretty and the practical. But, right now, we're in a tug between them, and the designers are winning.

Perspective: It's only 15 years since the first popular graphical browser came along, and the commercial Web (Amazon, eBay, and so on) followed. The 'Net is still young. It's a sophomore in high school, not even old enough to get its driving permit. So, some patience is required, along with as much innovation as we can stand.

✔ *Bloggers have to write even shorter, pithier pieces because the readers are on the move.*

I don't agree. Years ago people said blogging should be short-form, yet long-form blogs often did better than the short kind. The trick is to make them easy to read. People tweet and re-tweet most of my blog posts, and nearly all those posts are hundreds or even thousands of words long.

✔ *Bloggers need to make sure they have longer content available, because readers are sometimes killing time and are willing to drill down deep.*

That's true. I sometimes go to a long blog post before I get on the train and then read it underground, on my iPhone.

✔ *It's essential to have good-looking multimedia content to take advantage of the new smartphones that play video so well.*

No. You need interesting material. Good beats fancy every time. This is not to say that multimedia is bad, just that it won't be the only thing. TV didn't obsolete text. Nor will smartphones.

✔ *Multimedia content has to be stripped out because of the still-shaky data connections and the whole Flash controversy.*

Well, it needs to be optional — gracefully added and subtracted as bandwidth requires.

✔ *People are searching for immediate, useful information on their mobiles.*

Of course. In fact, in the long run people will be publishing their own demand selectively to markets on the fly — "I need a stroller for twins in White Plains in the next two hours. Who's coming through?" — without having to do that within the silos of eBay, Amazon, or Craigslist. (And this isn't a knock on those. Just an observation that we need an open marketplace as well as these closed ones.)

Q: Facebook's growth on mobile has been absolutely shocking — 600 percent last year.

Thank a killer — and very simple — Facebook iPhone app.

Q: Does this qualify as blogging?

No. Facebook is still a closed and private silo — or a giant walled garden. In this respect, it is still AOL 2.0.

Q: Is this kind of growth going to continue? Or are we going to get sick and tired of playing in Zuckerberg's garden and head off to more bespoke social communities?

We'll always head back in an open direction, away from beautiful but limited closed spaces.

(continued)

(continued)

There is a market ecosystem at work here. We have the Facebooks and Apples creating vertical apps and devices that create new categories (or vastly improve old ones) and show much of what can be done there. Then we have the Googles and open-source communities working horizontally, doing openly what closed systems prevent.

Q: You once described being an "alpha blogger" as being akin to being an "alpha paramecium." Does that make an alpha mobile blogger an alpha virus? Or a paramecium with legs?

The latter, I suppose.

What I meant there was that blogging is essentially a personal act: a one-man or one-woman show. It is social in the way all of us are social — humans are social animals — but it is not a collective activity.

Humans are also mobile animals, and phones are far more popular than computers for a good reason: They're more personal, more conversational, and you can carry them in your pocket.

The problem with blogging is that it is essentially a text activity. Given the difficulty of writing while walking or driving, blogging is likely to remain mostly a sitting-still activity as well. But there are endless possibilities here: speech-to-text, audio and video postings, mashing up work by other people. . . .

Q: Is being able to file live reports from out in the field such a big deal? Outside of a few high-profile successes, is this really that big of a selling point for a blogger?

The appeal of photography and video is that there's no limit to what you can do with them. Few of us imagine we'll be filing live reports, but knowing we can is not a trivial consideration. Most of us don't expect to be dialing 911 either, but knowing we can is a good thing.

Q: How often do you read blogs on your mobile?

Every day, usually several times a day.

Q: Under what circumstances and what are you looking for?

Usually, I'm following links in tweets, simply because they're interesting to me.

Q: What do you think is going to be a big growth area in mobile blogging over the next couple of years? What's going to take off that's just started getting traction?

The biggest thing will be video. The ability of anybody to upload, mash up, and edit video is going to put a big stress on existing systems, which are built with a bias for bandwidth in the downstream direction. This stress can break in one or both of two ways. One is resistance from the carriers, which would rather persist in their few-to-many entertainment industry dreams (TV moving to the 'Net, and available only to subscribers). The other is carriers (and other parties, such as municipal fiber systems) embracing users as producers and a wide-open marketplace where everybody can supply ideas and content to everybody else. There is far more economic vitality in the latter than the former.

Q: What is on your wish list? Is it an actual established business model for content creators?

That's one of them. See EmanciPay at `http://cyber.law.harvard.edu/ projectvrm/EmanciPay`.

Also,

- Grass-roots growth of municipal and regional broadband utilities — rising tides that lift all boats.

- Preservation of the 'Net as an open, simple, end-to-end style system that's NEA: Nobody owns it, Everybody can use it, and Anybody can improve it.

- Success of open mobile devices running on Android, Symbian, and other operating systems that no one company controls.

✔ Evolution of journalism from the exclusive province of the few into the standard practice of the many — with a sense or moral purpose and balance and purpose in the course of It. For a little on that, see my post at `http://blogs.law.harvard.edu/doc/2010/04/21/write-and-wrong`.

I could go on, but that's probably more than enough.

Q: Or is it the continuing creative chaos, where it's possible for people with a compelling message to make up a revenue stream on the fly?

Well, it's that too.

Chapter 10

Mobile Marketing and Social Media

*T*he only phone advertising you used to have to think about was the pesky telemarketers calling you right when you sat down to dinner. These days, advertising can be beamed to that device in your pocket wherever you go, whenever advertisers want to reach you. But before you chuck your phone into the nearest landfill, remember that you're probably reading this book because you're interested in having a mobile Web site of your own and that you want people to come and see what you've poured so much time and energy into.

Getting page traffic is a complex subject, one that has fueled innumerable books, Web sites, seminars, and blog posts. One of the most basic ways is to use advertising to make people aware that your site exists and to give them a reason to come there.

Of course, another reason to know about mobile advertising is that you're a content publisher and you want your stories, photos, videos, or songs to earn some money. Sure, you can do this by selling subscriptions (see Chapter 11, which is all about e-commerce), but adding advertising to your mobile site is a growing revenue stream.

Finally, if your mobile site is part of your overall business, and the whole point of all this is to get people to come to your restaurant, book a vacation, or buy your custom-painted T-shirts, you will most certainly want to start using mobile advertising.

In this chapter, we look at some early mobile marketing success stories and demonstrate how you can launch your own custom campaign using free or low-cost tools.

Understanding Mobile's Advertising Advantage

At first glance, advertising on mobile devices seems to be a losing game. The screens are tiny fractions of a proper flat screen TV, the connection to the Internet is far more tenuous than a cable modem or DSL line, and typing on the itty-bitty keyboards is comfortable only for leprechauns. However, the reality is that the mobile Web offers important advantages:

✔ **People take their mobile phones with them wherever they go.** Studies show that when you leave your phone behind in a restaurant, you probably realize it within an hour or two; however, most people take about a day to realize they've left their wallet with their ID, cash, and credit cards behind. This is how integral mobile phones are in people's lives.

✔ **Mobile phones offer one of the few times in modern life when you have the audience's undivided attention.** Think of the environment that most advertising gets tossed into, to sink or swim. The average teenager's room has a TV that she flips through channels on, a radio blaring, a laptop open to Facebook while instant messaging, glossy magazines open on the bed, and a video game console blasting aliens. Good luck breaking through that chaos.

In contrast, when that same teenager is on the bus to school, what does she do? She *cocoons* with her media — that is, she sits down, pulls out her mobile phone or media player, puts headphones in her ears, and plays music or a video. Even in busy and crowded environments, where visitors to your site may be distracted, researchers say that having the media player in her hand creates a special state of connection and concentration.

✔ **People trust content delivered via their mobile devices.** According to mobile marketing experts, that trust is built up from hearing your mom's voice come out of the device or relying on it to reach 911 when you witness a car accident.

That trust translates into a much better chance that your marketing message actually gets through. But don't just take that at face value; early research shows that, when done properly and integrated with other media, mobile advertising yields a return on investment that's surprising even seasoned advertising executives — a point we illustrate in the section, "Assessing the Impact of Mobile Advertising."

✔ **Mobile devices increasingly come with GPS built in.** With GPS, your mobile phone knows where you are (and can tell you where to go when you get lost). This also means that advertising can take advantage of that data to put in ads that are even more effective because of relevance — the advertising message reaches potential customers wherever they are. For example, a woman walks down a busy street when her phone suddenly lights up with a coupon for 20 percent off at the Starbucks up the block.

Similarly, restaurants can send mobile alerts at 11 a.m. on workdays to their most loyal customers (that is, those who have signed up to receive alerts and offers), inviting them to try the business lunch specials. The Pittsburgh Penguins hockey team started using mobile ads to alert rabid fans within a 10-mile radius of the rink that last-minute tickets had just become available, if fans could make it to through traffic in time to claim them.

Targeting your ads to appear where and when your customers need them transforms them from intrusive spam that everyone grumbles about into a useful service that solves a need. For instance, you might be glad to know

- Where the nearest tire repair shop is when your car blows a tire on the way to work

- Who can help you get a red wine stain out of a cashmere sweater before the stain sets in

- Where the nearest place is to get a refill on your allergy medication before you wind up in the hospital

Of course, this kind of targeting raises all kinds of privacy concerns, which is why so many mobile advertising practitioners talk about *opt-in* marketing campaigns. The Federal Communications Commission (FCC) and the major cellphone carriers (AT&T, Verizon, and Sprint) constantly work on establishing the rules and regulations for mobile advertising. Violations of the FCC rules can get you banned by the carriers, fined, or worse by the FCC. You can find an example of the codes of conduct at `http://mmaglobal.com/codeof conduct.pdf`.

In the upcoming sections, we take a look at what kinds of ads you need to check with your audience before you send them.

Checking Out the Types of Mobile Ads

Because the mobile Web has unique attributes and advantages, as we explain in the preceding section, mobile advertising sometimes works differently than traditional ads you see in print, on TV, or online. Here's a brief introduction to the most common types of ads, which you can explore in more detail later in this chapter:

- ✔ **Banner ads:** These ads are much like the banner ads you see all over the desktop Web. As a designer, the differences you need to understand are the ad's size, download speed, and placement. See "Creating Banner Ads for Mobile Sites" for details.

- ✔ **SMS messages:** Short Message Service (SMS), or text messages, are limited to 160 characters in length, so your advertising message has to be short and sweet. The messages can contain links to Web sites or *click-to-call messages* — you click the SMS so that your phone places a call. The section, "Launching a free SMS advertising campaign" explains the basics of setting up this type of ad.

- ✔ **CSC messages:** Common Short Codes (CSCs) are a series of numbers, usually five or six digits, to which a user can send a text message. A response message from an advertiser is sent back with information or content, or with a contest you can enter (for example, *American Idol* encourages viewers to text vote to a number corresponding to their favorite contestant to place their vote). The section "Connecting with Customers via Short Codes" explains how they work.

- ✔ **QR Codes:** Quick Response Codes, or 2D barcodes, look like the little jumbled checkerboard patterns used to track FedEx or UPS shipments. In 1994, Denso Wave created them to track auto parts because they can contain so much more data than traditional bar codes (such as the ones on packages in grocery stores).

    QR Codes work this way: Each code can contain up to 4,296 characters (or a string of 7,089 numbers). Users with cellphone cameras and the right software installed can take a picture of the QR Code, launching the phone's browser and redirecting to the URL contained in the code. Find out how to create your own QR Codes in the section "Offering Links and more with QR Codes."

- ✔ **Coupons:** Touted as "the coupons that you never forget to take with you," mobile coupons are attracting attention from major advertisers like Hollywood Video, 1-800-Flowers.com, Sears, Supercuts, McDonalds, and others. Juniper Research estimates that by 2011, about 3 billion mobile coupons will be redeemed for $7 billion in discounts. One of the big advantages is that mobile coupons can deliver demographic information about the users, in addition to motivating them to come to a store and make a purchase. You find details about coupon ads in the section, "Handing out Coupons via the Mobile Web."

✔ **Image recognition:** Image recognition advertising allows you to take a picture of something (usually an ad in a magazine or on a billboard) and send it to the publisher or advertiser. In return, you get exclusive content or prizes. The offer might be a ringtone, coupon, or anything else that can be sent directly to a person's mobile phone. See "Sharing Offers via Image Recognition" for more on this model.

Assessing the Impact of Mobile Advertising

Although mobile advertising agencies still debate the best way to measure how mobiles sway consumers to make purchases (is it intent to purchase after seeing an ad or do only dollars-and-cents sales figures count?), pioneers in the field report some compelling successes. Of course, the saying "The pioneers get all the arrows" also still holds true because detractors can point to ads that seemingly had no impact.

When mobile ads are targeted correctly and the campaign is well thought out, the response rates are much higher than direct mail or even Internet campaigns in which getting 0.1 percent of the audience to respond is considered success. Some mobile campaigns have response rates as high as 20 percent; basically, the ads are 200 times more effective than regular advertising.

Some notable examples of successful mobile campaigns include the following:

✔ The Stanislaus County Fair in central California was seeing sparse attendance during the middle of the day because of the hot sun during the day and concerts at night. By using mobile coupons, the fair was able to recruit young tech-savvy teens to show up in return for a $3 discount. Even in this rural market, the conversion rate on the coupons was 44 percent.

✔ The Gunstock Mountain Resort in New Hampshire started a program called JitterGram (basically, clever SMS messages) to get users to sign up for notices on lunch and happy hour specials, sales on ski clothes, and discounted lift tickets (that the resort used to drive traffic to the ski runs on off days). For each JitterGram sent to subscribers, the resort netted an extra $1,000 of business that day.

✔ In July 2009, Chicago's Shedd Aquarium tested the difference in response rates. In one TV commercial, viewers were sent to a Web site to register for a contest. In the other TV commercial, viewers we told to enter the contest by sending a text message to a short code.

The short code campaign generated 325 percent more entries than the Web-based call-to-action. Although the short code campaign ran only in 25 percent of the ads, it generated 52 percent of the total entries.

- Yamaha WaterCraft (the division that makes WaveRunners) ran a campaign in which people who texted WAVE to a short code or entered their mobile phone number into a form on the Yamaha mobile Web site were entered into a sweepstakes. Yamaha saw a 400 percent increase in the number of people who entered the sweepstakes (and also opted to receive more marketing information from Yamaha about their boats, motors, and Jet Skis).

- Lane Bryant started a program in which customers waiting in line at the cash register signed up for coupons and discounts to be delivered over their phones. When the customers walked out of the store, their phones lit up with text messages offering them special deals, such as cash back or a percentage off their next purchase. Nearly 20 percent of the customers re-targeted this way came back within two weeks to use the discount codes they were sent on their phones to make additional purchases.

- Reebok ran a campaign in which soccer fans could download pictures of their favorite players' jerseys and then send them to their friends via e-mail or SMS. This Gift a Jersey program led to Reebok vastly expanding its network of interested customers as well as a 14.6 percent increase in traffic to stores selling the real jerseys.

- When Volkswagen experimented with the launch of their redesigned GTI, it was determined not to spend a single cent on TV, print, or the Internet. Instead, Volkswagen licensed a driving game designed specifically to be played on the iPhone, and put its new GTI in it, with all the performance and handling characteristics of the real car. More than 2 million people downloaded the game, and the six best players won a free souped-up GTI. And in the ultimate measure of success, Volkswagen reported that the marketing cost per car sold dropped by 97 percent.

- PlayStation ran a mobile ad campaign for their Resistance 2 game. Out of 170,000 SMS messages sent, PlayStation got 27,000 people to click through and watch the video — about a 16 percent response rate.

For more great examples of successful mobile ad campaigns, check out Mobile Marketing Association's Web site at http://mmaglobal.com/resources/case-studies. You might even find some inspiration for the kind of mobile ad campaign that could work for you.

Creating Banner Ads for Mobile Sites

Every new medium is influenced by what came before it. The first movies were basically plays on film; directors plunked their cameras on tripods in front of a stages and called "Action!" Decades passed before anyone picked up a camera and moved it around or did any of the trick photography people now take for granted. When television came along, Hollywood figured it was just like radio — only with pictures. So directors took radio actors and stuck them in front of cameras, finding out in the process what the phrase "has a face for radio" means.

Banner ads came about through just such a process; early Web publishers took ads destined for newspaper or magazine pages, and then published them on Web pages (albeit with some enhancements such as simple animations that asked users to click to "Punch the Monkey"). The first impulse for mobile advertising was to take those existing banner advertisements from the Internet, shrink them, and stick them on the mobile Web. Although this may not be the most innovative approach, at this stage of development, it may be good enough (as long as the ads don't include the Flash animations, which are common to the desktop Web but won't work on many mobile devices). Of course, as mobile advertising evolves, banner ads will have to evolve and change with it.

All kinds of considerations come into play when displaying banner ads on a mobile phone. These include

- **Screen resolution:** Most often expressed as *screen width,* screen resolution refers to how many pixels wide the screen on the phone handset is.

- **File size:** Particularly crucial in mobile advertising because phones typically don't have the random access memory (RAM) and hard drive storage that computers do. Larger file sizes are risky on the mobile platform, because uncertain wireless connections can cause significant load time delays.

- **Phone processor speed:** Just like in computers, the speed here is constantly improving, which means that most phones can render and display video.

- **Software/operating system on the phone:** These include Opera Mini, Symbian, Windows Mobile, Android, iPhone OS, Moblin, and more every day. If you're designing an application instead of a Web site, you will need to create a different version for each operating system.

- **Functionality:** Clicking an ad on a mobile device can activate a script that causes your phone to make a call, launch an application, or go to a browser page.

At first glance, the technical challenges seem daunting: Handsets in the U.S. market have 31 screen widths coupled with different color depths.

The Mobile Marketing Association (MMA) has a chart that shows the recommended sizes in pixels for banner ads as well as the size of the graphic file. If you create a banner ad, you need to know and abide by these specifications.

Table 10-1 outlines what you find in the chart. The universal specification refers to basic banner ads that should display on most devices, while the supplemental specification is for banner ads that involve animation and that may have to be individually tailored to devices using content adaptation (see Chapter 6 for more on designing for different devices). The MMA is producing updated charts for the new wave of higher-resolution mobile device displays hitting the market; we have used the specifications for the 4:1 banner ads. A 4:1 aspect ratio refers to the relationship between the height and width of the ad, so that the ad is 4 times as wide as it is tall. Another common aspect ratio is 6:1; banner ads in this aspect ratio are therefore much wider than they are tall. You can download a PDF explaining these concepts in more depth at `http://mmaglobal.com/mobileadvertising.pdf`. You can see examples of the relative sizes and types of banner ads in Figure 10-1.

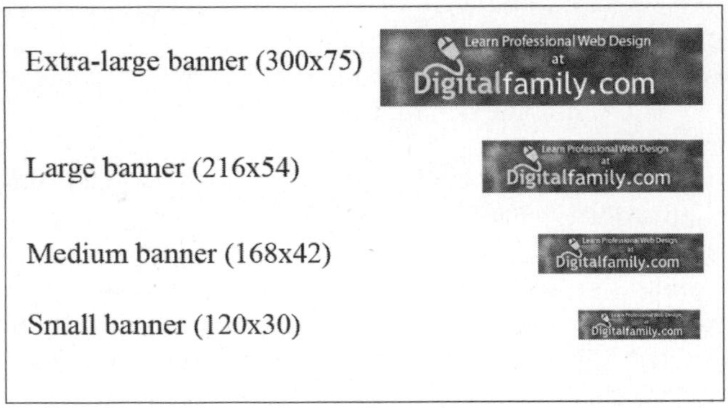

Figure 10-1:
Banner ads on the mobile Web look like pared down versions of the banner ads you see on the desktop Web.

Extra-large banner (300x75)

Large banner (216x54)

Medium banner (168x42)

Small banner (120x30)

Table 10-1	Mobile Web Banner Ad Units in 4:1 Aspect Ratio		
Banner Ad Type	**Size**	**Universal Unit**	**Supplemental Unit**
Extra Large banner (for phones with large screens, such as the iPhone or Droid)	300 x 75 pixels	GIF, PNG, and JPEG for still image Less than 5 kB file size	Animated GIF for animation Less than 7.5 kB file size
Large banner	216 x 54 pixels	GIF, PNG, and JPEG for still image Less than 3 kB file size	Animated GIF for animation Less than 4.5 kB file size
Medium banner	168 x 42 pixels	GIF, PNG, and JPEG for still image Less than 2 kB file size	Animated GIF for animation Less than 3 kB file size

Banner Ad Type	Size	Universal Unit	Supplemental Unit
Small banner	120 x 30 pixels	GIF, PNG, and JPEG for still image Less than 1 kB file size	Animated GIF for animation Less than 1.5 kB file size
Text tagline (usually a hyperlink, used as an ad on low-end feature phones)	Up to 24 characters for Extra Large Up to 18 characters for Large Up to 12 characters for Medium Up to 10 characters for Small		

The newest thing in mobile banner ads is the Adhesion product from Crisp Wireless. *Adhesion* is a banner ad that follows the user while he scrolls down the page — only unlike the other tagalong banners, this one disappears during the scrolling action and reappears only when the user comes to rest again. Adhesion is generating a lot of excitement in the mobile advertising world because one of the big problems with mobile banners is that the screen space is so limited that advertisers' messages appear onscreen only for a few seconds before the users move past them.

Reaching Out with Text Messaging (SMS)

Most advertisers use SMS as a way to contact their (potential) customers to alert them to a special event, offer, or opportunity. A lot of merchants see SMS alerts as a great way to maintain customer loyalty. Few see SMS alerts as a way to bring in new customers because the messages go out to users who have opted-in already to hear about the products, rather than to people who are unaware that the merchant even exists. Here are some ways that you can use SMS ads to drum up new business:

✔ **Promo ads:** These are short marketing messages, with no special links or functions included. For example:

> Special discount this week. Mention DigitalFamily.com and get an extra 50% off all training.

✔ **Site links:** Text messages that include a link that, when clicked, causes the user's phone browser to open and navigate to the advertiser's Web site.

- **Ad downloads:** These links download an ad to the phone. This download can be an audio file (usually a song), a photo, a video, or even a branded video game.

- **Appended ads:** These ads appear after some other kind of content. Think of them as the mobile equivalent of sponsorship, such as

    Packers 31–Vikings 10. These sports score alerts sponsored by DigitalFamily.com. Click here to get a 25% discount on all jerseys.

- **Voice call ads:** These ads use click-to-call functionality to deliver a prerecorded message. These are useful in situations when you want the impact of multimedia ads, but the data transmission network isn't reliable. You can either set the user's phone to make a call, or you can use a service that makes the calls (particularly useful in situations when incoming calls are free, and users don't use all their minutes). An example could be

    Click here to get a call back from Big Dave about tomorrow's surf report on Malibu Beach.

Most carriers charge mobile users for the text messages they send and receive. If you indiscriminately blast people with SMS, they may get charged money to see your ads. This can lead to very angry ex-customers, not to mention litigation from the FCC or cellphone carrier networks that have set up strict policies governing how cellphone users may be contacted.

You *must* get permission from your customers to send them SMS alerts. Usually this is done by having them text you an activation code from their cellphone or having them fill out a form that clearly expresses to them that they agree to receive text messages on their cellphones. An activation code is usually included in other marketing materials; common places such codes appear include posters outside concerts or sporting events, on soft-drink packages, in radio spots, at the end of TV ads, or on the back side of clothing tags. Typically, the message says something like "Text [a six-digit code] to [the advertiser's number] to receive news and special offers."

Finding an SMS campaign provider

SMS campaigns are much simpler to deal with than CSC (common short code) campaigns. Companies, such as the following, have lots of information on their Web sites about what you need to do if you want to run a large-scale SMS messaging campaign:

- **Clickatell:** www.clickatell.com Clickatell claims to be the first online SMS gateway; that means that they were the first to allow users to send SMS messages to mobile devices from desktop computers. They say they can send SMS messages to devices in more than 220 countries and territories around the world. They also sell short codes in six countries, including the United States.

- ✔ **txtwire:** www.txtwire.com Originally created specifically to take advantage of mobile marketing, txtwire has branched out to also provide emergency alert services for schools and local government. They are not as large as some of the other companies here, and they seem to be more open to working with small businesses.

- ✔ **TxtImpact:** www.smsgatewaypro.com This diversified company offers SMS applications to let people vote, enter contests, play trivia games, and much more. They also sell shared CSCs (ones that run only while your marketing campaign is running) as well as dedicated CSCs that would belong only to you.

- ✔ **iLoop Mobile:** www.iloopmobile.com They have slick templates for SMS marketing campaigns and aim their product offerings at large advertising agencies. While they are not an SMS gateway, they do work with bulk SMS providers and bundle the technical services with their professional consulting work in a way that may be attractive to people who just want a one-stop solution.

If you want to shop around, search for *SMS gateway;* new companies spring up daily.

Most reputable companies charge 5 cents or less per text message sent. But be aware that the rates these companies charge for advertising campaigns can vary wildly; some want as much as 50 cents *per customer* for each text message they send. Make sure you understand what you're signing up for before you start the campaign or you can wind up with a much more expensive bill than you expect.

If you want to get your feet wet, social media company Brightkite (http://brightkite.com) just rolled out a free service that you can use to send bulk SMS messages to as many as 25 people at a time. Brightkite was originally conceived of as a kind of location-based Twitter; that is, a place where people could quickly and easily upload where they were and what they were doing. Then, their friends could track them and see whether they were nearby for a serendipitous meet-up. Like many other social networking sites, Brightkite expanded its range of functions to include sending mass text messages and to allow the message receivers to message each other (and you). This may be enough for a small business to stay in touch with its most loyal customers.

As an added bonus, the Brightkite Group Text service allows you to use Facebook, Twitter, and Flickr to share the messages with friends — which may help your loyal customers and fans reach out to their friends. Although Brightkite imposes a 25-person limit on the number of people you can send an SMS message to at any one time, you can always have multiple groups. If your business scales up to the point that you send hundreds of text message ads, make the jump to a dedicated bulk SMS gateway anyway. You can also use Brightkite's iPhone or Android app to send these bulk SMS messages; these apps have their own sets of instructions to lead you through the process.

Launching a free SMS advertising campaign

To set up a free SMS text-messaging advertising service and send your first message, follow these steps:

1. **Open your browser and navigate to www.brightkite.com.**

   The Brightkite home page opens, as shown in Figure 10-2. This is where you log in to send SMS messages or to check whether any of your customers responded to the messages that you sent.

   If you already use Brightkite, skip to Step 6 and log in the way you always do. Otherwise, continue to Step 2 to create an account.

2. **Click the Group Text tab.**

   The Log In page opens.

3. **Click the Sign Up link, and on the page that appears, fill in your e-mail address, username, and password, and then type a security question answer.**

   For your username, use the name of your business, or if you promote your own services, use your name. Don't get too funky with your choice — you don't want to turn off your customers.

   The security question makes sure that automated bots don't take over the service by creating thousands of spam accounts.

Figure 10-2:
The Brightkite home page.

4. **Click the Terms of Service and Privacy Policy links.**

   Yes, reading these are tedious, but it's good to know what you're getting into, so make an effort.

5. **Click the Sign Up button.**

6. **On the Brightkite home page, click the Log In button and enter your username and password.**

   Your home screen appears with posts from users near you.

7. **Click the Group Text tab again.**

   The screen welcoming you to Group Text opens, with a short explanation of the features.

8. **Click the Start Conversation button.**

   A box opens on your screen with fields for you to fill out to send the text messages.

9. **Type the phone numbers for the people that you want to send messages to.**

   Press the Tab key to enter multiple phone numbers. And note that you enter the phone numbers without parentheses, commas, dashes, or periods. See Figure 10-3 for an example of how the text input field for the Group Text function looks when you are typing the phone numbers of your contacts into the fields.

10. **Type the short (fewer than 160 characters) message and click the Send button.**

    Congratulations! You just sent your first mass text message. You can also type the names of friends on Brightkite, if they have integrated Brightkite with their mobile phones. You can type in their names rather than having to remember their phone numbers if you have added them as friends on Brightkite. Because Brightkite is integrated with Facebook, if you have a Facebook page for your business, you can use that to contact your customers (if they have a cellphone associated with their Facebook account). You can also use your Facebook account to send out an SMS message to that person, rather than having to remember or know their mobile phone number.

Another way to build up your list of friends is to set Brightkite to show posts from people in a specified region. You can choose to find people who are anywhere from within 60 miles to 20 yards of your location. Take the time to fill out your profile so that people who friend you on the service learn about your location and what your business is about.

The first time you send a mass text message with Brightkite, test this process on your phone and on the phones of some close friends to make sure that it works the way you expected.

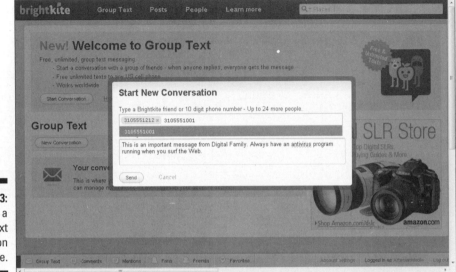

Figure 10-3:
Send a
mass text
message on
Brightkite.

When your customers receive the message, they can respond to you with a message of their own. Their messages are also sent to the other people on your SMS list, and you can monitor what they say about you or your business.

You can also *geo-tag* (include GPS data in your messages so that your location will show up on a mapping program like MapQuest or Google Maps) your messages to alert people to where you are, or send along photos for everyone to look at.

Connecting with Customers via Short Codes

To run an advertising campaign with CSC requires a lot of coordination; all the various carrier networks have to be notified and paid to allow the text messages sent to a number to go to the same place. Then the users have to be told that they need to send a text, to either opt-in to receive more content or to enter a contest.

To run a CSC ad campaign (such as "Text `Free Pizza` to JOESPIZZA to get a free Chicago deep-dish pizza delivered to your house"), you have to contract with a CSC reseller, who has contracts with all the major carrier networks so that your code works with all the phones in your area. These kinds of campaigns cost upward of $2,000 to set up and anywhere from $500 to $1,400 a month to maintain. They're that expensive because they require a lot of coordination to run across an entire country. In the list of SMS campaign providers shown earlier in this chapter, we included a couple of companies that also offer CSCs.

Offering Links and More with QR Codes

QR codes (or 2D barcodes) can appear on newspaper pages, signs, buses, business cards, or any object on which you can print a decent resolution image. These examples illustrate just a few ways these codes are used:

✔ In San Francisco, Scanbuy partnered with Citysearch to produce QR codes that were placed in the windows of 580 restaurants. Customers with the ScanLife software on their phones can point their phone cameras at the code in the window. As soon as the software recognizes the code, the phone displays a Citysearch review and information about the food and drinks available.

✔ Not to be outdone, Antenna Audio put QR codes at tourist attractions in San Francisco. Users can point their phone cameras at the codes and are treated to an audio tour of the site and an explanation of its history.

✔ Newspapers, such as the *Pittsburgh Post-Gazette,* run QR codes alongside concert reviews or sports stories. Readers can point their phone cameras at the code, and then their phones open a page where the reader can buy and download songs the reviewed band played, or browse through jerseys of teams that played in the game.

✔ Another very successful use of QR codes was done by the magazine *Get Married.* This magazine uses the *Microsoft Tag engine,* which makes it possible to create QR codes in color, rather than the black-and-white codes used in most QR codes. Another advantage is that with Microsoft Tags, you can turn almost any picture into a QR code, making the codes far more visually appealing. *Get Married* now includes Microsoft Tag QR Codes in nearly every ad in the print and online editions.

With the Microsoft Tag, anyone can create QR codes for mobile devices for free, which makes them an increasingly popular addition to everything from business cards to bumper stickers. For people to read your tags, they need a phone with an Internet connection and a camera, as well as the Tag Reader application installed on their phone. On the iPhone, after you install the Tag Reader app, when you point the phone's camera at any QR code, the phone buzzes in your hand, launches the Web browser, and takes you to the related content. Tag Reader already works with most smartphones and some feature phones. Find the most up-to-date details about Tag support at `http://tag.microsoft.com/resources/mobile-support.aspx`.

You can create colorful QR codes for free on the Microsoft Tag site, and you can even customize them with your own photos in the background. To get started:

1. **Open your browser and navigate to `http://tag.microsoft.com`.**

   The Microsoft Tag home page opens. As you can see in Figure 10-4, Microsoft is making a concerted effort to reach out to the hip, urban market that is the most connected with mobile technology.

2. **Click the Sign In link in the upper-right corner.**

   Microsoft Tag requires that you sign up with a Windows Live account. Although you can use this account to access other Microsoft products, you don't have to. If you already have a Windows Live ID (which you have if you've ever used Hotmail, Windows Live Messenger, or Xbox LIVE), you can use that to sign in. If you don't have one, you can create an account for free.

Figure 10-4:
The Microsoft Tag home page.

To create a Windows Live account, navigate to `https://login.live.com/` and follow the instructions there. If you sign in on the Windows Live page, Microsoft will place a cookie (a snippet of software code that is temporarily stored on your computer's hard drive, depending on whether or not you have your browser's security settings set to accept cookies) onto your computer that will keep you signed in to all Microsoft sites with that Windows Live ID. That means that when you navigate back to the Microsoft Tag page, you will remain signed in with your Windows Live ID (as long as you are doing it during the same browsing session that you were in when you created the Windows Live ID or during the same session that you were using when you signed in to Windows Live using your Windows Live ID and you haven't deleted your cookies). If you already have a Windows Live account, all you will have to do is sign in on the Microsoft Tag site, using the Sign In button and your existing Windows Live ID.

After you click the Sign In button next to your username, enter your password, and click the Sign In button again, the Manage Tags page opens.

3. **Click the Create a Tag button.**

   The Tag Manager page opens.

4. **Type the title in the Tag Title text box.**

   Start with something simple, such as **Test Tag**. When you run your own QR advertising programs, be more descriptive so that you can keep track of which QR codes correspond to what content.

5. **Choose what kind of QR code you want to create from the Tag Type drop-down list:**

   - *URL:* This is just a link to whatever Web site you want your users' phones to navigate to.

   - *Free Text:* You can have a secret message appear on the phone's screen; if you want, you can even protect that message with a secret password. This can be useful if you want to run a game, such as a scavenger hunt with clues.

   - *vCard:* This is the universal format for contact information that the user can then put into his electronic address book. Many people print these types of codes on their business cards in lieu of the increasingly diverse and complicated ways people have invented to contact each other.

   - *Dialer:* This is just a code that causes the user's phone to wake up and dial the number you specify.

   For this example, we create a code that drives users to a Web site, so as you can see in Figure 10-5, we chose `www.slightlyusedcats.com`.

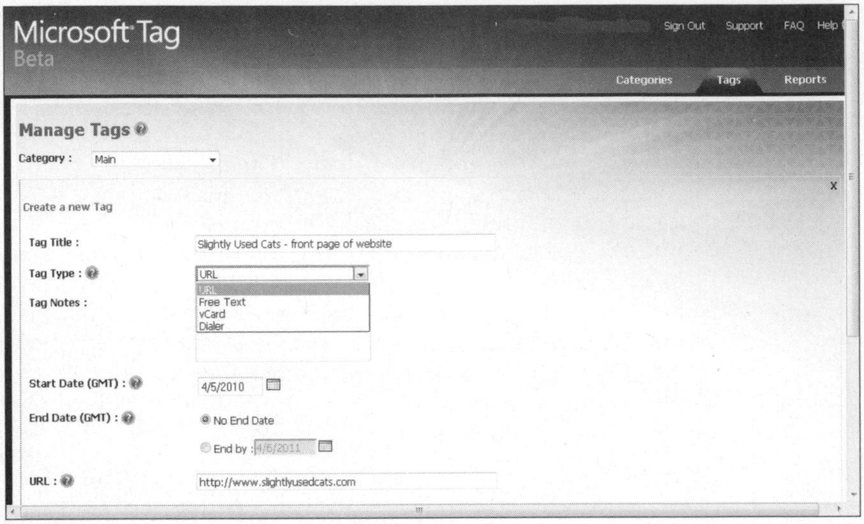

Figure 10-5:
You can
create QR
codes that
contain
more than
just a URL
link by using
the Tag
Type drop-
down list.

6. **Enter a brief description of the tag in the Tag Notes text box.**

   This reminds you what the tag does.

7. **Click the calendar next to the date to specify a different start date than the one shown.**

   This is available if you want the code to be posted somewhere but to not deliver its content payload until a certain date (such as a code, printed on concert posters to let fans buy tickets, that you want to coordinate with the date and time the tickets go on sale).

8. **(Optional) Choose an end date for the code.**

   You can either leave the code *open-ended* — the code always works — by selecting the No End Date radio button, or you can limit the time the code works, such as when the code is for a coupon or a special phone message, by selecting the End By radio button and then choosing a date from the calendar.

9. **Enter the URL that you want the users' phones to navigate to in the URL text box.**

   This can be the home page of your site or some special content on your site that you want the users to see, such as the menu for your restaurant or the map to your special super-secret party location.

10. **Click the Save button.**

    The Manage Tags page opens, showing you all the tags you have created.

11. **Under the Render heading, click the tag image to get an image file of the QR code you just created.**

    You can generate an image of the tag as a PDF, WMF, JPEG, PNG, GIF, or TIFF file, depending on your needs. You can also choose to have just the code or an image with brief instructions on how to use it, as shown in Figure 10-6, along with the URL of the Web site where users can download the app that reads these codes to their smartphones.

    That's it — congratulations! You just created your very own customized code.

To check how people respond to your code, log in via the Microsoft Tag home page and click the Reports tab. You see a summary of how many people have clicked your tag along with tracking and demographic information.

Figure 10-6: A Microsoft Tag code.

Handing Out Coupons via the Mobile Web

When customers use a printed coupon, you can only gather very limited information about them, such as what general zip code you distributed the coupon to (assuming your customers didn't share their coupons with someone from across town).

In contrast, when you use mobile coupons, you can track exactly who you sent that coupon to, how long it took them to redeem it, what kind of phone it was sent to, and all kinds of other demographic information that can help you make your marketing and sales efforts more efficient.

The capability of the mobile Web to deliver a coupon to the user exactly when and where it will do the most good creates an immediate and personalized call-to-action that results in instant gratification. Imagine reaching out to customers with discounts and special offers to tempt them while they walk past your place of business.

Research done by Michael Hanley at Ball State University shows two-thirds of college students (one of the most hard to reach and eagerly pursued demographics) will change their behaviors if they have coupon incentives. The top-three coupons they're most eager to use include at least one real surprise:

- ✔ Sit-down restaurants (because although college students may be broke, they're still hungry and like to impress their dates once in a while)
- ✔ Movies (again for dates or entertainment)
- ✔ Dry cleaning (because sometimes Mom just isn't available)

Scanning mobile coupons

There is, however, a major snag with mobile coupons: Because the coupon barcode appears on a phone's LCD screen, many older laser barcode readers can't process the information. Target recently spent tens of millions of dollars to replace all the scanners at their cash registers around the country for just this reason.

One way around this is to use other means to scan coupons. The mobile coupon companies are rolling out various small, point-of-sale terminals that can be used for coupons or for setting up toll-free numbers for merchants to call to verify and track coupons.

For example, Xtra Mobile Coupons (www.xtracoupons.com) ran a test campaign with Outback Steakhouse. In this campaign, Xtra provided the restaurants with a small terminal (about the size of an iPhone) that allows the server to read an eight-digit code on the customer's mobile phone screen and then punch that code into the coupon terminal to add the discount to the customer's bill. Outback is delighted with the program because it can map and track the zip codes that the customers are from and what times of day they come into the restaurant. Based on this information, Outback re-targets customers with incentives to come back. The technology has also helped Outback avoid the type of coupon fraud that bedeviled the Subway sandwich chain a few years ago.

Sharing coupons with mobile technology

The next wave of mobile coupons is likely to be driven by the growing inclusion of GPS functionality in mobile devices. Already, startups such as mobiQpons and Yowza!! show coupons based on the user's proximity to stores. Yowza!! even allows users to share coupons with their friends through social networking; thus, tying their coupons to the most popular use of the mobile Web today — updating Facebook and Twitter.

Creating free mobile coupons

You can try a free mobile coupon service to see whether it gets any traction and whether your customers like it. The following steps explain how to take advantage of the new technology platform created by MixMobi. MixMobi allows you to try its mobile coupon service for 14 days (and 5,000 page views). To continue after that costs $19.95 per month for the most basic plan. Follow these steps:

1. **Open your browser and navigate to** `http://mixmobi.com.`

   The MixMobi home page (see Figure 10-7) opens.

2. **Click the Free Trial tab.**

   The sign-up page opens.

Figure 10-7:
The
MixMobi
home page.

3. **Fill in the name of your company and your e-mail address, and then choose your time zone.**

4. **Pick a username and password, and then click the Create Account button.**

   The Account Dashboard page opens. Here you can manage your coupon campaigns. By clicking on the tabs, you can access a list of all the coupon campaigns you have running, schedule when coupons will be sent and when they will expire, track the redemption rates for your coupons, and, of course, pay for upgraded services on an account page.

5. **Click around the various pages to familiarize yourself with some of the features that will be available to you and then click the New Offer button in the upper-right corner of the page.**

6. **Click on the radio button next to "a template."**

   The other choices are to create a coupon from an existing offer or a blank offer. Once you have created a few coupons, you can choose from your existing offers, but if you're starting out, you obviously don't have any to choose from yet. The blank offer option is a real sparse, stripped-down layout that you can play with later, once you get the hang of using the more user-friendly templates that MixMobi has provided.

7. **Choose the layout of your mobile coupon from the Offer Template drop-down list or the gallery of templates below it.**

   You can mix and match pictures, text, logos, and message headers, and choose from a variety of layouts (see Figure 10-7 for a sampling of how many headers you can choose from). For now, just choose a simple image and code.

8. **Type the name of the coupon and a brief description of what it's for in the Name and Description text boxes, respectively.**

   As the page says, the description you type (or not) here is just for your internal use and will not be seen by your customers. It's just a handy way for you to be able to tell at a glance what the coupon is for.

9. **Choose the dates that the coupon is valid.**

   The default is to start today and run for a week. You can even choose the exact times the coupon is valid, which can come in handy when you want to have coupons *cascade* during a day — that is, to give 50 percent off to the people who show up first, 20 percent to the ones who are there an hour before closing, and 10 percent to the people who show up at the last minute.

10. **On the drop-down menu, choose which campaign this coupon is for, or click the New Campaign link next to the drop-down menu to create a new campaign.**

The first time you create a coupon, the default is "Your First Campaign." After you have created your first coupons, you can get more ambitious and click New Campaign to start creating categories to organize your efforts.

11. **Type tags relevant to what you create the coupon for.**

    Tags help search engines find and categorize stuff on the Web. For example, if you sell a cat in a hat, you could use tags like Cat, Hat, Apparel, Cute, Feline, and so on.

12. **Select the check box next to "list builder" if you want to add a field to your coupon where customers can send you their e-mail address or phone number.**

    Choosing this feature for your coupons will enable you to start building a mailing list of your best customers, or at least people who have responded to your special offers. When one of your customers registers, an e-mail will be sent to the e-mail address you used to open your MixMobi account.

13. **Next to Page Views Allowed, enter the maximum number of page views that you want to allow users of your mobile coupon to do. Leave this field blank if you do not want to limit the number of page views, although MixMobi says that their limit is 500,000 page views for your entire account.**

    This field is only crucial if you are running a large-scale mobile coupon campaign where you anticipate that hundreds of thousands of people are going to be responding to your offer, or if you have a lot of rich media (such as a video that takes up many megabytes of space) on the page that you are directing your users to.

14. **Click the Continue button.**

    The Edit Offer page opens to allow you to further customize your coupon. Here you can replace the text and images in the template with your own. The default for the images is a JPEG that's optimized for the Web and 320 x 305 pixels. If you have a picture of one of your products, make sure that when you resize it to use in this coupon, you use the Save for Web function in your image editor. For more about optimizing images for mobile, see Chapter 8 and Appendix B.

15. **Click on the drop-down menu under Offer Elements to find options that you can use to design your coupon, as shown in Figure 10-8.**

    You can choose to add design elements such as images, headlines, and descriptive text. Choose the category from the drop-down list and fill in the fields for that category. You can include any or all of the options. Each has its own fields for you to fill out.

16. **Click on the green arrows to the left of the elements that you have added to your coupon, and drag them up or down in the list to change the order they appear on your coupon.**

17. **Click the Save button to see a preview of how your coupon will look.**

    The updated coupon will load into the right side of the page, reflecting the changes and updates you have made.

18. **If you are completely satisfied with the way the coupon looks, click the Save and Close button to proceed to the Share page.**

    The Share page opens with links to the coupon you just created as well as buttons to send your coupon to friends, customers, and other contacts via Twitter or Facebook.

19. **Click the Clipboard icon next to the link to the right of the words Public URL to copy the link code for your mobile coupon.**

    If you run an SMS campaign (such as one created with Brightkite, discussed in the section "Launching a free SMS advertising campaign," earlier in this chapter), you can paste the link code for your coupon into the Group Text page on Brightkite. That will allow you to send this URL to people via SMS messages; they can then click on the URL in the SMS message to open their browser and navigate to the mobile coupon that you just created. Taking the initiative for distributing the coupon is a simple way to "close the loop" on this campaign.

Test the link code first by sending it to your own phone by using the Private URL so that you don't mess up your tracking statistics. After that, send the code to a few friends and see what they think about it.

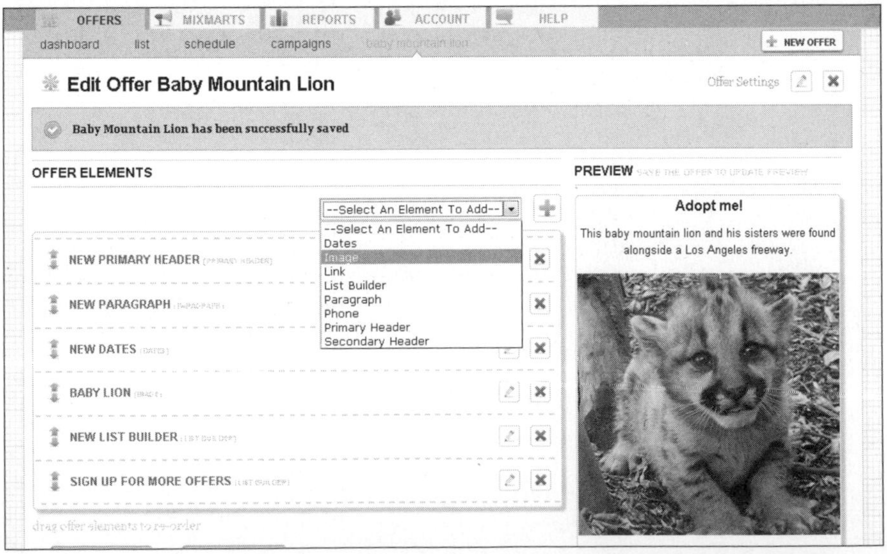

Figure 10-8:
Choose what elements you want to include in your mobile coupon from the Offer Template drop-down list.

Sharing Offers via Image Recognition

Similar to QR codes, image recognition advertising allows the user to take a picture of any object, including a print advertisement, send that image to a publisher or advertiser, and, in return, get exclusive content (wallpaper, ringtones, coupons, and so on). *Men's Health* and *Rolling Stone* were the first print publications to take advantage of this new product, which is attractive for publishers because it allows them to offer advertisers a chance to tie together their print and online ad campaigns in a seamless way.

This technology faces some initially daunting challenges. For instance, many cellphone cameras produce blurry, dim images, sending those images can be expensive or complicated, and the computing power required to process and recognize those photos is significant.

Among the companies making inroads with image recognition ads are:

- **GetFugu:** The mobile start-up company GetFugu recently launched its *See It* technology, which allows users to point their phone's camera at any modern corporate logo or sign, take a picture, and then be directed to that brand's Web site. The app also includes voice and GPS search functions.

  GetFugu claims that its technology has made the logo recognition process almost 90 percent accurate and that it can discern among such similar items as the Apple logo, the AT&T logo, and the Death Star from *Star Wars*.

- **Amazon:** Amazon tests its own image recognition engine and claims that if a user takes a picture of his dog, the phone responds by showing ads for dog food or flea medication.

- **Google Goggles:** This app runs only on the Android operating system, but it's gotten a lot of press because it has a great "wow factor." With Google Goggles you can point your phone's camera at almost anything and get more information about it. Point the camera at a label on a wine bottle, and you'll likely be directed to the winery or a wine distributor. Point your phone's camera at a building or other landmark, and you get information on the architect, the history of the location, or other details. You can even take a picture of someone's business card, and Goggles automatically enters that information into your contact database. This technology seems destined to become increasingly popular for all kinds of uses.

Advertising via the Power of Mobile Social Media

The number one use of the mobile Web is to participate in social media sites; after all, social media is all about communicating with your friends, and the one tried-and-true use of phones is to call friends, right? The statistics about how people use social media are enough to make advertisers perk up: Users spend about 2.7 hours a day on the mobile Web. Forty-five percent post comments on social networking sites, 43 percent connect with friends on social networking sites, 40 percent share content with others, and 38 percent share photos.

That's a lot of time and attention, but advertising over social media is still an extremely tricky thing. Advertising conferences are full of woeful stories of social media campaigns gone wrong, such as when Facebook tried to roll out a Beacon service that served up ads that mined all the things people had done on the Web and then offered suggestions. A businessman got all kinds of suggestions for expensive jewelry and racy underwear based on his recent purchases. Was he happy to see these ads? His wife certainly wasn't.

If you haven't been running social media advertising campaigns, the best way to begin is to start using the medium that you're going to be working in. People use social media — blogs, Twitter, Facebook, MySpace, YouTube, Foursquare, Brightkite, hi5, and dozens of others — as virtual water coolers or corner bars. Places to congregate and swap gossip, trade good-natured insults, flirt, plan outings, and generally commiserate. Using the traditional advertising techniques in this kind of milieu is like barging into someone's intimate private party and pulling out a briefcase full of samples; it comes off as rude and intrusive.

The best use of social media that advertisers have found so far is to use it to reinforce relationships and empower their best customers to say nice things about them to all their friends. Marketers talk about engagement (although there is a lot of disagreement as to what an engaged customer actually means) as the goal of forward-thinking campaigns to get people engaged in the brand or product you're marketing. The means to achieve this include SMS notifications, newsfeeds, integrated profiles, partner pages, surveys, competitions, games, widgets, and more. When you give your customers something that they like and then provide them with the means and encouragement to share it with all their friends, you can earn a lot of great buzz, but you also give up a lot of the power and control that come with more traditional forms of advertising.

When consumers get exclusive or early information, invitations to special events, promotions, or free stuff, they naturally feel like the advertiser has formed an intimate bond with them. And what do people like to do when they get something special? They like to brag to their friends. Make sharing information about your product easy for them to do, and you're off to a good start with a social-media marketing campaign.

The quickest and easiest tool for adding Facebook features to your Web site is available via the Facebook developer's page at `http://developers.facebook.com/docs/guides/web`. If you have some basic knowledge of HTML (you find an introduction to the Hypertext Markup Language in Chapter 4) and you aren't afraid of a few lines of code, you can download the files from Facebook and follow the instructions in the `Readme.mdown` file. Facebook Connect allows you to let your customers (who have experience with your product) click and post their enthusiastic recommendations to their Facebook pages. The service also lets users log into comment sections, forum boards, and other content using their Facebook profiles as their login identities, which saves them having to create new usernames and passwords.

Exploring Video and Other Rich Media Ads

With video on the mobile platform, the same forces that constrain other forms of advertising apply, only more so. So the dictum, "Never use four words when two will do," translated to mobile means that the traditional 30-second TV spots that advertisers shrunk to 15-second pre-rolls for the Internet get cut down to 7 seconds on the mobile platform. Any more than that and users get frustrated, or the ad interferes with the content users wanted to get to in the first place.

Even for a seven-second video clip, the challenges of serving targeted video ads to the mobile platform are still daunting. The restrictions on banner ads seem quaint when considering the demands of serving video or animated content to a cellphone. Consider the following hurdles:

- A humble, low-resolution YouTube video can take up 3–5 MB (megabytes) of space. An iffy cellphone connection or a dropped call means the mobile user never sees the content or the ad.

- The phone has to have enough processor power to render the video, and enough storage space and RAM buffer to hold the data until it's ready to stream.

- The carrier has to have a server backbone sufficient to deliver the files.

The tradeoff for the length of the ad is (at least in theory) a radical increase in effectiveness because the ad can be targeted to the user based on the time, location, browsing habits, and all the other data points available to a mobile advertiser. Marrying the mobile video ad with another content form has shown great results for companies, such as Mogreet and Vdopia (see Figure 10-9), as well as a recent interactive video product out of AdMob.

The AdMob Interactive Video Mobile Ad Unit product was bought by Google, a clear sign that Google sees a big future in the mobile advertising market. The considerable resources and expertise of Google mean that the AdMob ad product will probably get a wide market rollout. The technology allows users of iPhones and Droid phones to order products or get more information by simply tapping a button, a link, or even an image of a product on their mobile screens while a video is playing. It works like this: Imagine you're watching a movie and see a character wearing a really cool pair of sunglasses; with the AdMob product, you can pause the video, tap on the sunglasses on the screen, and a window pops up asking whether you want to learn more or order the merchandise on the spot.

This very sophisticated technology is still not quite ready for prime time and it will be complicated to make it all work because the ad servers will have to be able to interpret in real time the actions of a user (which item in the video the user is clicking on, for example) and then connect to one or more databases containing both the description of the product and the user's financial information to pay for it. Whether Google (or any other company) can make all these moving pieces work well together remains to be seen, but it seems promising.

The predictions are that mobile video will grow at the rate of 137 percent per year, and that it will comprise the single largest segment of global mobile data usage by 2013. Because advertising follows where the eyeballs are, most major ad agencies are feverishly working to prepare their creative directors and staff to take advantage of this shift.

Figure 10-9:
The interactive video company Vdopia specializes in crafting short, compelling pitches on mobile devices.

Advertising via Apps and Immersive Environments

The runaway success of Apple's iPhone App Store has been both a benefit and a nightmare for mobile advertising designers: It's a benefit because the market awareness that Apple's "There's an App for that" saturation TV campaign has created with the public, along with the widely publicized stories of 14-year-old coders becoming overnight millionaires when their quirky apps hit the big time, has finally made people take mobile advertising seriously.

The downside is that the App Store has sparked a frenzied gold-rush type mentality on the part of marketers who, in their panicked rush to not feel left out, have demanded that developers build apps for their products — no matter how absurd the resulting app is. Entire sessions at mobile advertising conferences are devoted to topics like "To App or Not to App?" and "How to Talk Your Client Out of an App." So before you rush toward apps as an advertising platform, make sure you've truly weighed the craze for apps against the drawbacks of investing time and resources into app development. Here are the key issues to consider:

✔ **The limited market reach of apps:** A truly well-designed mobile Web site can offer most of the functionalities that advertisers crave without having to custom-code an application — a process that then has to be repeated for each handset operating system. The iPhone, despite all the buzz, is still less than 5 percent of the market in the United States and far less than that worldwide. When you create an app for the iPhone, you freeze out the other 95 percent of the market. The same goes for apps that are designed for any of the other operating systems, such as Android, Symbian, BlackBerry, Palm, and so on. If you create an app, you need to create a different version for each operating system.

✔ **The competition among apps in the App Store:** Just about any human activity imaginable has had some bright coder try to produce an app to help do it better. But with more than 150,000 apps (and growing) in the App store, and many more on the way in the Android store, the idea of using an app to advertise your products is somewhat backward. Just to get people to become aware of the existence of your app, much less to download it and try it out, requires that you actually put money into advertising on other platforms. Thus, an app can become a net cost rather than a revenue-generator.

✔ **Ease of updates:** If you want to change an app, the user has to download and install updates for it. On a mobile site, however, you can simply update your mobile Web pages, and the user sees the new content the next time he visits your site.

Still, an app can do some things that provide advertisers with significant marketing opportunities. Notable successes include

- ✔ The Pizza Hut app allows users to register with their home address and login information and then build their own pizza using the touch-screen menus. People can add ingredients, choose the crust, and take advantage of special mobile coupons and discounts.

- ✔ Southwest Airlines lets you book and modify airline reservations, view flight status and flight schedules, and check your rapid rewards all from your iPhone.

- ✔ The E*Trade app allows investors to check stock prices, trends, and recent stories as well as place orders all from the same screen.

One emerging trend is that of *stub apps* — small applications that reside on the home screen of the mobile device and mainly open the device's Web browser and navigate to the mobile Web site of the app designer. To some developers, these combine the best of both worlds; because they're on the screen all the time, the mobile user is aware of it (the "out of sight, out of mind" paradigm is particularly powerful in the mobile world) and uses it more often. And because the content in the app resides on the mobile Web, it can be updated frequently, without requiring that the user download and install updates every time he wants to try something new and fresh.

Stub apps are also much cheaper to design and implement than full-fledged mobile apps, which start at about $10,000 and get more expensive from there.

The business of converting expectations: Interview with United Future CEO Scott Holmes

Mobile is an extension. Brands want to control their brand perception, and mobile is a part of that. When you talk about the scenarios that a consumer has with a brand's touch points, where does mobile fit? Mobile typically fits in

- ✔ **Utility,** such as Alaska Airlines in which you can check in using your phone

- ✔ **Push-pull** to give users some opportunity to sign up for some kind of redemption and reward

- ✔ **Entertainment,** whether it be some kind of game play, social interaction (because

that's a form of entertainment), your Facebook account, or highlights of the Super Bowl

If you accept that these are the three main areas, United Future looks at the utility first. Mobile advertising has to be done in the form of a reward. If you can check in sooner or check pricing on a product from Best Buy when you're in the store (versus making you go down the street or getting a quick validation on some type of local-based service or product), that has real utility and you'll use it. Things are becoming more common as people get used to the utility of a mobile device and the speed and connectivity. Very quickly mobile broadband will be just as fast as Internet connectivity.

United Future designs the mobile Web site for Holland America Line, which was developed to increase information and decrease the amount of confusion. Holland America Line really put a depth of information there because when booking a cruise, people plan six months out. People who go on these cruises have to go through pages and pages of choices in advance, planning everything from being on the Veranda deck to the Lido deck and the 57 excursion choices.

Holland America was very fearful of having too good of an online experience because it didn't want to disrupt its most important channel — travel agents. You never want to outsell your best salesmen. So United Future walked a very fine line between how much information to provide and how easy you could make a reservation or a conversion from researching a cruise to booking a cruise. United Future did such a good job that cruise bookings have gone up 191 percent. And most surprising of all, instead of resenting and fearing it, the travel agents started using the site as a tool. They now use the site as a one-stop shop to be able to explain to their customers on the phone what the difference is between the Veranda and the Lido and to say, by the way, here's your room. They have something to show the person in their office.

United Future is now building out the experience on the cruise. Now you can record your trip, not just with a video camera, but with your mobile device that's with you all the time.

People forget, though, that consumers don't adapt as well as companies would like them to. All this wonderful technology is out there, but how many people can take advantage of it? When does technology become a barrier? Companies have to make sure they aren't overdoing it.

When people encounter something while they're out of their home or office and they have their phones with them, eight times out of ten, they go to their calendar function and write it down. Isn't that strange? They add it to their to-do list. Your phone is your organizer. Philosophically, people still use the phone as an organizer, even though you can do all these things with it. People still instinctively come back to that initial use — it's what people are trained or programmed to do. A 13 year old doesn't do that with his phone, but that's a different story.

When Scott is in client conversations and strategic discussions, so many times people say, "We need a mobile app. We need an iPhone app." They saw the ads on TV, and they're in their heads. The first question Scott asks is "What is it that you're looking to achieve when the consumer uses that app?" Anything you want them to achieve, you can typically do it online, and if your Web site was semantic in nature, they could probably just type in your Web site.

What Scott tries to envision these days is what happens when advertising really goes to the mobile device. What's acceptable? United Future accepts banners on the Web page; it accepts pre-rolls and post-rolls in online video, but they're a little frustrating. Will you accept that on a mobile device?

Scott may not be the only one who thinks this way, but we say no. As a mobile user, it's going to cost you money for the data. So why sit through a pre-roll or a post-roll or anything? You want access to information right now; Scott's patience for advertising is teeny.

People skip commercials because the commercials don't mean anything to them. If a commercial meant something to you, maybe you'd watch it. If you're watching TV, you're relaxed and in a casual mode. If you're online, you're

(continued)

(continued)

in search mode. If you're on mobile, you're in a rush. What that means is that you don't want to be annoyed with an ad unless it's really, really relevant to you.

It's all about finding your niche audience. Television has a place. You can get the word out and do a mass approach, a roadblock. If you have the money, someone can reach you.

But then the next step is paying attention to what happens next. *Because ads are the business of converting expectations:* It's not a lead until somebody's interested, and it's not a sale until someone's been enticed and understands enough about the product and probably researched three other places to come back and purchase it.

After you convert them, did you give them something to make them a loyalist and part of your brand community? Mobile is about loyalists.

That's why mobile Web sites will become more and more important. After a customer decides to make a purchase, she's going to be in the store handling the merchandise, and she's going to do a last-second reality check, using her mobile phone.

Your mobile Web site has to validate that purchase.

The way you do that is to show them reviews and tell them that they're making the right decision. Maybe there's a service you can provide that provides more utility after the purchase is made — some added value.

The question then becomes how do people make this service on the mobile a loyalty service rather than an advertisement? Scott won't push ads on the mobile device. When you can do so much more on an interactive device like mobile, why settle for replicating the old TV interruptive advertising model? It's the equivalent of shovelware.

Chapter 11

Adding Mobile Commerce

· ·

In This Chapter

▶ Looking at how users adapt to mobile commerce

▶ Understanding the m-commerce basic building blocks

▶ Comparing m-commerce solutions

▶ Setting up commerce on a mobile site

· ·

Cellphone enthusiasts predict the day when your wallet, keys, and phone will all join together as the smartphones of the future fulfill all those functions in one. Outside *James Bond* movies, phones aren't quite magical open-sesame devices yet, but increasingly, they're turning into digital wallets.

For instance, cellphones are already taking on the functions of portable, virtual ATMs and credit-card processing devices. In Japan, commuters pay their subway fares by swiping their phones over sensors on turnstile gates, and use them to buy snacks and drinks from vending machines or convenience stores. Workers in the Middle East are paid via credits sent to their mobile phone accounts, which they then can transfer easily to their families in other countries. And in Los Angeles, street vendors are using iPhones to process credit cards for the lunch crowd.

Setting up a system that turns phones into offshore bank accounts is a task far beyond the scope of this book, but it demonstrates how quickly mobile is changing everything about commerce. For our purposes, let's define e-commerce as any kind of transaction that occurs via the Internet that involves money being transferred from one person, business, or organization to another. The transaction can be as simple as a teenager buying a 99 cent song on iTunes, or as complex as millions of donors around the world clicking a button to donate money in dozens of currencies to an international charity like the Red Cross.

M-commerce is essentially a subset of e-commerce, in that they both depend on the Internet to make the money go from one account to another. But what makes m-commerce different is that it can happen anywhere, not just in offices or on home computers. With m-commerce, people can take all kinds of actions involving money, such as transferring payments from bank accounts to mobile phones, from phones to bank accounts, and even from phones to phones.

In this chapter, we explore how mobile phones and other devices are increasingly used to sell things and transfer money, and we tackle how to set up your mobile Web site so that your users can buy your products and services, subscribe to your news feed, or pay to download digital goods, such as songs and videos.

Looking at How Users Adapt to Mobile Commerce

The advantages of having mobile commerce (or *m-commerce*) on your site seem, at first glance, rather esoteric. More than ten years passed before people felt comfortable buying and paying for items on their computers at home (and in the office, when the boss doesn't catch you on eBay). And still people tell scary stories about buying things online and then having their credit card numbers and identities stolen. Doing this over a phone, when (theoretically, at least) thieves can intercept radio signals, would seem to be a step further than most people are comfortable with.

And yet, the market indicates that m-commerce is growing rapidly:

- Retailers reported that sales to people using mobile phones were up 300 percent over Christmas 2009, and that people weren't just buying trinkets. Shoppers bought sailboats and Corvette sports cars for hundreds of thousands of dollars, using their phones to complete the transaction. Major chains, such as Pizza Hut, rolled out sites and apps that let you custom-build your pizza, type in the address you want it sent to, and pay for it from your phone.

- The worldwide market for m-commerce will hit about $120 billion by 2015, according to ABI Research.

- M-commerce growth in the United States has been stunning; mobile shoppers spent $396 million in 2008, tripling to $1.2 billion in 2009.

- More than half of shoppers now use their phones to check prices in stores.

- Nearly one in five shoppers in the crucial 18- to 24-year-old demographic has used a phone to buy products.

The advantage of m-commerce is that your customers can impulse-buy wherever they are, whenever the urge hits them. Your job as a Web developer is to make that process as safe and as smooth as possible so that they don't think twice or feel creeped-out and abandon ship before they hit the Confirm Purchase button. Think of m-commerce as the equivalent of having operators standing by to take your order; the only differences are that these operators never sleep or take breaks, and after you go through the expense of setting them up properly, they just keep working.

Understanding the Basic Building Blocks of an M-Commerce Solution

Whether you sell just one thing or have a site chock-full of thousands of items of all shapes, sizes, and prices, each store must have some of the same elements. The following sections guide you through the basics of how online commerce services (both for mobile and for the desktop Web) work so that you can better understand your options. We also tell you what to look for when you design a shopping system for your Web-based business.

Creating a mobile shopping experience: The front end

This *front end* of your site is where your customers shop and pick out what they want to buy. Whether you sell one item with a simple Buy Now button or you design a sophisticated shopping cart, think of your m-commerce site as your virtual showroom.

Just like in traditional brick-and-mortar stores, your goods in your mobile store need to be displayed in a logical, attractive manner, and your store needs to be laid out in a way that's clean and easy to navigate.

Everyone has wandered through a warehouse-style store at some point: You can easily get lost, the prices aren't always marked clearly, and no one's around to help you when you need them. Few things cost you more sales online than getting your customers lost in a sea of poorly organized links. You also don't want visitors to question your credibility because they feel they've wandered into a crummy junk shop with the merchandise piled in heaps. Even if they find something they like, they can't wait to get out.

Remember: Design is about making the site attractive and easy to use.

Imagining your target customers

One of the most valuable things you can do before creating your store is to step back for a second and imagine your target customers (the people most likely to spend money on your products). Don't just try to visualize who your target customers are — put yourself in their shoes. Where are they, and what are they doing when they come to your site on a cellphone? Anyone who's going to spend money while browsing a store on their mobile device is probably in one of five situations:

- ✔ **They're looking for a special deal while they're out and about.** For example, a couple on a date just found out that the restaurant they planned on eating at is closed and the movie they wanted to watch is sold out. Now they just want to order some takeout, go home, and snuggle in front of the TV. So they do a GPS-enabled search and find that your place is within two blocks and will have their food waiting by the time they arrive.

- ✔ **They're in a critical situation.** They absolutely need to buy your product and close the deal as soon as possible. For example, a diehard sports fan just got your text alert that a whole section of seats to the Super Bowl just opened. However, the tickets are going fast and probably will be gone by the time she can rush home — unless she places a bid on your site right this instant via her mobile phone.

- ✔ **They're impulse shopping.** Maybe they've trudged through snowdrifts past your billboard advertising tropical cruises for the last month. Today, the bus splashed them with a wave of freezing slush and muck. Shivering in their seats, they pull out their phones and punch in your travel agency's Web address.

- ✔ **They're in-store bargain-hunters.** Retailers are starting to notice that shoppers are whipping out their mobile phones and punching in product names and details to make sure that they're getting the best deal.

- ✔ **They're bored and killing time.** A group of 15 year olds decides to see what the new super-exclusive designer sneakers you just got in look like and how many chores they may have to do to earn themselves a new pair.

In each case, *immediacy* is one of the driving factors behind customers making a purchase with their phones. People buy things for all sorts of reasons, but when it comes to m-commerce, a lot boils down to just being in the right place, at the right time, with the right offer.

Following mobile design do's and don'ts

What makes m-commerce so exciting is that the mobile Web puts your store in your customer's pocket wherever they go. Before you get too excited by visions of round-the-clock shoppers, here are a few deadly design errors you need to avoid:

- ✔ **Don't cram too many things on your page.** The screen size is small, and even if you have hundreds of things you want to offer, if you try to put them all in one space, your customers can't figure out what they're supposed to click.

- ✔ **Don't use gimmicks, such as hokey animations and music to try to grab users' attention.** If they've made the effort to hit your mobile site, they're already interested. But they're also skittish — mobile shopping is still a new experience for most people. If your site looks like a 13-year-old girl's MySpace page, they're probably not going to trust that their financial information is safe with you.

✔ **Don't get cute and hide the prices from people.** Maybe your mobile customer is running up stairs, rushing into a meeting, or stopped at a traffic light. If they have to go through the whole checkout process only to find that your price isn't what they thought it was, they may never come back.

Guide customers, with just a few options per screen, until they're ready to make a buying decision. Mobile commerce in Japan is years ahead of the rest of the world; the online shopping site Rakuten is a particularly good example of how good mobile Web design can boost sales and profits. By designing for the mobile Web, they encouraged millions of users to shop using their mobile phones — and made hundreds of millions of dollars in profit.

The differences between the desktop experience and the mobile Web experience come into sharp focus when you look at how Rakuten appears when you navigate to the regular desktop site on a smartphone, as shown on the left side of Figure 11-1. Note how tiny the icons all look, how they all seem jumbled together, and how you can't really read any of the links. On the right of Figure 11-1 is Rakuten's site, as it appears when you go to the version that is optimized for the mobile platform. Note how having fewer choices (even if you can't read Japanese) makes it easier to figure out where you're supposed to click.

Figure 11-1:
The Rakuten e-commerce site (left) and mobile site (right).

Understanding your shopping cart needs

After your customers see your showroom and click through to read more detailed descriptions of your merchandise, you want to give them a shopping cart to put the stuff into. Why? Well, if you only allow people to buy one thing at a time, chances are they will buy *only* one thing and then leave.

If all you want to do is sell one thing at a time, add a PayPal Buy button or a simple Google Checkout Buy Now button and then you're done. You can find instructions in the "Creating a simple PayPal Buy button" section later in this chapter. The steps for adding a Buy Now button with Google Checkout are very similar to the steps for PayPal.

If you want to sell more than one item, you need a shopping cart that allows your customers to add and remove items while they move through your site's pages. Google and PayPal also offer a simple shopping cart solution that makes it easy to add these services with a minimal investment of time and no upfront costs. (See the section "Creating a simple shopping cart with Google Checkout," later in this chapter. The steps for adding a PayPal shopping cart are similar to Google Checkout.)

If you want a more sophisticated solution, consider one of the more advanced m-commerce options described in the "Comparing Mobile Commerce Solutions" section later in this chapter.

At the high end of these services, you'll find sophisticated options, such as shopping carts that integrate with existing inventory systems and features that allow customers to make comparisons among products, set up bridal registries, view recommendations, and more. To see a list of options across all these levels, read the section "Comparing Mobile Commerce Solutions." To read about more of the things you need to consider when choosing a shopping cart, see the sidebar "What to consider when choosing an m-commerce solution," later in this chapter.

Exchanging money with a checkout system

If everything else goes well, you ultimately guide your shoppers to the *checkout:* The place where the key action — money comes out of their accounts and goes into yours — happens. As you might expect by now, this is also where most of the second thoughts (or *cart abandonment*) happen. If you've designed your site well, you will overcome your customer's initial reservation to make a purchase and close the sale.

Your checkout must be as smooth and frictionless as possible; studies show that every 15 seconds of delay increase the chances of cart abandonment by as much as 25 percent. That is, if a whole minute passes for a mobile user (who moves around and has a short attention span) to get a response after clicking the Pay Now button, the odds of him just chucking the whole process approach 100 percent.

If your customers don't see what's happening, their fear overcomes their desire. You must not only use Internet-based security measures that use Secure Sockets Layer (SSL) technology (see the section "Securing transactions with your customers"), but also prominently reassure your customers that their financial information won't get stolen or misused. Nobody wants to risk a virtual credit card thief buying a pallet of yak vitamins just to buy a vintage concert T-shirt. We discuss this in a little more depth in the upcoming sections that discuss the back end of a site.

A good checkout system needs to

- ✔ **Total the cost of all the items in the potential customer's shopping cart** **including any tax and shipping costs.**

- ✔ **Allow the customer to choose shipping options.** Customers like shipping options — FedEx, delivery vans, in-store pickup, friendly kayakers, whatever.

- ✔ **Send the customer tracking information and a confirmation e-mail.** Pay attention to that confirmation e-mail because it's a great way to entice customers to come back and shop again, rate their transaction efficiency, or receive discounts by referring their friends.

Do some research. Go to your competitor's online stores and go through the buying process on as many mobile phones as you can get your hands on. Go to big online sites that have invested millions in perfecting the shopping experience, such as Amazon, eBay, Dell, and so on, and ask yourself questions every step of the way. Do you like the way the product's pictures are displayed and how the ad copy is written? What can you do better? What do you need to include? Take careful notes. If you start out armed with a clear vision of what you want and how you want to do it, you have a much better chance of coming out with a store that you like.

Amazon's shopping cart, shown in Figure 11-2, is a good model. This cart has both a large image of the item and a link to more images. The price is prominently displayed with a link to immediately check out and pay. And at the bottom of the cart is a suggestion to try to sell the customer some other items that go nicely with their selection. All the links are clear and easily understood, and the navigation at the bottom of the screen is unobtrusive.

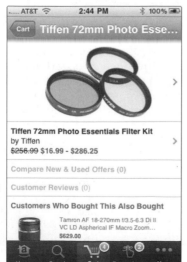

Figure 11-2: Amazon's shopping cart.

Working behind the scenes: The back end

Broadly speaking, the *back end* of your m-commerce site includes all the things that your customers don't see. Think of this as your stockroom where you store all your stuff on shelves, next to filing cabinets and order sheets. You use the back-end features of your m-commerce solution to

- ✔ Enter product and pricing information
- ✔ Manage shipping and tax options
- ✔ Configure any other features provided by the m-commerce service you use

The back end of your m-commerce site also has to integrate smoothly with your payment solution. If you choose a service like the Google Merchant (which is part of Google Checkout), you get everything you need in one easy package. If you want a more customizable shopping cart that offers mobile services, consider Magento (www.magento.com), but keep in mind that you have to integrate the cart features with a transaction service yourself (see the section "Comparing Mobile Commerce Solutions" for more on this option).

Google and PayPal offer many levels of service, so you can use Google or PayPal as an all-in-one solution for simple shopping sites, or you can use Google or PayPal just to handle the transactions if you use a more sophisticated shopping cart, such as Zen Cart, for the front end.

Securing transactions with your customers

Not to sound like a broken record, but security is one of the biggest hurdles m-commerce has to clear. Your customers watch TV ads about having their identities and credit card numbers stolen (particularly the ones that show little old ladies chortling in some gruff man's voice, bragging about all the expensive stuff he scammed by stealing granny's identity).

Here are the three main goals of security:

- ✔ **Protect your customer:** Customers who don't get robbed are much more likely to come back . . . and still have money in their pockets when they arrive.

- ✔ **Protect the merchant:** You want to keep your site from being used to launder money or having all your products drop-shipped to a P.O. Box in some prince's name.

- ✔ **Protect yourself:** If you're a Web designer creating m-commerce sites for clients, you don't want an angry customer coming after you with a lawsuit because someone hacked the system you designed.

If you're a designer and don't take security seriously, there could be legal ramifications. If credit card numbers and personal identities are stolen, expensive lawsuits could result. Depending on the kinds of contracts you develop with clients, you may be liable. Consult an attorney for the best way to protect your business and consider investing in a business insurance policy that covers online commerce.

The standard technology to protect transactions is *Secure Sockets Layer (SSL).* All the information sent between a computer or mobile phone and the payment site is encrypted. Options range from 128- to 256-bit encryption, but 128-bit is more than enough for most businesses. Banks and brokerage houses that transfer billions of dollars around the world use 256-bit security, but they pay a high price for that level of security, as well as the bandwidth and computing power that go along with a site built to securely manage such high-end services.

Think of mobile security this way: You don't need to hire a helicopter gunship to hover over your business to fend off robbers, but an alarm system and a good insurance policy are well worth the expense. Be safe, but not so paranoid you blow all your potential profits on security.

Inventory tracking and adjustment

The process of tracking and controlling inventory is something you're probably familiar with in the brick-and-mortar world, but in m-commerce, the process can get tricky. Here are some of the essential inventory functions to any good m-commerce system:

✔ You can add new products and services easily.

✔ You can adjust prices easily and have those adjustments applied globally to any mention of the same product.

✔ You can take things off the virtual shelves if you run out or need to do a recall for some reason. Make sure you can do this quickly and efficiently before you need to do so urgently. If you depend on a third-party solution to create and manage your online store, you may have to have someone else do this for you and you may not be able to control how long it takes them to get around to it.

✔ You get good records and can track the ups and downs in your inventory sales so you can figure out when to raise or lower prices or order more products from your suppliers.

✔ You have customer relationship management (CRM) features. A good CRM system tracks what your customers looked at, what they added to their shopping carts, and what they actually checked out and paid for, and then follows up and asks the customers how they felt about what they bought and allows them to write (hopefully glowing) reviews about you. Depending on how elaborate you want to get, and what your sales volume looks like, these services can get expensive. But when you can track what each customer buys and how they felt about it, you can start doing things (such as recommending related products and services) that can really increase sales.

Calculating taxes, shipping, and handling

After your customers buy your goods, the back end of your system needs some way of getting that merchandise to them. Whether you offer digital downloads, package your products in bubble wrap and cardboard boxes, or use a pizza delivery scooter, make sure it's clear to your customers what, if anything, you're charging them for delivery. If you offer multiple choices, such as rush services, make sure the m-commerce service you choose includes features to handle different shipping options (some are directly connected to common services, such as UPS and FedEx, to make things even easier).

Another charge that you need to be able to track and record is the amount of sales taxes you collect. Trust me, if you ignore this step, your accountant (not to mention the IRS) will have some very interesting things to say to you. And charging taxes isn't as easy as you might think because in most cases, you only need to charge taxes from those who live in your same state, and depending on your state, those taxes may vary from county to county. This can get complicated fast, and to ensure you're in compliance in your state, check your state business and sales tax requirements.

What to consider when choosing an m-commerce solution

There are a lot of factors that should go into choosing which m-commerce solution is best for your business, some of which may not have occurred to you. While we can't possibly anticipate all the needs of your business, the following are some questions you should answer for yourself; having a clear picture in your head of what is important can help you sort through the dizzying array of options in m-commerce solutions.

✔ How secure is the service against hacking, viruses, fraudulent transactions, and data corruption?

✔ What's the process and cost for rebuilding a store if your data becomes corrupted?

Keep in mind you may be responsible for not only your data but the data and security of your customers.

✔ Can you install, set up, customize, and administer the store yourself or do you need to hire a Web designer, programmer, or e-commerce specialist to help you?

✔ Is the store scalable? Can you add as many products as you like or is there a limit?

✔ How many customers can the system manage at a time? How does the service manage spikes in traffic?

✔ Can you easily import your current data into the system and then export your data at a later time?

✔ Does the software have application programming interfaces (APIs) that link to your legacy applications for inventory management and financial records? Will the software interface with the popular content management systems (CMS) or CRM?

✔ Does the store include a virtual shopping cart that allows online shoppers to browse through your store's inventory as well as add or remove items before logging in or checking out and paying for the items?

✔ Does the service handle all the different kinds of products, services, and digital goods you want to sell?

✔ Does the service support automatic reoccurring subscription payments? This is important if, say, you want to charge a monthly fee and automatically bill customers each month.

✔ Can you organize your products the way you want them within the shopping cart system? For example, can you group your products into categories and subcategories?

✔ Does the service support multiple sales tax levels and shipping cost calculations?

✔ What payment types (MasterCard, Visa, American Express, and so on) does the service support? Can you set up the system to work with your bank directly if you prefer to use its transaction services, or are you required to use a particular payment gateway or payment processing service?

✔ Can you modify the visual look of your store with customizable templates, and what additional software features are available?

✔ Does the store have integrated promotional tools? For example, can you easily offer sales on selected items or send coupons and customer notices via e-mail?

✔ Does the service support social networking and customer product reviews?

✔ Can you generate detailed reports of customer activity, inventory levels, and other data?

✔ What are the options to administer your store, such as processing orders, pricing, and modifying inventory? Some e-commerce platforms offer Web browser access whereas others may require separate software for each computer.

✔ How popular is the software, and is it time-tested or is it a new product without much history?

✔ Is the program an *open-source* solution (that is, it's free but may not have a company behind it that provides customer support)? If the service is open source, how active and responsive is the support community in addressing security patches, design templates, and software feature add-ons?

✔ What is the total cost of ownership and upkeep of your store? When you factor in all the expenses (not just the setup and transaction fees), what will the store really cost? Make sure to include costs for customization, Web hosting, updates, and customer support.

Comparing Mobile Commerce Solutions

When adding shopping carts and other e-commerce services to your mobile site, you can choose from many options. Many familiar brands, such as PayPal and Google, have made major efforts to migrate their online commerce technology to the mobile platform. And a crop of new companies are emerging, with dedicated mobile services that include everything from m-commerce to short messaging service (SMS, also known as text-messaging), mobile coupons, and other mobile features.

Choosing from four main flavors of mobile commerce solutions

With mobile commerce, you have a wide range of options. The following helps you appreciate the four main ways you can add m-commerce to your site, each with its own pros and cons:

- **A Buy button or simple shopping cart:** Google and PayPal offer one-click Buy buttons that make it easy to add the ability to sell one product, service, or digital good, such as a subscription or e-book, to your Web site.

  - *Pros:* You can complete this task in a few minutes and there are no upfront costs. Plus, everything you need is in one package, so you don't have to worry about setting up credit card processing or other transaction services.

  - *Cons:* You can sell only one item at a time, there are no shopping cart features, and you have few options about the way this button looks on your site.

- **A wide range of shopping carts combine mobile features with a payment service:** At the low end, Google and PayPal (see Figure 11-3) offer simple shopping carts in an all-in-one package. More sophisticated Web-based shopping carts, including Magento (www.magento.com), offer robust features but they come at a price, and not just in upfront costs and transaction fees. High-end shopping cart services can be complex to install and set up, but if you sell a lot of items, or need your online system to be integrated with your brick-and-mortar inventory system, you may find them well worth the cost. Dedicated shopping carts also require a separate transaction service to handle payment processing. For this part of the process you can use the transaction services provided by Google or PayPal. You may also be able to handle transaction processing with your own bank if it offers these kinds of merchant services.

  - *Pros:* You can better control how your merchandise is displayed, manage more products more easily, and even integrate online and offline inventory management. Some shopping cart services offer added features to help manage customers, product discounts, coupons, and so on.

- *Cons:* Using a shopping cart service requires considerable work to set up the software on your server and integrate it with your Web site. These services are also more expensive and generally only worth the added cost and effort if you sell at least a dozen products.

✔ **Dedicated mobile shopping carts:** A growing list of shopping carts and m-commerce services are designed specifically to work on the mobile Web. Some of the newest m-commerce companies are set up to do all the work for you; others offer shopping carts you can design or customize and build into your site yourself.

- *Pros:* Designed from the start for the mobile platform, you can expect companies such as asknet (`www.asknet.com`) and mPoria (`www.mporia.com`) to provide solid support for mobile devices and understand the unique challenges of the mobile Web.

- *Cons:* This is an exciting area of the mobile Web, but like any new technology, you won't find much history behind some of these companies, so it can be harder to compare customer reviews or find third-party help or tech support.

✔ **A completely custom-built cart with your own back end:** This is for the intrepid mobile Web designer only. If you want complete control over the look and functionality of your m-commerce site, as well as control over how the checkout and money-transfer process is handled, you can build your own integrated solution from the ground up. Most likely, you would need a team of experts to handle all the complex issues involved in such an undertaking.

- *Pros:* You have total control over the look and feel of the shopping cart. If something goes wrong, you can take matters into your own hands to fix it, rather than relying on someone else's customer service to pick up the phone or respond to e-mails. All the data about your customers and what they buy is under your control.

- *Cons:* You have to take care of every little nitpicky detail. If you miss something, only you can fix it. And if you're away and the site goes down while you're on vacation, you're out of business (at least until you can access your site again). You will need to have your own mechanism for transferring the funds, and maintain your own secure database for your customer's financial data.

Mobile commerce is evolving so rapidly that the companies listed here may well have added new features by the time you read this. Visit `www.MobileWebDesignBlog.com` for updates to the providers and services featured in this chapter and elsewhere in the book.

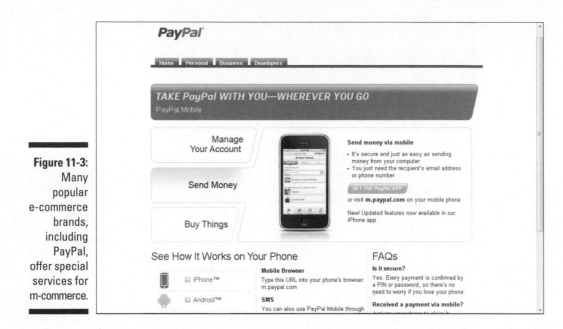

Figure 11-3:
Many
popular
e-commerce
brands,
including
PayPal,
offer special
services for
m-commerce.

For this chapter, we focus on the two simplest options. The nearby sidebar "Developing a custom system for mobile commerce" can help you get started with a custom solution if that's the route you need to go.

No matter what route you choose, the key points in the earlier section "Understanding the Basic Building Blocks of an M-Commerce Solution" apply because all m-commerce sites have some basic things in common.

Checking out m-commerce payment solutions

Most sites are best served by the latest online m-commerce tools, which combine the flexibility of displaying merchandise on your own site with offloading the heavy-duty banking and money-transfer functions to close the deal. Most Web designers agree that the best way for individuals and small to mid-size businesses to add m-commerce is to use a company that includes a shopping cart and transaction service or to combine a dedicated shopping cart with a transaction service. In this section, we introduce you to companies that offer m-commerce services.

Developing a custom system for mobile commerce

If you truly want to create your own custom-built site, look for more advanced books or other training specific to developing shopping carts, or consider paying for one of the services described in the "Comparing Mobile Commerce Solutions" section or hiring a contractor to take care of it for you.

To create such a system, here's what you need:

✔ You need to know how to use sophisticated functions in a dynamic programming language or technology, such as ASP.NET or PHP.

✔ You need the ability to integrate your system into a payment system in ways that require managing a secure server, SSL certificates, and other settings on your Web server.

Because all that gets complicated quickly, some great services solve all your problems at once, and if you like that approach, decide how much you want to be able to customize the design and what the services cost.

Major e-commerce sites, such as Amazon or eBay, have spent millions on developing custom shopping functions for their sites. If all you want is the simplest solution, you can list your goods on those sites and then simply include a link to that item on your mobile site. That's the simplest option, and the initial investment is minimal, but many people outgrow that option pretty quickly.

Amazon Payments

`http://payments.amazon.com`

This powerful and flexible payment engine allows users who are already familiar with, and trust, the Amazon brand to purchase goods from your Web site using their Amazon customer ID. The advantage is that Amazon has established itself as one of the biggest retailers on the Web, and its technological backbone is very strong.

The downside, however, is that your customers have to already have an account with Amazon; otherwise, they're forced to create one when they make their first payment. As you can see in Figure 11-4, the Amazon brand is all over every page (on the buttons, in the colors, and in the typography), which helps your customers know they're dealing with a reputable firm — but that also means Amazon promotes itself all over your site.

Still, if you sell digital downloads, such as ringtones, MP3s, videos, or pictures, Amazon's payment and pricing system is innovative and robust. And if you already sell your stuff on Amazon, it's very easy to integrate the links and payment system on your Web site because customers who have already paid with Amazon at your m-commerce store can buy with just one click. The Amazon site has detailed instructions for both amateurs looking for the simplest solution and seasoned developers looking to customize.

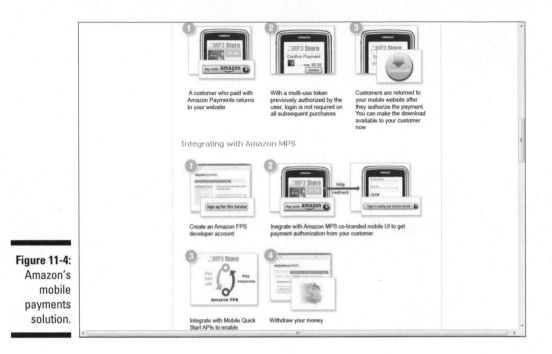

Figure 11-4:
Amazon's
mobile
payments
solution.

iTunes

```
www.apple.com/itunes
```

As of this writing, iTunes is still limited in what it sells, restricting anyone using the service to music, videos, and iPhone applications. You must submit your digital goods to iTunes for review before they can be listed on the site, and Apple's approval process can take a few days or even weeks.

But with more than 100 million credit card accounts on file (outnumbering even the 94 million Amazon customers or the 75 million PayPal customers), speculation is rife that Apple will extend its iTunes checkout processing technology to allow merchants to sell their stuff to customers who want to pay via their existing iTunes accounts. And iTunes provides digital goods for the iPhone, iPod touch, and iPad, so the combined audience is significant.

PayPal

```
www.paypal.com
```

PayPal is highly customizable and offers a wide range of services, broad international e-commerce support, and everything from simple one-click buttons to high-end transaction services you can integrate into most of the popular shopping cart services.

At the high end, you need quite a bit of technical coding skills to tweak PayPal's API to work with third-party shopping carts, but PayPal has been around for a long time, so you can draw on a large international developer network when you need help. At the low end, you can easily add PayPal buttons. See the section "Creating a simple PayPal Buy button," later in this chapter.

As with Amazon, the PayPal brand is the one your customers see on each Buy button when it comes time to make their payments.

PayPal has also created some extremely powerful and extensible technology to allow people to transform their cellphones into wallets. And because PayPal is owned by eBay, the integration between the two services is quite good. If you're selling your items through your eBay store, this may be all you need.

PayPal has also introduced an app for the iPhone that allows users to transfer money directly from one phone to the other, simply by bumping together the two phones.

Google Checkout

```
https://checkout.google.com/sell
```

Google has spent enormous amounts of time and money developing a whole host of other products and services to go along with its core business of being the top search engine on the planet. We discuss setting up Google Checkout later in this chapter because of the wide panoply of other products and services that Google has — most especially Google's recent acquisition of the mobile advertising company AdMob for $750 million. Spending that kind of money is a clear indication that Google takes the mobile Web seriously, and that it's going to continue to devote significant time and resources to ensuring that its existing products are mobile-friendly.

Google Checkout is easy to set up, and because it piggybacks on Google's massive network of server farms, it loads quickly — no matter where on earth your user accesses your m-commerce site from (not an insignificant consideration as billions of people come online via their mobile devices).

Like PayPal, you can use Google Checkout to add a Buy Now button to your site, to set up a simple shopping cart and transaction package, or to use Google for the transaction processing in combination with any number of shopping carts that are designed to work with Google. (Some shopping carts can be integrated with PayPal, Google, or both if you want to give customers the option.)

Similar to Amazon, if you use Google Checkout, the downside is that your customers have to already have an account with Google; otherwise, they're forced to create one when they make their first payment. The Google brand is what your customers will see when they make their payments; the buttons will have the Google logo on them, the color scheme will look like the color scheme that is used by Google, the words "Fast checkout through Google" will appear on the screen, along with a link that says "What is Google Checkout?" and leads to a page that is all about Google Checkout. Another possible downside for you may be that Google Checkout doesn't support currency in as many countries as PayPal. At the time of this writing, Google Checkout accepts U.S. dollars, euros, and British pounds sterling, but expect that list to grow over time.

Dozens of e-commerce shopping cart providers have made a special effort to make sure that they integrate cleanly with Google Checkout. If you want to use a more sophisticated shopping cart than the one provided by Google, you can view Google's recommended list of third-party vendors in the Integration Partners section on its Web site at `checkout.google.com/seller/integrate_cart.html`.

If you use Google Checkout, Google offers a couple other features that can tie into your Google Checkout system:

✔ Google also has a wizard that allows you to easily convert a Google Docs spreadsheet into a shopping cart. If you have a Google ID, you can use Google Docs to create a spreadsheet via the Web. Basically, in Google Docs, you fill the spreadsheet with any data you want to include about your products, including descriptions, pictures, pricing info, and so on. Then, run the wizard at `https://storegadgetwizard.appspot.com/storegadgetwizard/` to convert your spreadsheet into a shopping cart.

✔ Google Analytics allows you to track page traffic information, such as how many users come to your site, which items are most popular, and how long visitors spend on each page.

asknet

`www.asknet.com`

This large, international e-commerce company is based in Germany. asknet offers custom-built mobile sites and high-end m-commerce.

asknet is partnered with many Internet security companies and software retailers, and the company specializes in handling m-commerce across international boundaries. asknet provides support for multiple currencies, tax laws, delivery of goods, and customer tracking. Videos on their site (see Figure 11-5) explain how their service works.

asknet also has a network of warehouses that can handle fulfillment, so you can use it to store your merchandise and handle shipping around the world. asknet even burns CDs/DVDs, applies your labels, sticks them into jewel cases, and delivers them to your customers if you sell digital merchandise. As you might expect, asknet is far from the cheapest solution; it doesn't even list its prices on its site, but you can contact asknet for more information.

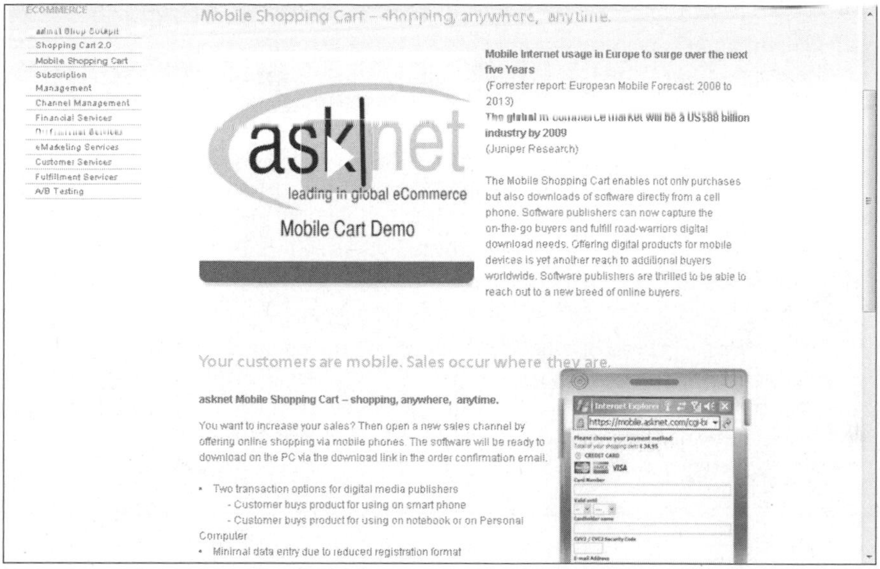

Figure 11-5:
asknet's
site.

CardinalCommerce

www.cardinalcommerce.com

Another high-end company that specializes in constructing the back-end payment solutions for major multinational corporations (see Figure 11-6), CardinalCommerce has made mobile a key part of its strategy.

CardinalCommerce's expertise centers on creating secure mobile banking and bill payment platforms for which it's been granted multiple original patents.

CardinalCommerce works with companies like Visa and MasterCard to build debit-based payment sites, and with international banks to develop identification and authorization systems for money transfers. Because CardinalCommerce built m-commerce sites for companies like SkyMall, 20th Century Fox, and Secure Vault, it obviously can handle many currencies. We assume this is one of the more expensive options, but CardinalCommerce doesn't publish its price list on its Web site.

mPoria

www.mporia.com

Designed from the ground up for the mobile Web, mPoria offers many great features, including secure checkout, site reporting, and real-time inventory management. This is one of the only dedicated mobile shopping carts we've found that you can customize and update yourself. And with prices starting at $20 per month, it's one of the most cost-effective options.

Open-source shopping carts for mobile

Many Web sites already use popular open-source shopping carts, including Zen Cart (www.zen-cart.com) and OS Commerce (www.oscommerce.com). Because they are *open-source,* they are free to download, but many people make money by charging to take the plain cart and make it look good.

The Web is full of design shops that make it their business to construct templates and themes that allow businesses to change the look and layout of their online stores. Some sites offer mobile store templates, but the forums and

bulletin boards of the open-source community are full of complaints from people who have tried to use these plug-ins. People have found that these templates either break their stores or require far more technical expertise than advertised.

However, thousands of software developers and coders are working on this problem, so if you already have a popular shopping cart like one of the above, plug-ins that you could try with your existing e-commerce solution may be hitting the Web every day.

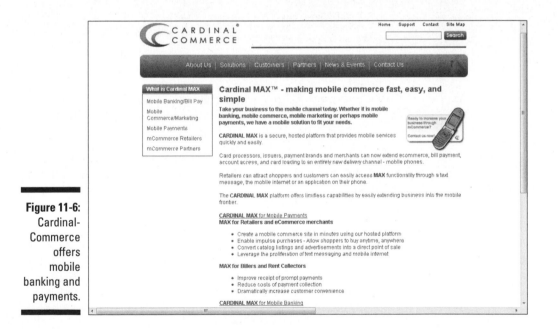

Figure 11-6:
Cardinal-
Commerce
offers
mobile
banking and
payments.

mPoria is a service for small to mid-level businesses that want to dip their toes into m-commerce but don't want to invest thousands just to get started. Prices range from $20 per month to $100 per month, based on the number of products in your online store. The pricing is based on 20–700 items per store.

mPoria offers a wizard that guides you through creating your own m-commerce portal, but it has some limits on how much you can customize the service. mPoria does have an automated process to help you build the site yourself (see Figure 11-7). However, the list of phones that are supported by mPoria's GoMobile! Sites (the sites that they custom-build for their clients) is incomplete, and it handles only U.S. dollars as a currency (although that may change as the company grows). At the higher levels of service, mPoria offers inventory tracking and other CRM tools.

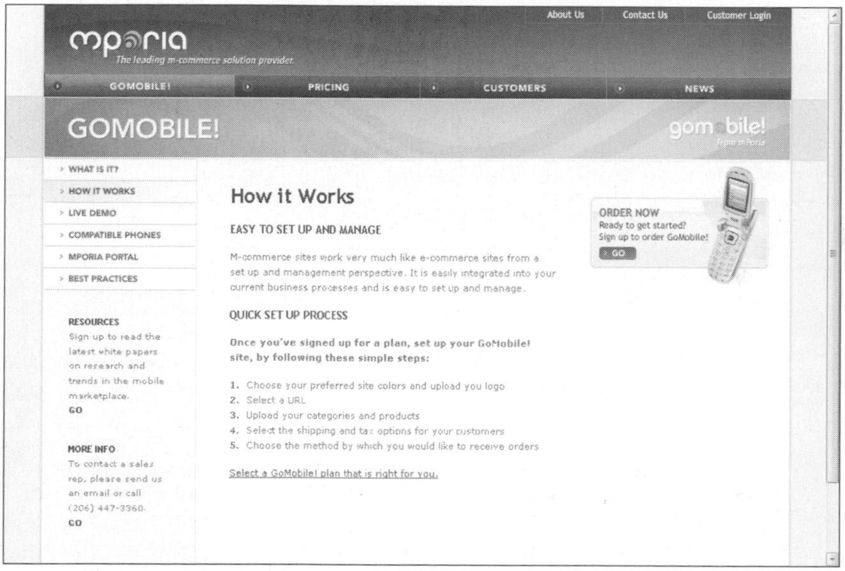

Figure 11-7: mPoria leads you through an automated wizard to create your mobile site.

Setting Up Commerce on Your Mobile Site

In this section, we guide you step by step through the process of setting up m-commerce with popular and easy-to-use services. You begin with the simplest option — adding Buy buttons with the popular PayPal service. You also discover how to create a basic shopping cart with Google Checkout. We guide you through the process of adding your Buy button or shopping cart to your mobile Web site using Dreamweaver and WordPress.

Both Google Checkout and PayPal offer simple Buy buttons, as well as shopping cart features, making it easy for anyone to sell products on a Web site with no upfront costs and a competitive transaction fee. Why would you choose Google over PayPal or vice versa? Two key differences: Google has a nicer interface design, but it doesn't support as many foreign currencies as PayPal. The PayPal interface is a bit clunky: Each time a user ads a product to the shopping cart, they are sent off to the PayPal site and have to navigate back to your site to add more products. However, you can send products to more countries using PayPal.

Creating a simple PayPal Buy button

The simplest and quickest option if you want to sell only a few products or services on your Web site is to create a PayPal button for each item you want to sell. Follow these steps:

1. **Open your browser and navigate to www.paypal.com.**

   If you have a PayPal account, log in here. If you don't have an account, click on the Sign Up link to establish an account, and follow PayPal's easy online instructions. Depending on what level of account you want to sign up for, you will need a valid credit card and your merchant account information handy.

2. **Click on the Merchant Services tab.**

   A page will open with many links to all the various actions you can take with your PayPal account, as well as links to various resources to help you run your online business.

3. **Click on the Website Payments Standard link in the box on the left side of the page.**

   The Website Payments Standard: Overview page opens (see Figure 11-8). This page allows you to choose from a couple other options, but for now, stick with creating a button for just one item at a time. PayPal also offers a Website Payments Pro service, but this requires that you register for a business account with PayPal and that you use an integrated shopping cart or build one with PayPal's APIs.

4. **Below the Sell Single Items heading, click the Create One Now link.**

   The Create PayPal Payment Button page opens with fields in it for the description of your item.

5. **Below Choose a button type, choose Buy Now from the drop-down list.**

   You can also create a payment button to sell your services, set up a subscription or recurring billing process, collect a donation, or buy a gift certificate. In this example, we make a simple button to sell one item.

6. **Type the item name in the Item Name field.**

   The optional Item ID field allows you to enter a tracking code for the item you're selling, if you want to use that number in your spreadsheets or inventory programs.

7. **In the Shipping section, fill in the amount you charge for the shipping and handling of your item.**

8. **In the Tax section, fill in the amount of sales tax and other applicable taxes you charge.**

9. **Choose how you want to be notified when someone has bought your item.**

You can be notified through your secure merchant account. If you select this option, your e-mail address doesn't appear in the button's HTML code. This may or may not be important to you. Some merchants want to appear as transparent and open as possible; others are afraid of having their e-mail inboxes overflow with spam.

If you choose to use your PayPal e-mail address, you receive a notification in your e-mail inbox every time someone buys something from you with this PayPal button.

10. **Click the Create Button button.**

    The You've Created Your Button page opens. In a panel in the middle of the page is the code for your PayPal button. Don't worry that the code looks like a lot of gobbledygook. You don't have to type this in anywhere.

11. **Click the Select Code button to select the button code.**

    The code is highlighted.

12. **Press Ctrl+C (on a Mac, ⌘+C) to copy the code.**

    You aren't done yet. . . .

13. **Depending on what you use to create your Web site, skip to the section "Adding a shopping cart to WordPress," or "Adding a shopping cart with Dreamweaver," later in this chapter. Start with Step 1 in each section.**

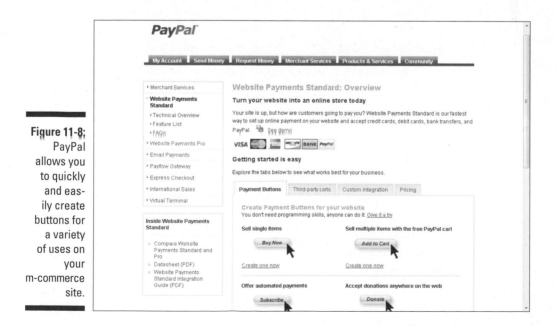

Figure 11-8:
PayPal allows you to quickly and easily create buttons for a variety of uses on your m-commerce site.

Creating a simple shopping cart with Google Checkout

Because so many people already use Gmail, Google Docs, or some other Web-based Google product, integrate Google Checkout. If you already have a Google account, you're halfway there. Also, Google Checkout has a special integration with Google AdSense, so you can easily advertise your products.

 Make sure that you have handy some basic information about your products before you proceed further. You need to know the names of your items, their prices, what options are available (size, color, weight, materials, and so on), and the URL where the picture of that item appears on your Web site. After you have that info, follow these steps:

1. **Open your browser and navigate to `http://checkout.google.com/sell`.**

   The sign-in page opens.

2. **Type your e-mail address and password.**

   If you've used Gmail, your username may already appear; if so, just type your password.

3. **Click the Sign In button and then follow the steps to either use an existing account or create a new one.**

   The Google Checkout page opens.

4. **Click on the Tools tab.**

   The Integrate Your Website with Google Checkout page opens.

5. **In the Google Checkout sign-in screen, enter your e-mail address and password, and then click the Sign In and Continue button.**

   The Tell Us about Your Business page opens. One of the somewhat annoying tics of Google Checkout is that it prompts you to enter your username and password at every turn. You may be prompted during several steps along the way to re-enter this information. Some of that is because Google times-out the sessions with Google Checkout to prevent you from leaving the screen open on your computer when you walk away from it and allowing someone else to quickly drain your accounts or hijack your site.

6. **Type the contact information, public contact information, and financial information for your business into the boxes provided on the page.**

7. **Scroll down to the bottom of the page and select the I Agree to the Terms of Service check box.**

   The Signup Complete page opens.

Note: Read through the Terms of Service. You must agree to them if you want to continue and use the service.

8. **Click the Google Checkout Shopping Cart link on the right side of the page.**

A page opens (see Figure 11-9) with fields for you to enter the details of your product.

9. **Choose from the following product types:**

   • *Simple* means that there's only one product, with no other options or prices, such as an antique vase.

   • *With Multiple Options* enables you to let your customers choose multiple options that are all the same price for a product, such as a T-shirt that can be white, blue, or black.

   • *With Multiple Prices* enables you to take a basic item and charge different prices, depending on the options that the customer chooses. This is the option shown in Figure 11-9 in which you can buy the snaggletoothed tabby with or without his jester's cap, which of course costs much more.

10. **Enter a product name in the Title field.**

11. **(Optional) Enter the URL where the image of your product appears on your Web site.**

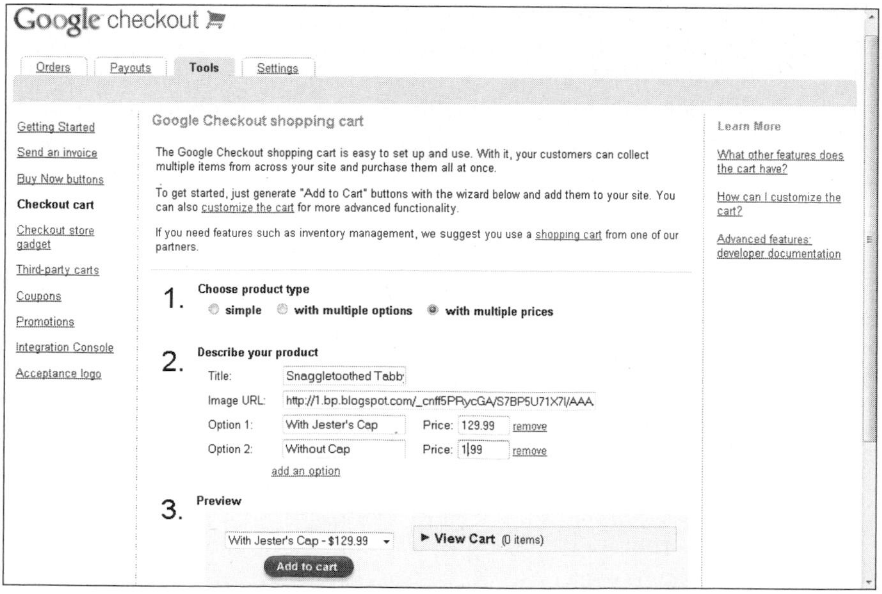

Figure 11-9:
Google
Checkout
has a very
simple inter-
face, and it
takes only
three steps
to create a
button.

Adding the image's URL causes a small thumbnail of the item to appear next to the item title and price in the shopping cart when your customer clicks to purchase it. Because this is just a little extra flourish, don't feel like you have to do this if it gets difficult or time-consuming.

 a. *To get the URL, navigate to where the item appears on your site and then right-click (on a Mac, Command+click) the photo of the item.*

 A menu opens with options that allow you to do many things with the photo.

 b. *Click Copy Image Location in the drop-down menu and then navigate back to the Google Checkout page.*

 c. *Click in the Image URL field and press Ctrl+V (on a Mac, Command+V) to paste the image URL into the field.*

12. **(Optional) Enter the options in the fields next to the words Option 1 and Option 2.**

 The default fields are Small and Large, but you can type whatever you want. If you have many options for the item, click the Add an Option link and keep typing until all the sizes, colors, time lengths, or whatever other variables your item has are covered.

13. **Enter the price.**

 Next to each option is a field for the price associated with that option. Click the fields and then type the prices.

14. **Test your changes in the Preview box.**

 You can see what your shopping cart will look like by clicking the buttons in the Preview box. If you spot an error, go back through the previous steps and re-enter the correct information.

15. **When you have the description the way you want it, select the Yes, I Have Configured My Account to Accept Unsigned Shopping Carts check box and be sure to configure your account at some point.**

 If you haven't configured your account yet, you can come back and do it later; just make sure to select the check box here.

 Because the Google Checkout shopping cart works entirely in the Web browser, a visitor to your site can alter the pricing in Google Checkout when she places an order. Unfortunately, Google can't protect the secret key needed to sign a shopping cart, but you can get around this limitation by letting the shopping cart work without being signed.

 To accept unsigned carts:

 a. *Click the Settings tab and then click the Integration link on the left side of the page.*

       b. Deselect the My Company Will Only Post Digitally Signed Carts check box and then click the Save button.

16. To generate the code to add to your Web page, click the Create Button Code button.

A page opens with two boxes of code generated by Google. The top box contains the code that needs to be copied into your page where you want the button to appear.

17. Select the code and press Ctrl+C (on a Mac, Command+C).

The next step depends on whether you sell your items from a blog, such as WordPress, or from a static Web page that you've designed with a program, such as Dreamweaver. The bottom box contains the code that creates the cart; it needs to be pasted into the bottom of each HTML page, which we address in the two following sections.

18. Repeat these steps for each item in your store.

You have to go through these steps for each separate store item.

Adding a shopping cart to WordPress

Many site owners are migrating away from having a collection of static pages or using expensive, custom-made content management systems. Instead, they're opting for open-source solutions like WordPress. Yes, WordPress started as a free blogging-software solution; however, its widespread use has spurred legions of developers around the world to customize its source code to make it do all sorts of wonderful things.

When you use WordPress for your shopping cart, you need to know the pros and cons:

✔ **Pros:** WordPress allows a site owner to quickly and easily update the site's content; as the saying goes, "If you can type an e-mail, you can write a blog post." Adding the shopping cart buttons you create in the previous two sections to a WordPress blog is as easy as cutting and pasting.

✔ **Con:** Adjusting the look and functionality of a WordPress site can be tricky and requires expert knowledge of the programming language PHP.

To copy and paste button code into a WordPress blog post, follow the steps here. (If you use another CMS, such as Joomla!, Drupal, Movable Type, or Blogger, you can still use the basic concepts explained here to make the buttons show up next to your items.)

1. **Open a new tab in your browser and navigate to your blog's**
   Dashboard.

   This is the page where you compose new posts, control which widgets appear in your sidebars, or adjust your site's theme.

2. **In the Posts heading, click the Posts link.**

3. **Scroll until you find the post containing the item that you just created either the PayPal button or Google Shopping Cart for.**

   When you run your mouse pointer over the title of the post, a menu appears, with the options for editing that post.

4. **Click the Edit link.**

   The post opens in the familiar window that you use to type text and upload photos.

5. **In the upper-right corner of the editing window, click the HTML tab.**

   In the editing window, the text changes to the code view of the blog post.

6. **Click in your post where you want to insert the button for the item you want to sell and then press Ctrl+V (on a Mac, Command+V) to paste in the code for the button.**

   This is the code that you copied in Step 11 (for the PayPal button) or Step 17 (for the Google Shopping Cart) above. See Figure 11-10 for an example of what inserting this code will look like.

7. **Click the Visual tab to see where the button appears in your post.**

8. **If you don't like the button's placement, switch to HTML view, delete the button code from where you've placed it, and then repeat Step 6 to put it in the new location.**

9. **When you have the button where you want it to appear, click the Publish button on the right to publish the page. (If you are editing an existing page, the Publish button changes to an Update button.)**

10. **(For Google Checkout) Click to return to the tab in your browser where you got the code you just placed in the blog post.**

    This is the page where you got the code for your shopping cart. You're going to have to get one more piece of code to make this work in your WordPress blog.

11. **Select the code in the bottom box on the page and press Ctrl+C (on a Mac, Command+C); click to return to the tab where your WordPress blog's dashboard is still open in your browser.**

    The bottom box is the one with the heading that reads "Add this code only once for each html page, just before the </body> tag."

12. **In the Appearance panel on the left side of your Dashboard, click the Editor link.**

    The Edit Themes page opens in your browser. In the middle panel is the code for your blog. On the right are the various templates controlling how the elements of your blog (such as the header, the sidebar, or the comments) appear.

13. **On the right side of the page, click the Footer link.**

    The PHP code for the footer that appears on every page of your blog appears in the middle panel.

14. **Scroll until you see the `</body>` code and then click the line above and press Enter (on a Mac, press Return).**

15. **Press Ctrl+V (on a Mac, Command+V) to paste the code here.**

    This code allows every page on your blog to know how to handle the buttons and Google Checkout shopping cart. This piece of code has your Merchant ID number in it and the currency you use.

16. **Click the Update File button and then test your work by clicking the name of your WordPress blog at the top of the Dashboard page.**

    Test how well your button works by going through the order process — right up to placing an order to yourself from your site.

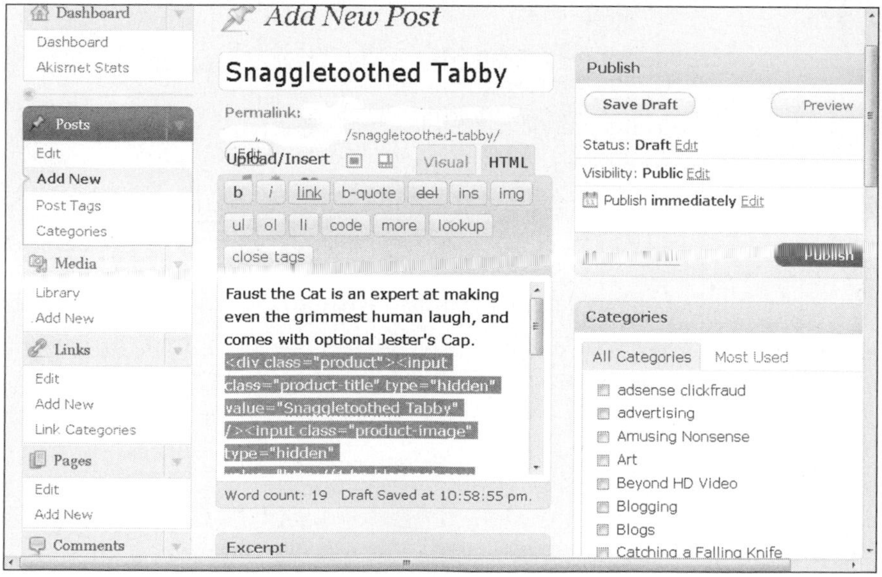

Figure 11-10:
Make sure that you choose the HTML tab before you paste the code for your button into your WordPress post.

Adding a shopping cart with Dreamweaver

If you sell your merchandise through a static site, insert the button(s) by using whatever tool you used to construct the site. In the example here, we will show you how to use Dreamweaver, the industry-standard tool used to create custom Web sites. To insert a button with Dreamweaver, follow these steps:

1. **Open the page of the item using Dreamweaver and then click the Split button at the top of the workspace.**

   This opens the dual-panel view, where you see the underlying code and the page's design.

2. **Click the page where you want the button to appear and then press Ctrl+V (on Mac, Command+V) to paste the code for the button into your page.**

   Again, this is the code that you copied in Step 11 (for the PayPal button) or Step 17 (for the Google Shopping Cart) above.

3. **Return to the tab in your browser where you created the shopping cart code, and then select and copy the code in the lower panel.**

   Press Ctrl+C (on a Mac, Command+C) to copy the code.

4. **Return to Dreamweaver, scroll to the bottom of your page, and find the `</body>` tag.**

5. **Click just above this tag and press Ctrl+V (on Mac, Command+V) to insert the code.**

   This code needs to be added to each HTML page that you have the shopping cart button on (see Figure 11-11 for an example of what inserting the code in Dreamweaver will look like). If you have multiple pages, put this code at the bottom of each page. It's helpful to use the Split view when you paste in the code for your button, not only so you can control exactly where it goes in amidst your other page elements, but so you can get a sense of how it fits into the rest of your page design.

   If, however, you have multiple items on one HTML page, return to your browser to generate the other buttons for the other items on your page.

Figure 11-11:
Dream-
weaver's
split view
helps you
insert the
code for the
shopping
cart.

Part IV
The Part of Tens

"Sometimes I feel behind the times. I asked my 11-year old to build a Web site for my business, and he said he would, only after he finishes the one he's building for his ant farm."

In this part . . .

In this part, you find ten mobile interface challenges and opportunities, and ten real-world examples of great mobile design. Use these great tips and real-world advice to take your mobile Web site to the next level.

Chapter 12

Ten Quick Tips for Mobile Design

*1*f you're looking for a quick reference to some of the biggest do's and don'ts of mobile Web design, this chapter is for you. We cover most of these tips in greater detail in other chapters of this book, but this collection of ten mobile interface tips gives you a quick overview of the most common issues you're likely to face while you create a mobile version of your Web site.

Design for Distracted Surfers

We're sure you'd never surf the Web while you're driving, and everyone would be a lot safer on the roads if no one else did, either. Unfortunately, the fact that we even have to write that is an indication of one of the biggest challenges in mobile Web design — distracted surfers.

Keep in mind that when people visit a mobile site they're often doing something else at the same time, and they're often under pressure to find information quickly.

Here are a few quick tips to make your mobile site easier for distracted visitors to use:

- ✔ Make key information, such as your address and phone number, easy to find right away.
- ✔ Make all links big and easy to click.
- ✔ Use text and background colors with good contrast so that your mobile Web site is easy to read, even in low light.

Surf the Web on Many Mobile Devices

To appreciate the challenges of the mobile Web, surf to your Web site on a mobile phone. But don't stop at one phone, especially if you have an iPhone or Droid. These phones may get all the headlines (and a majority of the traffic on the mobile Web), but they're not the only phones likely to visit your site — they're just the ones most likely to make your site look good, even if it's not optimized for the mobile Web.

Don't let these smartphones fool you with their relatively sophisticated features that make many desktop Web sites look good (or at least good enough). Those same sites viewed on a BlackBerry or, worse, a RAZR, may be completely unreadable.

Although you can test your mobile site using online emulators (see Chapter 7), the best way is to hold a device in your hand so you can see how it feels and looks.

Visit a mobile phone store and be really nice to the salespeople while you test your sites on their phones. Better yet, compare notes with friends and family. Ask people to visit your Web site on different phones and watch what they do, how they find their way around (or where they get lost), and how hard it is for them to get to the information they need when they interact with your site.

Set Up Mobile Web Addresses

So that everyone with a mobile phone can easily get to the URL of your mobile site (by typing as little as possible), set up multiple mobile addresses and direct them all to the mobile version of your site.

Until a clear winner appears in the mobile URL game, use the most common addresses to increase the odds that your visitors find you on their first try.

The following are among the mobile addresses in common use on the mobile Web:

✔ m.*yourdomain*.com: Recommended for ease of typing

✔ wap.*yourdomain*.com: A common address for sites created using the WML, Wireless Markup Language)

✔ *yourdomain*.com/mobile: Common alternative because of the easy server setup

✔ *yourdomain*.com/i: If you create a version specifically for the iPhone

✔ *yourdomain*.mobi: Requires registering the .mobi version of your domain name, which many sites don't seem to bother with

Whatever you do, drop the www. — no one should ever have to type those three letters and that dot again on the modern Web.

Create a Virtual Demo or Showcase

Consider what's most important for your audience. If you don't have a physical location but want to use your mobile site to showcase your work, create a portfolio that displays well on a small screen. Then, the next time you're at a party or business event, your mobile phone will be everything you (or your sales and marketing staff) need to give an impromptu demo of your products or services anywhere, anytime.

Location, Location, Location

Most people who surf the desktop Web are in an office, school, library, or cybercafé. Mobile Web surfers can be anywhere, including in front of your restaurant, office, or store, right now, or worse, lost on the road trying to find you.

As you consider how to design a mobile version of your Web site, consider not just how to make things smaller but also how to best present the information most likely to be useful to someone using a mobile device, wherever he is.

One of the most common uses of mobile phones is still the most obvious — making phone calls. So make sure your phone number is easy to find on the first screen of your mobile site, and include your street address and links to maps for those who may get lost on their way.

Including a link to a Google map is a great way to make it easy to find you, but for best results, make sure you link to the mobile version of Google Maps.

Both Yahoo! and Google let you prioritize searches for local matches on their mobile sites. Take the time to optimize your mobile site and make sure to include location-specific keywords, such as the names of the cities, states, and even local neighborhoods you serve.

Optimize for Low Bandwidth

The smaller screen size isn't the only thing that limits how well you can display images and multimedia on a cellphone; bandwidth also places limits. Although a growing number of mobile users take advantage of the faster 3G and 4G networks, most are still restricted by very slow connections.

The same challenges of limited bandwidth that throttled the early Web slow the mobile Internet, which lags far behind the high-speed DSL and cable modem connections that are common ways to access the Internet from computers.

When you design the mobile version of your site, the following tips can help your site reach visitors with a low bandwidth:

- ✔ Get ruthless with your images and multimedia files, limiting your mobile site to a precious few images that help tell your story and adding visual interest.

- ✔ As you streamline your site, replace banners and button images with text links, which work on any device.

- ✔ Give careful consideration to how you include multimedia. For example, don't put video or audio files on the front page of your mobile site. Instead, link to multimedia files so they're optional for mobile browsers, and include warnings about how big the file is and how well it will display on different devices.

✔ If you're designing for the lowest-level mobile phones, try to keep the total size of your front page to 7k or less. Yes, you read that right, 7k — that's one tiny image and a few links, and that's all folks.

Follow the YouTube Mobile Video Model

Point any Internet-enabled device that supports video at www.youtube. com and you quickly see that the biggest site for video on the Web has made mobile a priority.

YouTube uses the MP4 video format for mobile users, and that makes all the difference between a video you can watch anywhere, anytime and a blank screen on mobile phones that don't support Flash (a common video format used by YouTube only for desktop devices).

To fully appreciate YouTube's mobile adaptability, compare the early iPhone model with one that runs on the new 3G network — YouTube delivers two versions of the same video to accommodate the bandwidth difference. The result is that YouTube videos look a bit choppy in their heavily compressed versions for mobile devices with limited bandwidth, but they don't take all day to get there. On a fast 3G iPhone, the higher-resolution version of the same video plays smooth and clean over the faster connection.

Follow YouTube's model when you add videos to your site and avoid video formats that aren't well supported by mobile devices. If you want to make the process of publishing video to your site really easy, upload your videos to YouTube and then embed them into your mobile Web pages using their simple embed code — it's as easy as copy and paste, and you can rest assured your videos will play on most mobile devices thanks to YouTube's careful attention to the mobile Web. Already YouTube is starting to roll out video using the new HTML5 options covered in Chapter 5.

You find more information about video and other multimedia options in Chapter 8.

Follow Standards and Use Style Sheets

Desktop browsers, such as Firefox and Internet Explorer, are surprisingly for-giving when it comes to errors on Web pages. You can miss a close tag here or add an extra quotation mark there, and much of the time your pages still look okay.

Browsers that can handle code that's not written quite correctly have to be bigger programs with more complex code. You just can't run a browser that sophisticated on a mobile device. That's why following standards and testing your work carefully are more important than before you launch a mobile site. You find tips and links to some great sites where you can test your pages in Chapter 7.

Here are a few quick suggestions for creating clean, standards-based mobile sites:

- **Separate content from style:** Use Cascading Style Sheets and well-written semantic code to design clean pages that work well on many devices (you find instructions in Chapters 4, 5, and 6).

- **Use alt tags behind images:** Alternative text is text that you include in the alt attribute of the image tag (which we cover in Chapter 5). Alt text displays when images are turned off or can't be seen by the user. This simple addition as you insert images into your pages helps ensure that your designs are clear and understandable to everyone.

- **Use HTML heading tags:** The HTML heading tags <h1> through <h6> are well-recognized tags that create a hierarchy of information on your page. Your most important headline needs to be formatted with the <h1> tag, your next level of headlines with the <h2> tag, and so on.

- **Follow the W3C mobile guidelines:** The World Wide Web Consortium sets the standards for the Web, and they have a lot to say about designing for mobile devices. Check out www.w3.org/mobile to read more about standards, and test your site in the validator at http://validator.w3.org/mobile/.

- **Validate your code:** Mobile Web browsers are notoriously unforgiving about errors in markup. To make sure your mobile site won't fail to open on a phone because of a typo or missing quotation mark, make sure to run your URL through the W3C Validator at http://validator.w3.org.

Don't Make Anyone Type or Click Much

Even on the best mobile devices, typing and clicking links can be a real challenge. Therefore, make links big and easy to click for mobile visitors, and don't overload any page with too many options.

The best approach is to lead users through a series of simple choices, limiting the options to no more than five to seven big links at any stage, and direct visitors to increasingly specific sets of links until they find the information they need.

Avoid drop-down lists, or anything else that uses AJAX or JavaScript around links, because many mobile devices don't support these advanced Web technologies, making these links impossible to use.

Some information, such as contact information, should never be more than one click away, and in many cases, including your phone number on the main page of your mobile site is good practice — after all, you know your visitor has a phone handy.

Prepare for Fast Updates

The Internet increased the speed with which people share news and gossip around the world, and the advent of the mobile Web has accelerated the rumor mill.

As you create a mobile Web site, make sure you build it in a way that's easy to update, preferably from your mobile device and computer. There are many great online services that can help you update your Web site or blog using a mobile device. In Chapter 9 you find resources for blogging from a mobile device, and in Chapter 8 you find online services that make it easy to upload photos and post them automatically.

While you're at it, make it easy for visitors to your site to send you information from their mobile phones as well. Services, such as Picasa, featured in Chapter 8, make it easy for anyone with the right login information to upload photos to your site. Picasa works with Google Maps so it can even add geocodes to photos to show exactly where the photos were taken.

The mobile Web provides a powerful vehicle for individuals, businesses, and organizations to present their side of any story and get the word out quickly when tragic events, bad press, and other crises arise. But don't wait for an emergency to find out whether you're prepared to add new information to your Web site quickly, and don't fool yourself into thinking that just because you don't manage a daily Internet newspaper, you don't have to worry about speedy updates. Today, your staff and key constituents are more likely to have access to a mobile phone when disaster strikes than to a desktop computer. Don't wait for an emergency to prepare — host a training session, set up a mobile phone emergency drill team, and make sure the people who matter to you are prepared to use mobile devices to coordinate efforts and collect information from the field today.

Chapter 13

Ten Great Mobile Sites

Creating the best design for the mobile Web isn't easy, especially if you want your site to work on a wide variety of devices. The sites featured in this chapter illustrate some of the best early adopters on the mobile Web, complete with screenshots so you can see how the site designs vary across devices.

The sites selected for this top ten list won their place in history for creating Web sites that look great on everything from an iPhone to a Motorola RAZR. The sites featured in this chapter win points not only for their mastery of mobile technology but also for their innovative and effective presentation of information within the constraints of the small screens of mobile phones. Creating a great mobile Web site, such as the ones we feature in this chapter, requires more than just mastering a few new technical skills and cramming information onto a small screen. What makes the mobile Web different is that it requires an almost Zen-link ability to concentrate on all the tiny details, while at the same time remaining cognizant of the bigger picture. Only by having a strong grounding in the technical limitations and expanded functionalities of the mobile Web will a designer truly be able to give the user the right content in the right place at the right time — and then go a step further to ensure that the site functions on the device each visitor uses.

For each site, we include a screenshot of the desktop version (taken in Internet Explorer 8, on a computer monitor set to a resolution of 1024 x 768) and screenshots taken on the iPhone 3G, BlackBerry Bold 9700, and Motorola RAZR V9x.

We chose these phones because they represent the main categories of devices on the market today: a touch-screen phone (the iPhone), a smartphone (the BlackBerry), and a feature phone (the RAZR). With every device, we entered the URL for the site's home page and let the site redirect us to the version it thought best for the phone we were using. (You find out how to set up a site to redirect visitors like this in Chapter 6.)

Comparing the designs on each device in this chapter can help you figure out how best to take advantage of the limitations and features of each phone type.

Over the coming months and years, these designs are sure to evolve, and the list of favorite mobile sites is sure to grow (we already have a longer list of great examples than we could ever include in this book). Keep up with our favorites and send us yours via the e-mail link on our blog at www.mobilewebdesignblog.com.

Facebook Keeps You Connected

www.facebook.com

Perhaps not surprisingly, one of the best designed sites for the mobile Web was created with the goal of helping people connect with each other. You can take your friends from your home computer to your office to any mobile device you have with you when you sign up for an account on Facebook. The Facebook site performs well on everything from the simplest low-end feature phones to the latest smartphones to touch-screen phones, with a special version optimized for each type of phone, as shown in Figure 13-1. Facebook reports that more than 100 million people access their site via the mobile Web, that those users are twice as active as non-mobile users, and that more than 200 mobile operators in 60 countries are trying to make sure that their users can access Facebook on their mobile devices. And yes, of course, Facebook has an iPhone app with additional features.

The premise of this book is that every Web site needs to be optimized for mobile devices, and some may warrant an app as well. Facebook is a great example of a company that does both well.

The team at Facebook understands that mobile technology facilitates a dramatic cultural shift as people rely more and more on cellphones to connect *IRL* (that's *in real life* for those who don't text much). Yes, most still want to get together IRL at least once in awhile, and that's part of why Facebook has become such a popular part of the Internet. The addition of mobility to Facebook makes it easier than ever to stay in touch all the time no matter where you are and to hook up almost anywhere when you're in the same neighborhood.

Figure 13-1:
Facebook
is optimized
for each
phone.

BBC Sends News Around the Globe

www.bbc.com

Serving a diverse international audience, the British Broadcasting Corporation (BBC) recognized earlier than most the importance of creating a mobile version of its Web site that would work on a variety of devices. An early player on the mobile Web, the BBC succeeded in creating one design that looks good on a wide variety of devices — no small feat for a site that's updated around the clock with breaking news. In Figure 13-2, the designs vary across all three types of phones, but they all are quite different from the desktop version. Like most news sites, the front page of BBC.com is packed with stories, photos, and advertising when viewed on a desktop computer.

Figure 13-2:
The BBC design varies from desktop to mobile, and among different phones.

On the mobile phone version, the site is stripped to the bare minimum, with just three tiny photos and links to quickly follow the top stories or navigate to the section that most interests you with just a few clicks. The most dramatic difference between the desktop and mobile version is hard to appreciate in the black and white figures in this book. The desktop version is red, and the mobile version is blue — a popular color among mobile designers because blue displays well on many devices under a wide variety of lighting conditions.

Google Wants to Know Where You Are

www.google.com

Google, the most popular search engine on the Internet, pays close attention to the explosive growth in wireless Web surfing. Google has not only optimized its designs to work well in a variety of devices, but it also produces different search results when you search the mobile site. Although Google guards its search algorithms closely, the search giant favors sites that are optimized for mobile devices when delivering results to mobile phones. In Chapter 2, you find a few tips for optimizing your mobile site to score better in Google and other mobile search engines. (You find the URLs for several other mobile search engines on this book's online Cheat Sheet; see the inside front cover for details.)

In Figure 13-3, you can see that Google's minimalist design requires little adjustment on the mobile Web. Most sites limit the amount of information they present in the mobile version, but Google, king of the We Love Whitespace home page, actually added text to the mobile version that's not on the desktop Web site.

In the iPhone version, you see My Location: Off followed by a Turn On link. If you click the link, Google asks you to confirm that you want to turn on this feature, which uses geo-location technology (either GPS or triangulating via the signals from the cell towers) to enable Google to provide location-specific information when you search.

Anytime you want to collect information through a Web page, especially something as potentially revealing as the exact location and movements of your users, take a lesson from Google (a company that has faced its share of controversies over privacy) and ask permission first.

Figure 13-3:
The Google search engine offers special location options on its mobile site.

Dictionary.com

www.dictionary.com

You can clear off the bookshelves and empty your student backpack because soon you'll have every reference manual you could ever need in the palm of your hand. Start with Dictionary.com (and don't forget Wikipedia, a non-authoritative but still useful site when you want to start exploring a topic, which has also been optimized to display well on mobile devices).

In Figure 13-4, you see the difference in designs at Dictionary.com. In this case, the designers stripped the site to its core function — looking up words. The focus in the mobile version is the search field, and most of the other information visible on the home page of the desktop site can be found only by following links deeper into the mobile version's site.

If you include advertising on your pages, you may want to pay special attention to how Dictionary.com delivers ads. On the RAZR and the BlackBerry, a small banner ad is included in the page design. Although you can't see an ad in the iPhone screenshot, when you open the Dictionary.com site on an iPhone, a full-screen ad loads and then you move on to the home page.

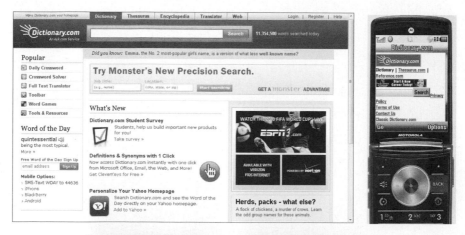

Figure 13-4: Dictionary. com is an example to follow if you want to efficiently include ads on your mobile site.

Discovery Channel Creates a Sense of Wonder on Any Platform

www.discovery.com

From popular television shows, such as *Deadliest Catch, MythBusters,* and *Dirty Jobs,* to games, blogs, and other Internet-only content, the team at Discovery Channel works hard to make sure you can interact with their award-winning content anywhere, anytime. In Figure 13-5, you can see that stripping this highly interactive multimedia site to just the core elements wasn't easy.

Figure 13-5: The Discovery Channel site becomes a bare-bones site that still delivers key content on the mobile platform.

On Discovery mobile, you don't find all the cool features of the desktop version — the main part of the desktop site rotates through a series of full-screen, rich media content related to each of its shows. On the mobile versions, especially on a low-end feature phone, you find a much more limited set of links and very few images, but you can still access key content and keep up with Discovery Channel's most popular shows.

The Wall Street Journal Serves Its Well-Heeled Audience on Any Phone

`www.wsj.com`

Internationally respected as a carefully researched news source on business and the economy, *The Wall Street Journal* (WSJ) was an early player on the mobile Web. The newspaper's readership, made up primarily of business executives and financial experts, serves an audience that's likely to carry the latest in mobile gadgetry.

An unusually high percentage of readers of *The Wall Street Journal* is likely to have BlackBerrys, and the designers created a special version for these smartphones (see Figure 13-6). Like many sites, WSJ delivers the desktop design to the iPhones, also shown in Figure 13-6. The iPhone can display most Web pages without requiring special markup, and many iPhone surfers prefer the desktop version (one of the reasons it's considered good practice to include a link to the desktop site from any mobile version you create). Although the experience isn't as rich, you can still access the WSJ's stories even on a low-end feature phone, as shown in Figure 13-6.

Figure 13-6:
Knowing
its readers
are likely
using a
BlackBerry,
*The Wall
Street
Journal*
offers a spe-
cial site for
those users,
as well as
a nice look
on other
phones.

Share Photos with Anyone on Flickr

`www.flickr.com`

One of the most popular places to share photos on the Internet, Flickr has devised the magic formula to maintain its impressive collection of interactive features while still being accessible from a variety of mobile devices (see Figure 13-7).

From the high-resolution images you can access with a desktop computer to the stripped-down version for feature phones, Flickr makes it as easy to upload photos as it is to download them. Since so many phones now come with cameras, it's a natural fit for Flickr to empower you to share all the snap-shots you take.

Figure 13-7:
The Flickr photo site enables visitors to share photos via any type of phone.

YouTube Brings Video to (and from) the Masses

`www.youtube.com`

Unfortunately, a large percentage of video on the Web is completely inaccessible to mobile devices because it's presented in the Flash video format, which isn't supported on many mobile devices, including the iPhone.

All the more reason to admire YouTube for figuring out how to deliver different versions of its videos, optimized to play well on nearly any mobile device on the planet. In Figure 13-8, you see a video clip from one of author Janine Warner's training videos. Thanks to YouTube, this video plays on the lowly feature phone almost as well as the iPhone.

If you want your videos to display well on a mobile device, uploading them to YouTube and then linking to them from your mobile site is an easy shortcut to ensure that your video looks good to a broad mobile audience. (You can read more about adding multimedia to your mobile designs in Chapter 8.)

Figure 13-8: The YouTube video-sharing site enables visitors to play video on any type of Web-enabled phone.

Checking Flights on American Airlines

www.aa.com

The American Airlines site offers rich, interactive features, including the ability to check your gate while you run through the airport to catch your flight. (Assuming you can juggle your carry-on bags and your phone while you dodge and weave through the airport.)

The *form tag,* which creates search options and other interactive features like the ones at AA.com, works fairly consistently across most mobile devices. But anything you can do to more easily allow visitors to fill out forms, such as offering multiple-choice options instead of requiring users to type a lot of data, makes it easier to interact with your site on a mobile device. (You find a list of form tags supported in mobile markup languages in Chapter 5.)

When you look over the four versions of AA.com, shown in Figure 13-9, note that the mobile versions offer just a few options — the things you're most likely to need if you're about to catch a flight. Note that on the desktop site, making a reservation is the most prominent option on the home page. If you scroll down the page on the mobile versions, you find links that take you to a page where you can make reservations.

When you adapt a site for the mobile Web, determining what content is most useful to someone on a mobile phone is often the most challenging and most important part of the job.

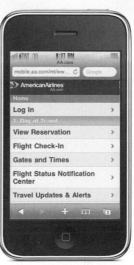

Figure 13-9:
The American Airlines mobile site pares down content to just what visitors need on the go.

Mobile Web Design Blog

www.mobilewebdesignblog.com

Of course your authors' Mobile Web Design blog (see Figure 13-10) is optimized for a wide range of mobile devices. We include the process by which to install and activate a simple plug-in that makes WordPress blogs mobile-friendly in Chapter 9.

For updates, and a list of great online resources, visit the Mobile Web Design blog on your favorite device (or desktop computer).

Figure 13-10:
The Mobile Web Design blog on a desktop or, of course, optimized for mobile devices.

Testing in DeviceAnywhere

Special thanks to the great team at Device Anywhere. We used the DeviceAnywhere online service to test all the sites in this chapter and to take all the screenshots of mobile devices that you find in this book.

DeviceAnywhere makes it possible to access a long list of devices. After you open the device in the DeviceAnywhere software on your desktop computer, you can access any page on the Internet as if you were actually using the phone. You can even make phone calls, play music or games, or send text messages. You can read more about testing sites on mobile devices, and about using DeviceAnywhere, in Chapter 7.

Appendix A

Interviews with Mobile Experts

*I*f writing about the Web is like shooting at a moving target, writing about the mobile Web is like trying to hit a cheetah in full stride. The contradictory claims, promises, criticism, and grandiose world-conquering rhetoric can be hard to sort through. This is why we reached out to high-level mobile experts to get their perspectives on what the mobile Web really is, what it's good for, and where it's headed.

Patrick Collins, CEO, 5th Finger

www.5thfinger.com

The company name — 5th Finger — is a mobile Web pun; it refers to the thumb, which is the digit most people use to tap SMS messages on their smartphones. 5th Finger designs mobile marketing campaigns and sells in-store mobile commerce tools that allow shoppers to check prices and comparison shop.

Q: What are the biggest mistakes people make when getting started with the mobile Web?

Short-term thinking is really dangerous in mobile. Because even an effective iPhone app, when you launch with a three-month test budget and leave it alone, is going to fail. You have to look at your mobile Web presence as an ongoing program to talk to the consumers.

People who come to us are generally pretty passionate about mobile already. In fact, I find a very high correlation between the success of a mobile campaign and the passion of someone who's leading it. Passion is one of the biggest drivers; when you find people [who are already knowledgeable and enthusiastic], that makes creating a marketing campaign a lot easier because the question isn't "Should I do it?" but "What's the best way of locating a certain segment?"

Every week someone comes up to us wanting an app. You can choose to talk the client off the ledge or run with it.

Q: What are some tools you use to help people figure out how they should use the mobile Web?

We approach this question by just trying to understand what a client's objectives are. Often you can use reason and statistics to help them understand why they should or shouldn't go down that route. The most common one is asking them, "Who are your consumers, what are they using, and how are they using it?" Okay, so if they're 50-year-old females, they're not going to be a large proportion of iPhone app users, so you might want to think about that.

In addition to the user base, we look at the existing marketing mix [to see what advertising channels the clients are spending money on at the present time]. If the existing marketing mix has a heavy amount of TV spending, we try to figure out how we can utilize that. If there's a heavy amount of online spending, we figure out how to use that. We find that most clients are at least somewhat attuned to what they can achieve or what mobile can do.

Often, clients have already done the homework, but you also want to take that step back, make sure you get the objectives, and do some basic planning on the fly. The clients we love let us do a planning session with their team. We just get amazing outcomes from that process and really try to understand which divisions and which people in the company view mobile differently. A lot of people approach mobile through the lens of, "Well, we don't do much advertising, not on mobile anyway; we don't have an iPhone app, and therefore, we don't do mobile." But it's quite a lot more than that.

Q: What kinds of missed opportunities just make you cringe?

Well, start with the fact that only one in four of the URLs that went up during the Super Bowl — which, mind you, is $2 million for 30 seconds — were mobile-friendly. When you think about where the people are going to access the site from, that makes absolutely no sense.

People are at Super Bowl parties with their friends, and when they see these ads (which are some of the most-watched ads ever), they hopefully want to follow up. They're going to whip out their mobile phone and do a search, and 75 percent of the time, they're going to find . . . nothing.

What a waste.

We just ran an ad campaign for a major pharmaceutical company during the Oscars. There was a text-to-call action: "Text *this word* to *this number* and your phone automatically dials *this number*." We spent a lot of money setting up the program. When the ad came on, this SMS messaging program was only onscreen for like the final half a second in the bottom-left corner. The ad was in such fine print that you couldn't even see it. Then they said, "Why did we get only 150 entries?"

Niles Lichtenstein, Director, Velti Plc, formerly Managing Director, Ansible

www.ansiblemobile.com

Ansible, Interpublic Group's full service mobile marketing agency, specializes in building mobile Web sites that work across a broad spectrum of mobile devices. Ansible also custom-builds applications and manages mobile marketing and advertising campaigns.

Q: Because you work with apps and mobile sites, which do you think is more useful?

We joke around and say that the iPhone app is like the TV ad. Just like every client wants to see his brand on TV, now everyone wants to see their icon on an iPhone; it's just one of those things. We really do focus on the mobile Web though. Our slogan is "no phone left behind."

If someone is just dead set on having an app, we recommend she builds a mobile Web site that will reach more or less all platforms, and just put an iPhone *stub* (an app that basically just opens a browser and navigates to the mobile Web site) on it. That gives you the app you want and a way you can actually scale it relatively well across different platforms. Then you reach that larger audience.

Q: What are the various levels of experience you can build to use the mobile Web, starting with the cheapest ones that don't require everyone to have an expensive phone to access the site?

We're working with one auto company and with dealerships closing and cutting back on staff; their questions were, "How do we still service the customers; how do we get people information about the cars around them when they're on the lot?"

If the customer has a text plan, he can text a code from the sticker in the car. The phone then rings, and an automated voice response message "walks" him around the car and explains everything in it. That's just with your most basic phone.

If the customer has a phone that can access the mobile Web, you can actually pull up the mobile Web, see the car videos, look at some of the specs, get some information, and enter your e-mail for a sign-up brochure.

If that customer has a phone with a compass (more phones have those these days), we can kick the experience up to the next level. We can put in an augmented reality layer so that while the customer walks around the car, messages pop up that say, `this is a hemi engine`, and so forth.

The idea that more people can participate if we actually think about it and go through that planning session is pretty important. There are ways to get it done.

Q: What's been your biggest recent success with a mobile Web site?

We recently launched Intel's corporate site, and during the Super Bowl, the commercial launched where the Android comes up to the lunch table. We knew that not many people in the middle of a Super Bowl party were going to whip out their laptops. But still, we set a record that day for the highest total of people looking at the Intel site — for that day — because people were using their mobile phones, looking and searching for Intel, trying to find the commercials.

We worked hard to prepare the site for that traffic. We knew there was this audience — a large audience — that was going to be captivated by the Super Bowl and was going to look for the site.

If they had all gone to this Intel site and had gotten redirected to a crappy situation, maybe it's so commonplace that it's okay. But you lose that engagement. You lose that whole entire opportunity to capture the conversation past that Super Bowl ad.

Ajay Luthra, Senior Director of Advanced Technology, Home and Networks Mobility, Motorola

www.motorola.com

Motorola's RAZR phone was a breakthrough device in the early '90s, and is still the most sold handset in the world. Motorola's global presence gives it insight into trends outside the U.S. market, and it is working hard to build smartphones, like the Droid, that are designed to take advantage of the mobile Web.

Q: What are some of the things Motorola is learning from the global market that would surprise people in the U.S.?

Our world is changing at an exponential rate; many of us thought we knew where it was going, but we always get surprised. There are 4 babies born every second in the world, but there are 32 mobile devices sold every second.

That's right. Mobile devices are growing at eight times the speed of human population.

And more and more phones can access the mobile Web and play multimedia. Most of our old business was more like broadcasting. When we got very excited about interactivity, it was video on demand. That's about it. Nowadays we get excited about capturing video and then sending it and interacting with the people after we send around the video.

I still remember quite clearly when I was watching the announcement of a new Pope on TV. Thousands of people were watching in St. Peter's Square, which is thousands of years old. And in that historic spot, at that historic moment, thousands of hands went up with their cellphones — to take pictures.

Q: All this mobile interactivity is nice, but what does that mean to companies that want to make money off the mobile Web?

How content will be monetized on mobile still isn't clear. We talk with our customers all the time; sometimes it's a very heated discussion. One way to monetize is through a subscription system; the other is advertisement.

But good gosh. How many advertisements can one person see in one day and keep in one's head? It reminds me of those travels where I go through 20 airports and when I come back, I have no idea whether I was in Bangkok or France — where in the world was I?

There's the same problem emerging now with advertising. I see so many that I've become like my kid who automatically tunes me out. The only time I pay attention is when someone texts me to say, "That was a cool ad," and I say, "Well, let me go back and see."

I could easily say that we'll send more ads, but we're getting saturated. So people are trying to work on subscription models.

We're seeing a slow but very steady shift in the way that people think about advertisements on TV. It all started with DVRs that allow you to skip all the ads. You get used to skipping the ads and boring parts and finishing the whole thing in 20 minutes.

So the issue has come that if they aren't watching the ads, what's the worth of them?

Q: What are some other trends you see in the rest of the world that haven't hit the U.S. yet?

We're seeing more companies working to embed the ad inside the content — either on the boundary or literally inside the content so that you can't skip over it [unlike what the TiVo and other DVRs allow users to do with TV ads]. We tried a lot of interactive things, but when you're watching TV, it doesn't work too much or too well.

People aren't really that interested in seeing an ad and then going and buying the thing, unless you're watching a really boring program. And if you're watching a boring a program, why are you watching that program? So we've tried a lot of things — but it hasn't been too successful so far.

We see a lot more adoption of video being distributed, especially in Japan. Even in a country like India, I was surprised. About five years back, I saw a cricket match on a cellphone in India. We're seeing a lot more there than in the U.S. or Europe.

When people ask me why mobile is moving so much slower in the U.S. than it is in Europe, I say, "Well there are a lot more lawyers here in the U.S. than in Europe. There are a lot more silos here because of that."

In India, there are even bigger silos. The market there has grown more like a tangled vine in which regional warlords have created their own network, and so there's this jumble of disconnected networks trying to come together.

Thomas Ellsworth, CEO, GoTV

www.gotvnetworks.com

GoTV specializes in delivering video content to mobile phones; it offers the content through both the mobile Web and branded apps. Companies trying to crack the "TV anywhere" puzzle face the steepest challenges in the mobile content realm.

Q: What are some of the changes in the market that make it feasible to build a business out of delivering video to mobile phones?

The best estimates I've seen say that in the U.S., 15 percent of the market uses smartphones, with about 280 million subscribers. We have a long way to go with smartphones, but we've gotten a lot of heat and buzz, thanks to the iPhone changing the game for everyone else. Google reacted very well with their Android. Now you have a platform that you can *monetize,* or charge a small subscription for.

So start with that. Only 15 percent of the U.S. carries a smartphone. And 33 percent of that is *enterprise-class* BlackBerrys, meaning those users may or may not be allowed to buy applications and other things because they're salespeople at a pharmaceutical company or working for the government, and their rate plan doesn't allow them to buy ringtones, songs, or anything else. If I'm being generous, I'll say that two-thirds of the smartphones can even run apps or other content. That's about 10 percent of the mobile subscribers.

With only that, think of all the heat and buzz we've generated in the last 18 months. We're just getting warmed up with how effectively priced smartphones with unlimited data plans allow the consumers to do something.

If you look back on the last year only, there have been some starts and stops. But if you look forward, you have huge, huge handset makers that are speaking in the hallways at industry conferences. They say that by 2013, we'll be 50 percent smartphone platforms, dominated by Android. Now, you step back and think that's three years from now. Right now, when you look back at video advertising, 2009 was a year of testing, emergence, and rumors. But from this point forward, you have audiences.

If you have great content and an audience that's willing to pay for it, you have an audience that an advertiser would be willing to pay to be a part of.

Q: What kind of advertising works on video on mobile phones?

For video ads on the mobile, you have to take a cue from television networks that have done a really good job with the floating network promos in the lower-thirds of the screen. You also have to put the ad in context — an ad for Wrigley's 5 gum probably doesn't fit on Discovery Health, where there's a quick clip from a dentist talking about the danger of cavities. So the context has to be there.

A video ad needs to create a positive, strong impression without being a negative, interruptive impression. To do so, you can integrate the sponsor into the programming, or you can respect the consumer while making a strong impression with a seven-second [ad] at the beginning and maybe a four-second [ad] at the end. There's a variety of things you can do to test [what kinds of ads work best].

A ton of phones can deliver a really nice experience to the user. It's up to content creators and advertisers to make effective impressions and ensure that we don't cause a negative effect on the viewer or advertiser. You don't want transitive property of blame, for the consumer to say, "Aw, not another ad for Bud Light. I hate those guys now."

Q: So is there also room to charge people to watch video on their phones? Sort of like a mobile pay-per-view model?

The notion that the Internet is free is a false notion. People know that they pay a monthly recurring charge to get their mobile access. And on top of that, they pay some dollars to get the Wall Street Journal application, and then there will be ads nested around that and some of them will be video. We're all going to experiment, but the consumer inherently understands that ads and a subscription are part of the game.

I wish it was a year from now, and we had another 20 million people buying applications with smartphones they love, hopefully under a 3G umbrella and Wi-Fi at home, that provide them just wonderful access to do whatever it is that they want to do.

Our biggest challenge is time. We wish it'd go a little faster because we've spent four years preparing GoTV and building a business in this space. And now we're in a great spot and are just trying to drive forward.

Soren Schafft, General Manager of North America, Fox Mobile Distribution, a Unit of Fox Mobile Group (FMG)

`http://foxmobile.com`

Fox Mobile Group takes the content from all the Fox properties (such as Fox News, 20th Century Fox movies, FX Network, and so on) and decides which pieces are appropriate for delivery via the mobile platform.

Q: Is there any generation gap between older users and kids who have grown up attached to their mobile phones?

I was talking to a neighbor, and he was complaining about how many text messages his daughter sends. So I tried to console him; I told him that our research shows that girls in that age group do a lot of texting. How many did she send? He said, "700." I said, well, we see that kind of usage in Scandinavia; some girls hit that every month.

He said, "That was yesterday."

Kids don't watch TV anymore. They watch the Internet; they watch short-form videos. They do a lot of social networking and online games. The way they engage and experience content is really different. So we have a studio that creates content, and we do short-form series.

When we show the sizzle reels (short teasers that show off the best moments of the shows) for these series to our staff, the younger viewers have completely different tastes from what I would've expected.

Q: How do you pick and choose what content you try to move into the mobile realm?

It depends on who you are and what your objectives are. For a number of content creators, it makes sense to do only an iPhone and Android app. For others, it makes sense to create a broad-based inventory for as many devices as you can and to get repeat users to that inventory so you can monetize that through advertising, cross-selling, and upselling.

It depends on the type of content you have, the type of distribution reach you have, and how you want to take advantage of the core assets you have as a company.

Within five years, we're going to see content that was originally created for a mobile phone move up the chain and become a hit sitcom.

Q: How does Fox plan on monetizing its content on the mobile platform?

I think if you look at where the revenues are generated, it's all about usability, user experience, and engagement. Those are real key issues. If you're engaged in some service that brings you closer to a brand, something that you enjoy, or something you are interested in, that is a value. In that case, advertising isn't a detriment.

If you're into the more advanced services, some of the programs we're putting together have the advertising mixed in with the programming — similar to what you see on *30 Rock,* where it's just contextually integrated.

What we're trying to do is contextual integration of experiences where users are, based on what things they like to do, and engagement of users in the world and environment that they enjoy. In terms of growing the business and engaging customers, that's really the thing to focus on.

Greg Pinter, Founder/Director, NetInformer

www.xtracoupons.com

Mobile coupons are billed as "the coupon you never forget at home" because they live on your cellphone. NetInformer's product, known as *Xtra! mobile coupons,* works to make sending coupons to phones as easy as opening envelopes that arrive in the mail.

Q: Is there really a market for coupons on mobile phones?

Obviously, I think the mobile Web is the wave of the future, and we've seen strong indications that that's the case. To back that up, the story of one of our customers — Shoe Station — comes to mind. Shoe Station is an online and brick-and-mortar shoe store in the South. We added mobile coupons to their existing TV and newspaper ads.

They saw a great big turnaround. People walked in with these mobile coupons on their phones. Shoe Station came back to us within two days and said, "We want to continue with the coupon because it's so phenomenal." Their database now has more than 5,000 people that they can send mobile coupons to.

All this can be geo-targeted to people in a state, in a zip code. We're working on targeting people who are walking down a specific block, but for right now, most of our clients seem comfortable with just getting as specific as zip codes, which fit in with the direct-mail paradigm that they're familiar with.

Q: We keep hearing about targeting — is it really that big a deal?

The future looks like this: Apps will allow merchants to know when you walk into a mall and if you've opted-in previously to receive special offers, and then, these apps will send special offers right to your phone as you walk by. I don't want to get blasted like in the movie *Minority Report,* but when I walk into the mall, I want to get the offer of the day from one of the stores that I'm interested in.

You're going to be tying information about the things that you're interested in to what you see so that you can filter the things that you don't want. That's going to drive up the value of that advertising; publishers will make more money, and the consumer will be a lot happier because she's not getting bombarded with stuff she doesn't care about.

Q: But is any of this applicable to the average, small, or mid-sized business?

Well, the restaurant down the street is a client of ours. The dad owns the restaurant, and the son runs it daily. Perfect small business snapshot. One day, the dad comes in to check how the new mobile coupon campaign is doing and asks, "How many coupons did we give away today?"

It was $700. The dad's jaw dropped; he almost had a heart attack. But the son said, "Yeah, but we had a $10,000 day instead of $5,000."

The dad shakes himself, and then says, "Well, okay. I don't mind giving away $700 if I made an extra $5,000."

Q: Where do you stand on the whole mobile Web versus device-specific apps battle?

My take is that mobile advertising is going to have to reside both on the mobile site and the mobile apps designed for the individual devices. On one side, the Google model is willing to put everything into the cloud (that is, all the content and the ads exist only on internet servers). You put out a book-marked badge that brings the coupons into whatever site you're on via the mobile Web.

But depending on the device, I think in the near-term, it'll be easier to bring up an app. If you're looking for ValPak to send you a package in the mail once a month, you know where to look for that. That'll be like the app.

When you get down to it, there's not much different that can be done with an app than can be done with a Web page.

Chris Cunningham, Co-Founder and CEO, appssavvy

www.appssavvy.com

The runaway success of Apple's App Store has made having your very own custom-built application the first thing that people want on the mobile Web. At the center of this maelstrom are companies like appssavvy, which has learned crucial lessons from the work it's done for major companies.

Q: How do you deal with people who just want an app because everyone else seems to have one?

What we try to do is take a step back and answer the following questions:

- ✔ Why do you want to get into this space?
- ✔ Are you planning on supporting it for a while?
- ✔ Do you have content to provide users?

To bring a brand or company to mobile, our advice is don't look at mobile as just mobile; look at it as an extension of the platform.

Because mobile is daunting and overwhelming, I have to educate my clients and my colleagues on it. Mobile is really just an extension; it's just another platform to leverage. A lot of what we do is the education process because so much of this is so new.

Q: What has been the biggest evolution that you've seen happen on the mobile Web?

The way that the Internet has supported itself so far is through the banner ad. You're supposed to click the banner that some media agency displays that's hopefully targeted and maybe has a rich media component. You then go to a Web site that some creative shop spent millions of dollars building.

That model is just broken; it doesn't make any sense. People don't want to go to Web sites to look at content. They want to hang out with their friends.

Prior to smartphones, before the Android and iPhone, there was really nothing there as far as the mobile Web. There was nothing to be excited about from a mobile perspective, but that's changed drastically. They are providing a true value, a true resource for people. To see a brand come with such a strong presence, that looks beautiful, shows just how far mobile has come and how much opportunity there is.

Q: What are some of the big challenges of building an app that you don't get with the mobile Web?

The thing to remember is that the problems with integrating all your content into an app are bigger. On a Web site, if you want to change and integrate a piece, you just change it and upload it, and it's live.

With Apple, if we want to significantly modify the interstitial [ads that appear between content in applications], we have to go through an Apple approval process, which can take anywhere from one week to three weeks. So you have to build in at least a month. You also have to factor in the amount of time it takes to get your advertisers on board, which can take 30–90 days or a year. Our largest advertiser took a year to develop and cultivate.

Right now, everyone keeps talking about Apple and the iPhone because that's where designers and developers can go to make a business and generate revenue. Android is making a surge, and although developers had ignored it, it's starting to get traction. Maybe in the future Android will dominate, but right now, the truth is Apple is going to be the dominant player for the foreseeable future.

Mobile should always be part of a multi-platform strategy. All the content should be promoted across every platform you can to increase adoption and usage.

Tom Limongello, Head of Business Development, Crisp Wireless

www.crispwireless.com

Crisp Wireless builds advertising products for both apps and the mobile Web and also has its own technology to allow companies to track how well their ad campaigns are working.

Q: Why have you concentrated on the mobile Web rather than on apps?

The thing with apps is that after the first month, the amount of time spent with them by the average user just plummets. However, the mobile Web grows and grows. This year, 30 percent of the people in the U.S. use the mobile Web regularly, and that's going to go up to 35 percent in 2011. As you look at Nielsen stats, by 2011, more than 50 percent of the U.S. is going to be using smartphones. iPads and all the other types of devices will only contribute to the growth of the mobile Web.

So, what are the top mobile Web sites? Obviously Google, Yahoo!, Facebook, and portals are huge on the mobile Web. But you may not know that The Weather Channel, CNN.com, and MocoSpace are also huge. This is some tremendous reach. Other than maybe Pandora and Facebook, no apps have the kind of traffic that a good mobile Web site will have.

Q: What are some of the things that you're doing on the mobile Web to compete with the functions that apps offer?

Most people think that the most engaging ads and content for wireless have to be within applications. But we've built ads that can run on the mobile Web, such as the photo gallery for Ford that looks like Cover Flow in iTunes. Or we have an in-banner, data input, full screen ad for the Hampton Inn in which you can actually book a room. If you go to CNN.com's mobile site, you can see an Intel ad that actually allows you to drag and drop the features you want in your new CPU chip into an area that has multiple-choice questions appear within that ad.

We also offer Adhesion, which is a happy medium between a full-screen takeover and a standard MMA (Mobile Marketing Association — the group that sets the standards for the sizes of mobile advertisements) banner.

There's nowhere near as much flexibility in applications as there is on the mobile Web. On the mobile Web, if I want to make a change to my site, I can make it tomorrow. I don't need to go through Apple, Google, or whoever it might be.

Q: Can you provide an example of one of the sticking points with apps?

When applications are provisioned, they have a *software development kit* (SDK; a list of rules and processes for building the app) for serving ads and rendering ads within the application. That SDK is rigid.

The SDK doesn't allow expansions beyond the 350 pixel by 50 pixel placement, it doesn't allow full-screen, and it doesn't allow other things [like changing the multimedia or interactivity]. So if an advertiser comes along and wants to do something innovative on the ESPN.com application, they'd have to modify the SDK and modify the application to support new and innovative ad units.

Q: Is anyone bridging the gap between apps and the mobile Web?

Right now, the ones that are doing the best are the ones who aren't winning the race, such as Palm. They're probably the closest to app-mobile Web convergence that you can get.

You're actually seeing the ability to basically download a Web site and have features enabled with HTML5 so that you can do the things that you're supposed to be able to do only within an app. Eventually, you'll just have Web features built into something like an app wrapper.

Users don't like to be taken off the site that they're on. The more seamless you can make that transition from app to mobile Web and back again, the more likely that the user is going to stick around. Because of the load times, crashes, and the inconvenience of getting back to where they were, users usually abandon the process.

Appendix B

Optimizing Graphics for the Mobile Web

• •

*M*aking sure your images download quickly is even more important for the mobile Web than for sites designed for desktop computers. If you're familiar with using a graphics-editing program, such as Adobe Photoshop or Fireworks, to create graphics for the Web, you're a step ahead. If not, in this appendix, you find out how to convert images for the mobile Web, discover the best image formats to use, and discuss how to optimize images for faster download times.

We use Adobe Photoshop CS5 in the examples in this appendix, but because the features we use are nearly identical in both Photoshop and Photoshop Elements, you can use these same instructions to complete these tasks in Photoshop Elements. (See the nearby sidebar "Comparing Web graphics programs," in this appendix, to read more about the differences.)

Creating and Optimizing Web Graphics

The most important thing to keep in mind when creating images for the Web — especially the mobile Web — is that you want to *optimize your* images to make your file sizes as small as possible so that they download as quickly as possible.

How you optimize an image depends on how the image was created and whether you want to save it as a JPEG, PNG, or GIF. You find instructions for optimizing images with Photoshop in the sections that follow, but the bottom line is this: No matter what program, format, or optimization technique you choose, your biggest challenge is finding the best balance between small file size and good image quality. Essentially, the more you optimize, the faster the image downloads, but the compression and color reduction techniques used to optimize images can make them look terrible if you go too far.

Comparing Web graphics programs

Most professional designers strongly prefer Adobe Photoshop, although we have to say we've been impressed with Photoshop Elements, which is a "light" version but offers many of the same features for a fraction of the cost. The following is a list of some of the most popular image-editing programs on the market. All these image programs are available for Mac and Windows:

✔ **Adobe Photoshop:** (www.adobe.com/photoshop) By far the most popular image-editing program on the market, Photoshop is a widely used standard among graphics professionals. With Photoshop, you can create original artwork, edit and enhance photographs, and so much more. Photoshop has a wealth of powerful painting and selection tools, special effects, and filters that enable you to create images far beyond what you can capture on film or create with many other illustration programs. Photoshop includes special tools for optimizing Web graphics, and because Photoshop and Dreamweaver are both Adobe productions, switching between the two is easy.

✔ **Adobe Photoshop Elements:** (www.adobe.com/elements) If you don't need all the bells and whistles offered in the full-blown version of Photoshop, Photoshop Elements is a remarkably powerful program

— for about a sixth of the price. If you're a professional designer, you're best served by Photoshop. But if you're a hobbyist or small business owner and want to create good-looking images without the high cost and learning curve of a professional graphics program, Elements is a great deal and well-suited to creating Web graphics. Like Photoshop, Photoshop Elements includes special tools for optimizing graphics for the Web.

✔ **Adobe Fireworks:** (www.adobe.com/fireworks) Fireworks was one of the first image-editing programs designed to create and edit Web graphics. Originally created by Macromedia, the program is now part of the Adobe Web suite and is fully integrated with Dreamweaver. Fireworks gives you everything you need to create, edit, and output Web graphics, all in one well-designed product. Although Fireworks lacks many of the advanced image-editing capabilities of Photoshop, Fireworks shines when creating Web graphics.

If you have an Internet connection and want to do basic image editing for free, visit www.gimp.org or www.photoshop.com/express. Both sites let you edit and optimize images online without purchasing a software program.

As a general rule, do any editing, such as adjusting contrast, retouching, or combining images, before you reduce their size or optimize them because you want to work with the highest resolution possible when you edit. Also, resize an image before you optimize it. You find instructions for resizing an image in the following section and instructions for optimizing in the sections "Optimizing JPEG images for the Web" and "Optimizing images in GIF and PNG formats," later in this appendix.

Resizing graphics and photos

Resizing is important for two reasons: The images must be small enough to display well on a mobile screen, and you want them to download quickly to a user's phone or other mobile device. The smaller the image is, the faster it downloads.

Although you can change the display size of an image in a Web page by altering the height and width settings in Dreamweaver, you get much better results if you change the physical size of the image in a graphics editor, such as Photoshop.

When you alter an image's height and width in the HTML code (via the Height and Width settings in Dreamweaver), you simply instruct a Web browser to display the image in a different size. Unfortunately, browsers don't do a good job resizing images because browsers don't change the image itself but just force it to fit in the assigned space when the browser loads the page. If you set the image to display larger than its actual size, the image is likely to look fuzzy or distorted because the image doesn't contain enough pixels for all the details to look good in a larger size. If you set the code to display the image smaller than it is — a more likely scenario on the mobile Web — the image may look squished, and you're requiring that your users download an image that's larger than necessary, making them wait longer and using more of their bandwidth allowance (which not only costs time on the mobile Web, it can cost your visitors money for data usage as well).

Reducing an image's size for use on the Web requires two steps. First, reduce the resolution of an image, which changes the number of pixels in the image. When you work with images for the Web, you want to reduce the resolution to 72 pixels per inch (or ppi). (If you're wondering why 72, see the sidebar that's appropriately named "Why only 72 ppi?") Second, reduce the image's physical size by reducing its dimensions. You want to size your images to fit well in a mobile browser window and to work within the design of your site.

Follow these steps to lower the resolution and reduce the image size in Photoshop (in Photoshop Elements or Fireworks, you follow a similar process, but the specific steps may vary):

1. **With an image open in Photoshop, choose Image⇨Resize.**

   The Image Size dialog box opens, as shown in Figure B-1.

   If you don't want your original image to lose quality (or you just want to play it safe), make a copy of your image and resize the *copy* for your Web site.

TIP

2. **To change the resolution of your image, deselect the Resample Image check box at the bottom of the Image Size dialog box.**

   For best results, always deselect the Resample Image check box when you change the resolution.

3. **Highlight the number in the Resolution field and replace it by typing** 72.

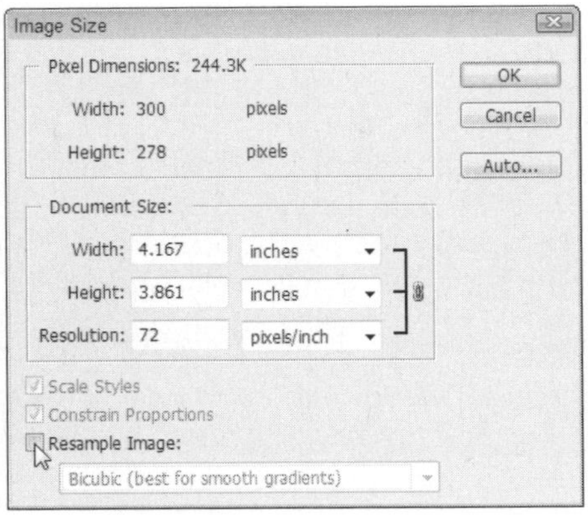

Figure B-1:
To best pre-
pare your
images for
the Web,
change the
resolution
to 72 ppi so
the images
download
faster.

Image Size

Pixel Dimensions: 244.3K

Width: 300 pixels

Height: 278 pixels

OK

Cancel

Auto...

Document Size:

Width: 4.167 inches

Height: 3.861 inches

Resolution: 72 pixels/inch

☑ Scale Styles
☑ Constrain Proportions
☐ Resample Image:
Bicubic (best for smooth gradients)

4. **Select the Resample Image check box.**

   With the Resample Image check box deselected, you can't change the pixel dimensions, so it must be selected when you change the image size.

5. **Enter a height and width for the image in the Height and Width fields, respectively.**

   As shown in Figure B-2, we reduced the image size to 278 pixels wide.

6. **(Optional) Select the Constrain Proportions check box at the bottom of the dialog box.**

   Any changes you make to the height automatically affect the width (and vice versa) to ensure that the image proportions remain constant. We prefer to work this way, but if you want to change the image and not maintain the proportions, you can deselect this check box.

7. **Click OK to resize the image.**

   If you want to return the image to its previous size, choose Edit↪Undo. Beware that when you save the image, the changes are permanent.

Why only 72 ppi?

When you save images for the Web, you save them at a resolution of 72 ppi. Most computer monitors and mobile device screens display no more than 72 ppi, so any resolution higher than that is wasted on the Web because you'd make your visitors download more pixels than they can see. Although some of the new smart-phones, including the iPhone 4, have higher image resolutions, most designers still set the ppi to 72 for the mobile Web. However, if you want to print an image, you want all the pixels you can get, usually at least 200 ppi or higher, which is why most images you see on the Web look terrible if you try to print them in a large size.

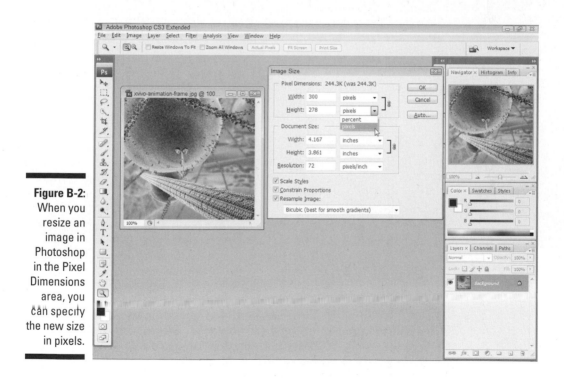

Figure B-2: When you resize an image in Photoshop in the Pixel Dimensions area, you can specify the new size in pixels.

Using Actions to automatically resize images in Photoshop

If you're only working on a few images, resizing and optimizing each image individually enables you to find the best settings for each image. However, if you're working with a bunch of images and you need to resize them into multiple different sizes, the minor benefits of optimizing the settings for each image are probably not worth the time. That's where Photoshop's Actions (macro scripts that automate a series of steps) can really come in handy.

The following steps walk you through creating a macro to automatically resize images in Photoshop:

1. **Save the images you want resized into a separate folder on your desktop.**

   The macro resizes all the images in any one folder. Unless you want all the photos on your site given this treatment, it's best to work with only the ones that you want to deal with now. Consider creating an Images to Be Resized folder (or name it something like that) so that it's easy to find when you go through these steps.

2. **Create a new folder for the resized images.**

   Consider naming the folders according to the width of the photos so you can more easily keep track of which photos go with each version of your mobile sites. In this example, we name the folder 300 and save it in the Golden Gate folder to keep track of a collection of images of the Golden Gate Bridge that we resize to 300-pixels wide.

3. **Launch Photoshop.**

   You can use other image-editing programs, but the steps may vary.

4. **Choose Window⇨Actions.**

   The Actions panel opens.

5. **From the bottom row of the Actions panel, click the Create New Action button.**

   The Create New Action button is the second button from the right, just to the left of the trash can.

6. **Type a name for your new macro.**

   We suggest using the pixel size in the title so you can quickly find and use this macro later. For example, we call this macro Resize to 300px.

7. **Click OK.**

The red record button appears at the bottom of the Actions panel. You are now recording.

TIP

This step starts recording the macro, which means that every action you perform is saved so that it can be replicated by the computer when it runs the macro. From this point on, if you make a mistake, don't panic! Just stop running the macro by clicking the stop button, return to this point, and start over.

8. **Choose File⇨Open and then select one of the images you want to resize.**

   The image opens in the workspace.

9. **Choose Image⇨Image Size.**

   The Image Size dialog box opens.

10. **Enter the new width or height you want in the Width and Height fields, respectively.**

    To maintain the proportion of your images, make sure that the Scale Styles, Constrain Proportions, and Resample Image check boxes are selected, and you need only to enter a height or a width, but not both.

11. **Click OK and then choose File⇨Save for Web and Devices.**

    The Save for Web and Devices dialog box opens.

12. **Specify the settings you want for the folder of images you're converting.**

    You find instructions for optimizing images in the "Saving images for the Web: The basics," section later in this chapter as well as in the sections on optimizing JPEGs and GIFs.

13. **Click the Save button and then select the folder where you want to save your resized, optimized images.**

    In this example, we select the Golden Gate 300 folder we created in Step 2.

14. **Click OK and then choose File⇨Close.**

    Including Close in the macro is important because you don't want to overload your computer's RAM by having all these image files littering your desktop.

15. **Click the Stop button in the Actions panel.**

    The Stop button is square and is the button farthest to the left on the bottom of the Actions panel. (You can relax because the computer no longer records your every move.)

16. **Choose File⇨Automate⇨Batch.**

    The Batch dialog box opens, as shown in Figure B-3.

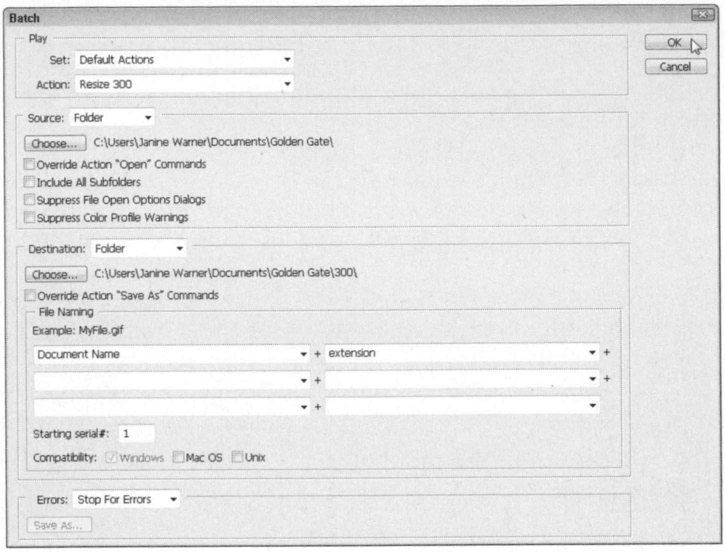

Figure B-3:
The
Photoshop
Batch dialog
box includes
many
options you
can specify
when creat-
ing Actions.

17. Choose the macro you just created from the Action drop-down list.

Many other macros come with Photoshop and are included in this drop-down list.

18. From the Source drop-down list, choose Folder, and then click the Choose button below Source and select the folder that contains the images you want to resize.

19. In the Destination drop-down list, choose Folder, and then click the Choose button and select the folder where you want the automatically resized images to be saved.

Again, we select the folder named 300 (which we created and saved in the Golden Gate folder in Step 2).

The rest of the settings in this dialog box are optional. If the macro doesn't run smoothly — for example, if it hesitates when opening the images or warns you that you're changing the color profile — you might solve problems by selecting the Suppress File Open Options Dialogs check box or the Suppress Color Profile Warnings check box.

20. Click OK to run the macro.

Photoshop automatically opens each image and executes the recorded steps. If your computer is really fast, this is like a slide show for hummingbirds; if it's a little slow (or if you have a large number of high-resolution images to process), this might be a good time to get a nice cup of tea.

After you create an Action, you can use it over and over again, simply by specifying different folders of images to be resized.

Choosing the best image format

One of the most common questions about images for the Web concerns when to use GIF, PNG, or JPEG. Table B-1 provides the simple answer.

You can use transparency in both the GIF or PNG format, a great trick for making the background of an image invisible so that it seems to "float on a page." Unfortunately, not all mobile devices support transparency in GIF or PNG files. You can still use transparency, and it will work on many mobile devices, including the latest smartphones, but if you do use transparency, we recommend you design your pages so that they still look okay, and are readable, if the background color is displayed.

Table B-1	Image Formats for the Web
Format	*Best Usage*
GIF (.gif)	For line art (such as one- or two-color logos), simple drawings, animations, and basically any image that has no gradients or blends. The GIF format also supports transparency.
PNG (.png)	PNG generally produces better-looking images with smaller file sizes than GIF for the same kinds of limited-color images. Most mobile devices support the PNG format, but some older feature phones only support GIFs. Before you choose this format, make sure that your target audience can support it. The PNG format also supports transparency.
JPEG (.jpg or .jpeg)	JPEG is the best format for colorful, complex images (such as photographs); images containing gradients or color blends; and any other images with millions of colors.

Saving images for the Web: The basics

If you're new to saving images for the Web, the following basics can help you get the best results from your files, your image-editing program, and ultimately, your Web pages. You can

✔ **Convert an image from any format into the GIF, PNG, or JPEG format.** For example, turn all your TIF, BMP, and PSD image files into a Web-friendly file format.

✔ **Optimize images that are already in GIF, PNG, or JPEG format.** Even if your files are already in a Web-friendly format, following the instructions later in this appendix for optimizing images with Adobe's Save for Web dialog box further reduces their file sizes for faster download over the mobile Web.

✔ **Make image edits before you optimize.** When you edit, using the highest quality image possible is always best. Make sure to do all your editing, sharpening, and resizing before you use the Save for Web option. Similarly, if you want to make further changes to an image after you optimize it, you achieve the best results if you go back to a higher-resolution version of the image rather than editing the version that's been optimized for the Web. (When you use the Save for Web & Devices feature, Photoshop creates a new copy of your image and leaves the original unchanged.)

Optimizing JPEG images for the Web

JPEG is the best choice for optimizing continuous-tone images, such as photographs and images with many colors or gradients. When you optimize a JPEG, you can make the file size smaller by applying compression. The more compression, the smaller the image, but if you compress the image too much, the image can look terrible. The trick is finding the right balance, which you discover in this section.

If you have a digital photograph or another image that you want to prepare for the Web, follow these steps to optimize and save it in Photoshop (in Photoshop Elements or Fireworks, the process is similar, but the specific steps may vary):

1. **With the image open in Photoshop, choose File⇨Save for Web & Devices (or File⇨Save for Web).**

   The Save for Web & Devices dialog box appears.

2. **In the top-left corner of the dialog box, click either the 2-Up or 4-Up tab to display multiple versions of the same image for easy side-by-side comparison.**

   In the example shown in Figure B-4, we clicked the 2-Up tab, which shows the original image on the left and a preview of the same image as it will appear with the specified settings on the right. (If you're working with a horizontal image, the previews appear one above the other.) The 4-Up tab, as the name implies, displays four versions for comparison.

3. **On the right side of the window, just below the Preset drop-down list, choose JPEG from the Optimized File Format drop-down list (see Figure B-4).**

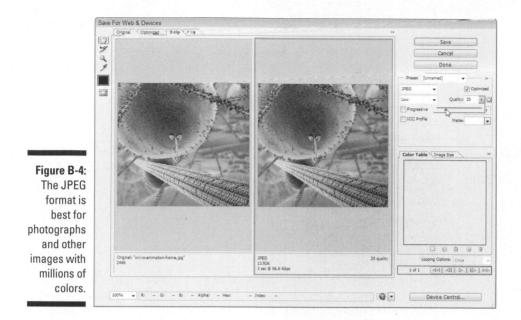

Figure B-4:
The JPEG
format is
best for
photographs
and other
images with
millions of
colors.

4. **Set the compression quality.**

   Use the preset options Low, Medium, High, Very High, or Maximum from the Compression Quality drop-down list. Or use the Quality slider just below the Quality field to make more precise adjustments (see Figure B-4). Lowering the quality reduces the file size and makes the image download more quickly, but if you lower this number too much, the image looks blurry and blotchy.

   Photoshop uses a compression scale of 0–100 for JPEGs in this dialog box, with *0* the lowest possible quality (the highest amount of compression and the smallest file size) and *100* the highest possible quality (the least amount of compression and the biggest file size). Low, Medium and High represent compression values of 10, 30, and 60, respectively.

5. **Specify other settings as desired (the compression quality and file format are the most important settings).**

6. **Click the Save button.**

   The Save Optimized As dialog box opens.

7. **Enter a name for the image and save it into the images folder in your Web site folder.**

   Photoshop saves the optimized image as a copy of the original and leaves the original open in the main Photoshop work area.

8. **Repeat these steps for each image you want to optimize as a JPEG.**

At the bottom of the image preview in the Save for Web & Devices dialog box, Photoshop includes an estimate of the time required for the image to download at the specified connection speed. In the example shown in Figure B-4, the estimate is 3 seconds at 56.6 Kbps. As you adjust the compression settings, the size of the image changes and the download estimate adjusts automatically. You can change the connection speed used to make this calculation by clicking the small arrow just to the right of the connection speed and using the drop-down list to choose another option, such as 256 Kbps for Cable Modem speed, but I prefer to keep this set to a lower speed, such as 56.6 Kbps to better reflect the lower connection speeds of many mobile phone users. Use this estimate as a guide to help you decide how much you need to optimize each image.

Optimizing images in GIF and PNG formats

If you're working with a graphic, such as a logo, cartoon character, or drawing that can be displayed in 256 colors or less, your best bet is to use the PNG format and reduce the total number of colors used in the image as much as possible to reduce the file size. (If you're concerned about visitors using very old mobile phones, use GIF instead.)

To help make up for the degradation in image quality that can happen when colors are removed, GIF and PNG use a dithering trick. *Dithering* involves alternating pixels in a checkerboard-like pattern to create subtle color variations, even with a limited color palette. The effect can smooth the image's edges and make it appear to have more colors than it actually does.

To convert an image to GIF or PNG in Photoshop, follow these steps (in Photoshop Elements or Fireworks, the process is similar, but the specific steps may vary):

1. **With the image open in Photoshop, choose File⇨Save for Web & Devices (or File⇨Save for Web).**

   The Save for Web & Devices dialog box appears.

2. **In the top-left corner of the dialog box, click the 2-Up or 4-Up tab to display multiple versions of the same image for easy side-by-side comparison.**

   In the example shown in Figure B-5, we chose 4-Up, which makes it possible to view the original image (displayed at the top of the dialog box) and three different previews of the same image.

3. **Select a preview image to begin changing its settings.**

   Changing the preview images in the 4-Up view enables you to compare an image with up to four color settings, as shown in Figure B-5.

4. **On the right side of the dialog box, just below the Preset drop-down list, choose GIF or PNG from the Optimized File Format drop-down list.**

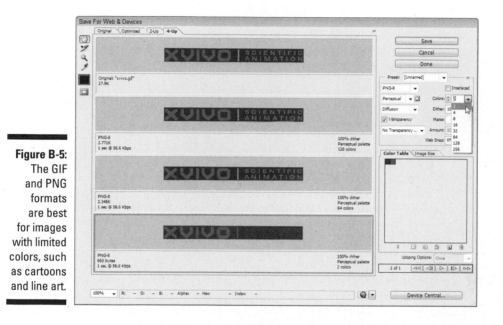

Figure B-5:
The GIF and PNG formats are best for images with limited colors, such as cartoons and line art.

5. **In the Colors box, choose the number of colors (see Figure B-5).**

   The fewer colors you use, the smaller the file size and the faster the image downloads. But be careful; if you reduce the colors too much (as we have in the bottom-right preview in Figure B-5), you lose details. The ideal number of colors depends on your image; if you go too far, your image looks terrible.

6. **(Optional) If you want to maintain a transparent area in your image, select the Transparency check box.**

   Any area of the image that was transparent when you created the image in the editor appears transparent in the preview window. If you don't have a transparent area in your image, this setting has no effect.

   Transparency is a good trick to make text or an image appear to float on a Web page. That's because a transparent background doesn't appear on the Web page. You can select transparency as a background option in the New File dialog box when you create a new image in Photoshop or Photoshop Elements. (*Note:* Transparency does not always work on older feature phones, but is well supported on most smartphones.)

7. **If you select the Transparency check box, also specify a Matte color.**

   You want the matte color to match the background of your Web page so that the dithering along the transparent edge blends in with the background. If you don't specify a matte color, the transparency is set for a white background, which can cause a *halo* effect when the image displays on a colored background.

8. **Specify other settings as desired.**

   The remainder of the settings in this dialog box can be left at their defaults in Photoshop.

9. **Click the Save button.**

   The Save Optimized As dialog box opens.

10. **Enter a name for the image and save it into the images folder (or any other folder) in your local site folder.**

11. **Repeat these steps for each image you want to optimize as a GIF or PNG for your site.**

Trial and error is a great technique in the Save for Web & Devices dialog box. In each of the three preview windows, displaying optimized versions of the graphic in Figure B-5, we used fewer and fewer colors, which reduced the file size with increasingly degrading effect.

The version displayed at the top of the dialog box is the original, which has a file size of 27.9K. Reducing the image to 256 colors dramatically reduced the file size to 2.771K but made little noticeable change to the image, as you see in the version shown second from the top. In the third version in the list, the image is reduced to 64 colors, which brought the size down to 2.346K but still made little change to the quality of the image. In the bottom version, we reduced it to two colors, which made the file size only 660 bytes, but the image quality suffered so dramatically you can no longer read the text *Scientific Animation*. Although it's harder to tell in the black-and-white reproduction in this book, all the color and details disappeared. In this last case, the savings in file size are clearly not worth the loss of image quality.

Index

• *Y* •

• *Z* •

Notes

Business/Accounting & Bookkeeping

Bookkeeping For Dummies
978-0-7645-9848-7

eBay Business
All-in-One For Dummies,
2nd Edition
978-U-470-38536-4

Job Interviews
For Dummies,
3rd Edition
978-0-470-17748-8

Resumes For Dummies,
5th Edition
978-0-470-08037-5

Stock Investing
For Dummies,
3rd Edition
978-0-470-40114-9

Successful Time
Management
For Dummies
978-0-470-29034-7

Computer Hardware

BlackBerry For Dummies,
3rd Edition
978-0-470-45762-7

Computers For Seniors
For Dummies
978-0-470-24055-7

iPhone For Dummies,
2nd Edition
978-0-470-42342-4

Laptops For Dummies,
3rd Edition
978-0-470-27759-1

Macs For Dummies,
10th Edition
978-0-470-27817-8

Cooking & Entertaining

Cooking Basics
For Dummies,
3rd Edition
978-0-7645-7206-7

Wine For Dummies,
4th Edition
978-0-470-04579-4

Diet & Nutrition

Dieting For Dummies,
2nd Edition
978-0-7645-4149-0

Nutrition For Dummies,
4th Edition
978-0-471-79868-2

Weight Training
For Dummies,
3rd Edition
978-0-471-76845-6

Digital Photography

Digital Photography
For Dummies,
6th Edition
978-0-470-25074-7

Photoshop Elements 7
For Dummies
978-0-470-39700-8

Gardening

Gardening Basics
For Dummies
978-0-470-03749-2

Organic Gardening
For Dummies,
2nd Edition
978-0-470-43067-5

Green/Sustainable

Green Building
& Remodeling
For Dummies
978-0-470-17559-0

Green Cleaning
For Dummies
978-0-470-39106-8

Green IT For Dummies
978-0-470-38688-0

Health

Diabetes For Dummies,
3rd Edition
978-0-470-27086-8

Food Allergies
For Dummies
978-0-470-09584-3

Living Gluten-Free
For Dummies
978-0-471-77383-2

Hobbies/General

Chess For Dummies,
2nd Edition
978-0-7645-8404-6

Drawing For Dummies
978-0-7645-5476-6

Knitting For Dummies,
2nd Edition
978-U-470-28747-7

Organizing For Dummies
978-0-7645-5300-4

SuDoku For Dummies
978-0-470-01892-7

Home Improvement

Energy Efficient Homes
For Dummies
978-0-470-37602-7

Home Theater
For Dummies,
3rd Edition
978-0-470-41189-6

Living the Country Lifestyle
All-in-One For Dummies
978-0-470-43061-3

Solar Power Your Home
For Dummies
978-0-470-17569-9

Available wherever books are sold. For more information or to order direct: U.S. customers visit www.dummies.com or call 1-877-762-2974. U.K. customers visit www.wileyeurope.com or call (0) 1243 843291. Canadian customers visit www.wiley.ca or call 1-800-567-4797.

Internet
Blogging For Dummies,
2nd Edition
978-0-470-23017-6

eBay For Dummies,
6th Edition
978-0-470-49741-8

Facebook For Dummies
978-0-470-26273-3

Google Blogger
For Dummies
978-0-470-40742-4

Web Marketing
For Dummies,
2nd Edition
978-0-470-37181-7

WordPress For Dummies,
2nd Edition
978-0-470-40296-2

Language & Foreign Language
French For Dummies
978-0-7645-5193-2

Italian Phrases
For Dummies
978-0-7645-7203-6

Spanish For Dummies
978-0-7645-5194-9

Spanish For Dummies,
Audio Set
978-0-470-09585-0

Macintosh
Mac OS X Snow Leopard
For Dummies
978-0-470-43543-4

Math & Science
Algebra I For Dummies,
2nd Edition
978-0-470-55964-2

Biology For Dummies
978-0-7645-5326-4

Calculus For Dummies
978-0-7645-2498-1

Chemistry For Dummies
978-0-7645-5430-8

Microsoft Office
Excel 2007 For Dummies
978-0-470-03737-9

Office 2007 All-in-One
Desk Reference
For Dummies
978-0-471-78279-7

Music
Guitar For Dummies,
2nd Edition
978-0-7645-9904-0

iPod & iTunes
For Dummies,
6th Edition
978-0-470-39062-7

Piano Exercises
For Dummies
978-0-470-38765-8

Parenting & Education
Parenting For Dummies,
2nd Edition
978-0-7645-5418-6

Type 1 Diabetes
For Dummies
978-0-470-17811-9

Pets
Cats For Dummies,
2nd Edition
978-0-7645-5275-5

Dog Training For Dummies,
2nd Edition
978-0-7645-8418-3

Puppies For Dummies,
2nd Edition
978-0-470-03717-1

Religion & Inspiration
The Bible For Dummies
978-0-7645-5296-0

Catholicism For Dummies
978-0-7645-5391-2

Women in the Bible
For Dummies
978-0-7645-8475-6

Self-Help & Relationship
Anger Management
For Dummies
978-0-470-03715-7

Overcoming Anxiety
For Dummies
978-0-7645-5447-6

Sports
Baseball For Dummies,
3rd Edition
978-0-7645-7537-2

Basketball For Dummies,
2nd Edition
978-0-7645-5248-9

Golf For Dummies,
3rd Edition
978-0-471-76871-5

Web Development
Web Design All-in-One
For Dummies
978-0-470-41796-6

Windows Vista
Windows Vista
For Dummies
978-0-471-75421-3

Available wherever books are sold. For more information or to order direct: U.S. customers visit www.dummies.com or call 1-877-762-2974.
U.K. customers visit www.wileyeurope.com or call (0) 1243 843291. Canadian customers visit www.wiley.ca or call 1-800-567-4797.

DUMMIES.COM®

How-to? How Easy.

Go to www.Dummies.com

From hooking up a modem to cooking up a casserole, knitting a scarf to navigating an iPod, you can trust Dummies.com to show you how to get things done the easy way.

Visit us at Dummies.com

Dummies products make life easier!

DVDs • Music • Games • DIY • Consumer Electronics • Software • Crafts • Hobbies • Cookware • and more!

For more information, go to **Dummies.com®** and search the store by category.

Making everything easier!™